FRUITS OF EDEN

OTHER BOOKS BY PATRICIA DAMERY

Farming Soul: A Tale of Initiation. Fisher King Press, 2010.
Second edition with a foreword by Robert Sardello. Napa, CA: Leaping
Goat Press, 2014.

Snakes. Napa, CA: Leaping Goat Press, 2014.

Marked by Fire: Stories of the Jungian Way, co-edited with Naomi Ruth
Lowinsky. Carmel, CA: Fisher King Press, 2012.

Goatsong. Carmel, CA: Fisher King Press, 2012.

FRUITS OF EDEN

Field Notes * Napa Valley 1991–2021

PATRICIA DAMERY

Group discounts are available (10 or more copies).

Contact dyane_sherwood_press@icloud.com

Book Design: Dyane Neilson Sherwood and Elijah Satoru Wood

Published in 2022

DANCING RAVEN PRESS is an imprint of Analytical Psychology Press

280 Elm Street, Oberlin, OH 44074-1504, United States

https://analyticalpsychologypress.com

ISBN: 978-1-958263-07-5 paperback, black and white interior

ISBN: 978-1-958263-03-7, paperback, color interior

ISBN: 978-1-958263-05-1 hard bound, color interior

Library of Congress Control Number: 2021953527

for Donald

and

for Judy

CONTENTS

Foreword

Landscape is the first born of creation.
John O'Donohue, *Divine Beauty: The Invisible Embrace*[2]

THE NAPA VALLEY IS the location of Patricia Damery's soul journey. Her fierce defense of this fecund and pristine landscape describes a path that all who are deeply troubled by the trajectory of exploitation of the land might want to learn from—and follow. I personally witnessed the glee with which developers in the valley celebrated its newfound popularity when I overheard a conversation between young entrepreneurs. One young man breathlessly recounted to a companion that the Napa Valley now surpassed Disneyland as the most frequently visited location by tourists in California. The specter of auto and bus traffic into the valley is surely not the Edenic vision of those who would protect and preserve its natural integrity.

Damery's narrative is structured like one of the ancient oak trees she has encountered along her life's path. An ever-radiating architecture of stories, intricately woven into a single person's soul journey, this branching oak of Damery's life weaves together personal history, mythic resonance, science, politics both global and local, history, and, most importantly, the psychology of living in harmony with nature.

In *Fruits of Eden* Damery explores her personal awakening to a deep relationship with the natural world. The flora, fauna, spirits, personages, and ecosystem container, seen with keen observation and deep relatedness, propel this journey in a kind of reverse Dantean trajectory. From the Eden of childhood, complete with the friendship of a stately oak, even while tinged with the background fear of nuclear contamination and war, to an adulthood characterized by an evolving awareness of the fragility of the ecosystem and the need to fight for its continued healthy existence, Damery's ever-expansive consciousness, a transformative individuation, offers us hope.

What are the archetypes of landscape? Surely Mother Earth, Gaia, is among them. When scientist James Lovelock, in his search for how one might detect life on a planet, recognized Earth as a living, breathing entity, governed by a reliable homeostasis, he named this entity Gaia. Gaia is also the mother of the Titans and therefore the grandmother of all the gods. She is our archetypal primeval first ancestor. Her power is limitless and terrible. What humans do to her Earth, she will answer with unflinching response. Along with this power comes the source of life, of sweetness, and another archetype of landscape, Eden. Longing for Eden is endemic among us. Patricia Damery traverses a life from Eden to the witnessing

LEFT: **Strawberry Creek Oak** (© Deborah O'Grady)

of its demise at the hands of human intervention. Among the signals, the victims of this assault, are trees she reveres.

How does one person find solace in a natural world that is ever threatened? How can an individual consciousness hold the multitude of conflicting conditions—of beauty and health, of threat from disease and the unconscious exploitative greed of late capitalism? In this book, we witness grace under pressure, a continuous willingness to sacrifice personal pleasure for engagement, and ultimately, a deep love of life in all its daunting contingencies.

Patricia Damery's journey, so beautifully articulated in *Fruits of Eden,* with its multitude of interlocking stories, reaches deep into the psyche, showing us how one person's life story brings forth so many valuable, necessary episodes. She invites us all to find the strength, determination, and generosity to unearth our own path to both the consciousness of our relatedness to earth and our willingness and energy to stand up for those values that protect the planet and thus all life. Her story embodies the holding of the opposites that produces the third, the transcendent function, a necessary development that allows forward movement amid the conflicting presence of both beauty and peril, a conscious way of hope.

DEBORAH O'GRADY

INTRODUCTION

Fire, Water, and Climate: What Unites Us

As the sun set, the winds rose. Like demon's breath, the air was slick and hot. The goats' hooves gouged the ground as I corralled them into their barn. Although the National Weather Service had issued warnings of high fire danger, I was focused on our upcoming trip to Portugal the next day. When I opened the bedroom window to the east, I noticed a plume of deep crimson smoke striated in orange, mushrooming into billowing blackness on the ridge across the valley. I called Donald, who was watching TV. By the time he came to the window, the fire had spread south, outlining the ridge top. Within minutes golden flames flowed like lava down the entire eastern ridge.

Within the next hour, the western sky behind us reddened with the second of three fires started that night. What was happening? Panicked, we led the bucking goats and llama down our three-quarter-mile driveway to the pickup of a friend waiting to transport them to an animal evacuation center. We gathered our dog and ourselves and followed the pickup into the hopeful safety of town. Before we left, I wandered through the house we had built together, grabbing a few items and saying goodbye to our home.

That first night the Atlas Peak Fire in Napa County burned six people alive. Helicopters airlifted people trapped at the end of the six-mile, dead-end Soda Canyon Road, a road that is the focus of the contentious permitting of Mountain Peak Winery. Of the 163 residences on the road, 82 percent of them burned over the next days; 72 percent were completely destroyed. Three fires, which all began that night, burned 6300 homes in Napa and Sonoma counties, killing 29 people. Until the next year when wildfire wiped out the town of Paradise, California, these fires would be declared the biggest and deadliest wildfire in California history.

This is a love story: for my husband's and my beloved ranch upon which we have farmed grapes and lavender for almost forty years, now threatened by a neighbor's proposed winery event center; for my husband as he sinks into the fog of dementia; and for those individuals whom I have come to know well through this advocacy. Their friendships are the diamonds formed through the chaos, greed, and ignorance of these times.

October 10, 2017, Atlas Fire (© Stuart Palley via ZUMA Wire)

It is also the inside story of a group of citizens working to awaken local county government to the challenges of our changing climate and to the need for action that ensures resiliency. Since the 1976 Paris blind tasting, which put Napa Valley wines on the map, the wine industry's success has also led to the county's greatest challenges. The county had the foresight in 1968 to form the first ever zoning designation of Agricultural (Ag) Preserve, limiting development in our rural valley lands. A few years later the hillsides were legally protected by the zoning designation Agricultural Watershed (AW). (The Appendix offers an overview of pertinent land-use ordinances and ballot measures.)

Through the years some in the wine industry have systematically eroded these protections. Since the early 1970s, the number of wineries has grown from less than two dozen to over five hundred today. Emboldened by its successes, the industry has effectively eclipsed the power of the elected and appointed governing officials through campaign donations. Valley land has been planted out with vines, and now the industry looks to the hillsides for future vineyards and remote wineries—impacting the often fragile, wooded watersheds. Water supply has been impacted as vineyard irrigation drains groundwater and runoff from vineyard erosion silts in the Napa River and our municipal reservoirs.

This is the David and Goliath story of citizen groups challenging significant corporate and wealthy interests to bring balance between agriculture and our wild lands, between the aspirations of monied interests for their visions of wineries and vineyards and of those of the workers and community residents for living wages, affordable housing, clean air and water, and health.

Because of human actions, we are experiencing the beginnings of unprecedented climate disruption. It will take human action if we are to survive. To meet these challenges, we are being called to develop our relationships with each other and with the planet. This is, after all, a crisis of consciousness. I take the Dalai Lama's words as my guiding star: "It probably has been many lifetimes since we have had such an auspicious conjunction of conditions favorable to progress along the path of higher being."[3] The path of conscious activism offers that opportunity.

When my husband Donald and I applied for biodynamic certification, we received a series of Google Earth pictures of our ranch from Demeter USA,[4] each from a higher elevation, until the last image pictured dark blue Earth against the backdrop of luminous starry space. The image of remembering the needs of Mother Earth acts as a guiding star embedded deep within my soul whether I am deciding to replant lavender near the oak savanna or making public comment at a Planning Commission hearing. Life on Earth is a web of abundance, but now, *especially* now, with responsibilities attached.

"We have lived by the assumption that what was good for us would be good for the world," Wendell Berry writes. "We have been wrong. We must change our lives so that it will be possible to live by the contrary assumption, that what is good for the world will be good for us. And that requires that we make the effort to know the world and to learn what is good for it."[5]

The author and her husband, Donald Harms

CHAPTER 1

The Light of Nature

I AM HAUNTED BY a photograph I took of my husband Donald during our early years at the ranch. It was taken on one of our daily walks up the old wagon trail to the building site of our new home. Everything is captured there—the arresting bloom of absolute presence of the day. Donald's painter pants glow white against the golden green of early spring grass; his dog Elsie's white fur also contrasts against the grass in juxtaposition to my large black poodle Cincinnati. Donald was then sixty-three, younger than I am now. When I study the photograph, I remember the happiness of those days. Moving to the ranch was like coming home to something so big that I knew I would have my ashes spread here, that I would always be here. Yet deeply embedded in that photo is the thorn of prescient grief: *These days are precious, and they will be gone. This season will pass. These dogs will die and so will we.*

Donald and I met through a dating service, Perfect Strings, which preceded the current internet dating sites. The cover was connection through classical music. He was the first person I met; I was his last. I was drawn by the fact that he was an architect and by the sensitivity of his responses to the questionnaire; he, by my statement "In my next life I want to be an architect" and by the disclosure that I subscribed to *Parabola* magazine. I have no recollection of our preferred music choices.

At the time, I lived on Atascadero Creek in Sebastopol. When Donald arrived for our first date, I watched from the boys' upstairs bedroom window as he unfolded his very tall frame from his Honda Prelude, which I would soon discover was full of Elsie's hair. As he got out, he brushed himself off for several seconds. Later that evening I remember his stooping to examine the front door handle, which often stuck, saying he would fix it. In retrospect, I see how important these moments were in the decisions we made.

The sixteen years difference in age made us both cautious. We were in different life stages: I was a single mom of two sons, Jesse, eleven, and Casey, nine; his four children were about the ages of my brother and youngest sister, his grandson two years younger than Casey. We began slowly, testing the waters by spending Sunday afternoons over the first nine months walking the shoreline of Salmon Creek with our dogs, talking of geometry and architecture,

LEFT: **The Milky Way** (Adobe Stock Photo)

of life. He had had two difficult marriages and was gun shy of a third. I had been alone for two years and the main breadwinner for many years in my previous marriage. In addition to the overlap of common interests, the prospect of having a working husband was very attractive to me. What I did not anticipate is the experience when two energetic *in*dividuals join. We had opportunities we would never have had alone: building our home, developing a biodynamic ranch, travel, and, for me, walking the trails of our ranch with our goats every day, partaking of the beauty as if it were milk.

During those early years with Donald, I felt I had somehow wandered into heaven, and it frightened me. Instinctively I knew I had entered the realm of the gods, a transgression for which mortals are punished. I struggled to find a way to comprehend what I was perceiving. The light emanating from the first shoots of grass and from the tiny unfolding leaves of black oak hurt my eyes; it was that brilliant. It was as if a rheostat were slowing turning up the light within what I saw. But I also *felt* the glow of it in the hot interior of the compost pile, *smelled* it in handfuls of fragrant, transformed earth, and *heard* its resonance at dusk and again in the early hours of the morning when coyotes whooped in the woods near the pond.

Each day of those years, Donald and I walked the trail from the ridge through the ravine where birdsong was an echo and slender bay laurel allées through the summer-dry creek. We acquired two pygmy goats, and they, too, walked with us, their Swiss goat bells melodically announcing their every step. In those woods silenced by foliage and full of goatsong, we felt the *axis mundi,* that cord attaching us to the center of the world.

I still do not know how much was the ranch and how much was our marriage. To see the gold in the green, to rest in the coolness of a leafy cathedral near the top of the ridge—which Donald described as a great bowl—was synonymous with his shy grin that seemed to say, *I am so happy I married you!* My experience with Donald and our ranch was the most open-hearted and expansive that I had ever known.

On warm nights we would awaken at 2 A.M. to the mockingbird's song. Donald studied the patterns of repetition, which he said had a sequence. *Tweet, tweet, tweeettttt, oooohhhhhh, click, click, tweet, tweet tweeettttt, oooohhhhhh . . . .*—it all made sense. In the dark hours, I would awaken to find him designing our new home. One night he was determining the depth of the center of the arc from which he generated the curve of the vaulted ceiling of the master bedroom, the center of which now lies nine feet below our bed. We sleep within a sphere that he dreamed those many years ago.

The building of the house stretched us both. Through candlelight, lovemaking, and talking, we conceived a form, which Donald rendered. I witnessed the breadth of him in this process. Not only was he a creative architect, but he was also a builder. He directed the earthmoving of mountains of clay from what became the basement onto what became the north loop of the driveway. He poured the concrete windowsills he designed himself, placing them with a used forklift he bought from a roadside farm on his trip north to supervise the construction of an Ukiah maternity ward he had designed. He constructed our curved

*Donald creating the curved fireplace mantel from the mold his
daughter Genevieve cast from valley oak leaves.*

fireplace mantel from the mold his daughter Genevieve cast from valley oak leaves from one of the oak savanna trees south of the dining room. He mixed the paint for the windows and doors onsite—the green for the house, the orange red for the studio—and supervised the workers in the unconventional construction, knowing exactly what they should do and how they should do it.

And so, we built our home.

And the land! The ranch was a mile-long tail of property, starting at the valley floor and climbing back to the tip of the ridge. Although it was only forty-one acres, it seemed much larger. Surrounded by oak woodland, Donald bought the land in part to plant a vineyard on the eight acres closest to the valley floor. In the center of what became the vineyard was a kind of inholding in which the last remains of four families of settlers of the Napa Valley are buried, a peaceful spot graced by valley oaks and Lebanon cedars. Until I came along, Donald seldom walked into the back acreage.

When Donald bought the ranch in October 1982, the realtor had refused to show him the old pioneer house; it was that old and decrepit. Donald restored and repaired the porches and updated the bathroom and kitchen. When we married in 1994, saying our vows under a valley oak between the pioneer cemetery and the vineyard, we continued to live in the old house while we built our new home. Given the amount of dog hair and general bachelor-quality housekeeping, I informed Donald that I came with a housecleaner—the housecleaner who proceeded to clean his old Wedgewood stove so thoroughly that we could never get the handles back on quite right. Generously, Donald removed everything from the house; we painted and carpeted, put back only what we needed, stored or gave away the rest. For three years the two of us, two growing boys, two big dogs, and a mean cat lived in 900 square feet of rather primitive house—and I loved almost every moment of it.

I set about learning the names of the vegetation: toyon, with its red berries that ripen around the winter solstice; the tiny white fruits of California snowberry; and tangles of wild honeysuckle. My inner clock was set by the progression of the wildflowers: Milkmaid, the first to appear just after the new year. Then shooting star (February), blue-eyed grass, Douglas iris (March), lupine, California buttercup (April), cluster lilies, Neptune's trident, clarkia, yarrow (May), all punctuated by the bloom of mariposa lily in late May or early June. It took me years to discover we had two species of wild orchids: bog candle and lady's slipper, and that you had to look carefully in the right places at the right time to find them. Walking the trails each day I became acquainted with the plants' habits. Coyote bush blooms in October and November, when the buckeye butterfly visits; the buckeye tree yellows her leaves even in June, the first hint of fall. By July poison oak is a brilliant red. Valley oak loses her leaves in the storms of December and January, only to push tiny new leaves after a week of warm days in March—an event, I have discovered, that comes almost two weeks earlier than it did when I first visited the ranch in 1992.

Now I orient myself by the cycles of the trees and wildflowers, by the greening oak savanna south of our kitchen after the first two inches of autumn rain and by the stormy flooding of the ditches along the driveway in January. The beauty of the ranch opens me into something I had never experienced—the apprehending of *the light within*. I am wedded to this land. My love is not a general love of Earth, but a simple fiery love honed from *knowing* this piece of earth to which Donald and I belong. It is a love that also engenders a mother-fierceness to protect it.

My awakening presented itself in *light*. The mystery of the experience led me to medieval texts: the *lumen naturae*—the light of nature. Medieval alchemist Paracelsus says the *lumen naturae* comes primarily from the "star" of man and "leads us toward great wisdom."[6] "Now as in the star lieth the whole natural light, and from it man taketh the same like food from the earth into which he is born, so too must he be born into the star."[7]

Was I born into the star of myself during those years and so came to recognize it in the land? I think this experience is as close to apprehending the Holy Ghost as one can get and still be in a human body. "The light is of a kind that desireth to burn, and the longer [it burns] to shine the more, and the longer the greater . . . therefore in the light of nature is a fiery longing to enkindle."[8]

Training to become a psychotherapist, I was advised by my first clinical supervisor to follow what I loved above all else and that I could not go wrong, advice I have mostly heeded. Love leaves its crumb path, and I work to not let other agendas override it. Through attention to the bell of interest, a precursor of love, I have found my way.

Love, engendered in our marriage and, until recently, inseparable from our ranch, is what also brought me into the larger concern for Napa County and the world. Not that my love of the Earth wasn't there before. I grew up on a farm, and my father's love of the Earth and of farming is deeply embedded in my soul, as it is in all my siblings. But the risk of our ranch's demise has awakened me into another consciousness. Napa County is being bought up by the business interests of extraordinarily wealthy individuals and multinational corporations, a microcosm of national and global issues and the continued exploitation of the Earth as we face climate change beyond our wildest imaginations. But this is only the latest wave of "invaders." The Wappos—First Peoples—populated the Napa Valley, and our ranch, for millennia before the Spanish arrived. First Peoples were then killed off by disease, relocation, and Indian wars. Civil War–era style cannonballs can still be found in creeks on our mountainside. The newcomers knew little about how to live in balance with the land, seeing only a spot to farm and "own." This acquisitive consciousness so easily leads to exploitation. That, also, is the impetus for this book.

These days Casey and his wife, Melissa, and their two sons, Wesley and Sabien, ten and eight, live in the little house Donald and I lived in while building our current home. The boys often spend a night with us. Wesley is tall and thin for his age with long curly red hair. I sometimes have to remind myself which decade I am in; he looks that much like his father at ten. Sabien is stockier, also with long curly hair and a penchant for drama and storytelling. He has the greatest capacity to learn the habits of lizards and sand crabs by simply observing them. I have never seen an eight-year-old with so much focus, although I realize, as his grandmother, I may be biased. They both love the Earth as much as any of their predecessors.

Wesley is an early riser, as I am, as was my father. He loves that period just before the sun crests the eastern ridge and the display it affords. For those few moments, the madrone and redwood trees on Goat Mountain to the west reveal a golden orange hue, as if on fire. We call this the *golden moment*. Just as the flaming begins, I repeat a beloved Robert Frost poem:

> Nature's first green is gold,
> Her hardest hue to hold.
> Her earliest leaf's a flower;
> But only so an hour.
> Then leaf subsides to leaf.
> So Eden sank to grief,
> So dawn goes down to day.
> Nothing gold can stay.[9]

We call this the Golden Moment.

"Say it again, Grandma." Wesley leans his warm body against me in the cool breeze that always announces the coming of the sun.

I begin again, slowly, "Nature's first green is gold, / Her hardest hue to hold . . . "

He repeats it with me, tapping his index finger in rhythm, committing it to memory.

CHAPTER 2

What's Jung Got to Do With It?—
and Brown Pelicans

WHEN I MET DONALD in early 1992, I was in training to become a Jungian analyst at the C. G. Jung Institute in San Francisco. Candidates attend classes for four years and then consult with senior analysts for another few years before writing the final paper. When the time came, my senior consultant suggested an approach to the final paper. "Choose a series of your patient's dreams and string them like a pearl necklace," he advised. As I strung the dream pearls, I found that I was tracing my patient's story of Self, an image of unity within and without. Carl Jung believed individuation, a process whereby we become more ourselves, involves learning to listen to the Self and the unconscious it encompasses. Apprehending the wholeness of Self, whether that be of ourselves as we do in personal analysis or of the living organism of Earth, Gaia, is, in fact, a large part of this story. Consciousness comes through this listening. As a result, we are less likely to project unacceptable parts of ourselves onto others or to exploit them, recognizing ourselves as only a part of the whole.

This awareness of being part of the whole is critical to understanding the needed shift for confronting the challenges of climate change. Jung believed that we must learn to accept the many aspects of ourselves that appear personified in dreams. He stated the future of humanity is contingent on this work with the unconscious: "The world hangs by a thin thread, and that thread is the psyche of man. . . . *We* are the great danger."[10]

Dreams are a kind of crumb path into a parallel dimension that our noisy society too often obscures. The internet and television, the general busy-ness of life, the pressure to do more and more and more . . . all these stop us from musing, from meditative experiences in which we *listen*. We lose track of these other dimensions of reality that give meaning and act as guiding stars.

Jung addressed the importance of listening to these other dimensions through the vehicle of dreams:

Dreams pave the way for life, and they determine you without you understanding their language. One would like to learn this language, but who can teach and learn it? Scholarliness alone is not enough; there is a knowledge of the heart that gives deeper insight. The knowledge of the heart is in no book and is not to be found in the mouth of any teacher, but grows out of you like the green seed from the dark earth.[11]

Brown Pelican, Pelecanus occidentalis, using its wings for balance
(Photograph: Brian Lasenby / Shutterstock)

As I address my feelings about what is happening to the Earth along with my struggle to find an effective activism to protect it, I string strands of my own pearls: Letters to the Editor to our local paper I have written over the past decade; the story of my husband's and my changing relationship to each other and to our ranch and the path of activism this love inspired; and last, but certainly not least, some of my own dreams during these years I have been drawn to political action, constellations I orient by. A new animal totem arrived in a dream early on, that of the brown pelican. It has taken me years to begin to grasp its meaning. I start with that short dream:

December 9, 2014: I am being served a brown pelican on a plate, which is at once disturbing and disorienting.

CHAPTER 3

Beginnings

I was born in 1948, three years after the atomic bomb was dropped on Hiroshima. My father, Merle Damery, was a radar repairman on Tinian, the Pacific Island from which the atomic bomb was deployed. Although we were told that my father was on the island, my mother, Lois Damery, told us not to ask him about it.

In early 1958 when I was nine, four children were born to mothers in our country church. Three of those children were born with Down syndrome, two needing to be institutionalized as infants. My family was lucky: my sister Shelly, the fourth, had only a webbed right hand and webbed feet. One of our church elders, grandmother of two of these children, said we were being punished for falling away from God, a theory we did not want to believe.

It would be years before we heard of the clouds of radiation that blew our way from above-ground testing of atomic bombs in Nevada during the 1950s and early 1960s. Several of us wondered if the families impacted had been together at a church potluck one of those days that a cloud passed over central Illinois and Blue Mound, our small town, exposing all of these mothers to enough radiation to impact the developing fetuses.

When I was in sixth grade, my class was presented with beautiful, freshly printed, blue-bound science books. Their glossy pages had the inky smell that I loved. Included in the science book was the apocalyptic story about the death of the sun, written as a journal entry by a survivor who recorded his final cold, sunless days. I became phobic, unable to open the book to the page with the story, which progressed to fearing the sight of the book itself.

Soon after, in October 1962, the Cuban missile crisis gripped the country as we stood on the brink of nuclear war with the Soviet Union. I was terrified by the national hysteria of building bomb shelters. Even at age eleven I questioned this. If we survived an atomic blast, what would we come out to? I grew up anticipating catastrophic events.

On a personal level, catastrophes were happening too, beginning even at my birth when my mother almost died of milk fever, saved only because of the recent discovery of penicillin.[12] It was the beginning of a lifelong string of health problems and multiple hospital stays for her. Because we did not have an indoor toilet in our home until I was six (I was toilet-trained to an outhouse), she avoided using the outhouse because there were snakes in the pit and in the yard. She was, after all, a city girl used to indoor plumbing. As a result, she had numerous kidney infections.

When I was five, my younger sister Judy and I had to spend a couple of days with my cousin Dolores while our mother was in the hospital. Before that we had stayed only with our grandmothers. Although Dolores was a beloved cousin, this was a particularly lonely experience. I found the bottom of a broken cookie jar in the shape of a giant apple in the

My father's watercolor painting of the family farm, which had been in my family for over 150 years, painted while he was attending an art class taught by a neighbor, Lois Rice, in the 1960s.

junk pile, which I insisted on retrieving and keeping. Dolores made us nap, something my mother no longer required. I remember lying on the bed with Judy, both of us wearing only navy-blue underpants. Judy fell asleep immediately. I was wide awake in the humid summer afternoon, watching dust motes in the afternoon sun with no one to keep me company.

But most often Grandma Peabody stayed with us during our mother's hospitalizations, something Judy and I loved. She was our favorite grandmother. Once during such a stay when we were nine and seven, we waded in our rubber boots into our flooded chicken yard after a spring deluge. Of course, we got stuck, the gooey mud sucking our boots down until it almost covered the rims. In our attempts to get out, we pulled our feet out and into the soup of mud and dreaded earthworms. I remember screaming for Grandma, who was in the house taking care of our toddler brother, Mark. She walked to the edge of the chicken yard holding Mark, who appeared a little coy to Judy and me as he clung to her. Grandma was uncharacteristically frustrated and annoyed. "You can just wait until your father comes home!" she hollered. We were shocked to hear her say the words that woke the fear of God in our hearts. A long hour later our father arrived home and was, fortunately, amused and quickly got us out.

Also at nine, our mother became pregnant with Shelly and had to spend a fair amount of time in bed before and after. That winter our country doctor visited Mom in our home because she was too ill, and it was too cold to travel the fifteen miles to his office. I remember his remarking that anyone would be sick with the amount of noise we kids were making. During this time, my father learned to diaper babies and fry eggs (I still prefer crispy edges around the whites). Before this he had refused to do what he considered *women's work.*

Not only was Shelly born with a webbed hand that required a series of surgeries starting at age six months, but also my toddler brother developed a low-grade fever that we feared was leukemia. After two years of monthly visits to Barnes Children's Hospital in St. Louis, Missouri, we learned instead he had a rare condition caused by a worm normally found in dogs and pigs. This worm ended its life's cycle in my little brother's liver; he would be okay. But my mother's condition worsened. One dark evening before Thanksgiving we rushed her to the hospital as she hemorrhaged, the iron-smell of hot blood silencing us kids in the back seat as my father sped through the night. At the time that I began my period, my mother had to undergo a hysterectomy. She was admitted just as my grandmother, her mother, was being released after surgery for breast cancer.

My mother survived, living to the age of eighty, albeit with diabetes and several associated complications, but Grandma Peabody died within months of her surgery from complications after being given a transfusion of blood tainted with hepatitis. She had been like a mother to us, and we mourned her profoundly, often dreaming of her return.

My way of approaching the Earth and my relationship to Donald were formed by the pattern of fear and worry that shaped my relationship with my mother. I had held myself a little apart, thinking I could rely only on myself. Concurrently, I wanted to heal her, watching her food choices and nagging her to exercise, advice she ignored, which infuriated me. I am sure this influenced my entry into a healing profession. Years of personal analysis helped heal this wounding, and yet, my worry for my mother's survival created a kind of processing organ within my psyche. I feel it now: with Donald's slow decline, I once again feel that I am being left alone to face the ultimate abandonment: the threat to Mother Earth and her vitality. I struggle with wanting to hold myself apart so I feel less pain, and at the same time, I want to heal the Earth—or Donald. Yet, as I know from experience, if I stay open-hearted, even to the loss of life as I know it, I am brought into an intimacy with life. Grief, when fully experienced, paradoxically opens my heart.

Psychiatrist Carl Jung described the patterning I have with my mother as a "Mother complex." A *complex* is a feeling-toned pattern, often developed in childhood through trauma, in which parts of our psyche split off and operate autonomously, with only limited control by the mind. These patterns often appear in dreams as figures and situations that unconsciously organize our way of approaching the world. So much of early psychological work in analysis involves becoming conscious of and integrating these split-off parts of ourselves.

Complexes often reflect larger patterns, or archetypes, which transcend culture, in this case, that of the Mother archetype, with its many facets and polarities. Jung says of the Mother archetype:

> This is the mother love which is one of the most moving and unforgettable memories of our lives, the mysterious root of all growth and change; the love that means homecoming, shelter, and the long silence from which everything begins and in which everything ends. Intimately known and yet strange like Nature, lovingly tender and yet cruel like fate, joyous and untiring giver of life—*mater dolorosa* and mute implacable portal that closes upon the dead. . . . the mother carries for us that inborn image of the *mater nature* and *mater spiritualis,* of the totality of life of which we are a small and helpless part.[13]

Jungian analyst Nathan Swartz-Salant put it this way: the mother is the first mediator of God, of those divine energies from which we incarnate at birth. Our relationship with her influences us throughout the rest of our lives, consciously or unconsciously.[14]

My experience of the larger patterning of the Mother archetype was formed by these early experiences with my personal mother. There was not a day while my mother was living that I did not worry for her survival. I have to ask myself why. She was, after all, a vital woman. Large in body and spirit and with great *joie de vivre,* she was at the center of many community activities, full of life, and she had a wicked sense of humor. We shared the uncontrollable affliction of gales of laughter at mishaps: her getting "beached" in a glass bottom boat she had always wanted to ride and having to be rolled out "like a whale" (her words), her adventures in learning to drive Walmart's handicapped electric wheelchair as she knocked over displays at the end of aisles. One of the more serious of these occurred when my nine-year-old nieces lost their grip on her wheelchair at the top of a hill during a *Race for Life* fundraising event for breast cancer survivors (yes, she also had breast cancer) and her careening down the pavement out of control, hitting a curb, and being thrown unhurt into the grass, again in spasms of laughter.

But she was also thoughtful about all of us and sensitive to me. Once she asked me on a visit home, "If you were sick, would you tell me?" I lied, "Of course." But we both knew the horse had already left the barn on this one. After her mastectomy, she showed me her scar—I am sure to relieve my anxiety about her missing breast and to give me some facts on the ground in case I, too, suffered this disease.

When she died, my brother and two sisters and I compared notes: my brother and I had worried constantly for her health; my sisters did not consider this! We were surprised at each other's different realities.

I wonder about the connection between my entry to life, my mother's physical vulnerabilities, and the resulting psychological complexes that defined me in relationship—and now my worry about Mother Earth.

Too often the anxiety of anticipated grief separates me from that which is also most dear to my heart. My fear for my mother's survival, inflamed by the worm in my little brother's liver, my sister's hand surgeries, and then my grandmother's cancer and death, reinforced my sensitivity to the transience of the human relationship. I spent years in analysis addressing this. Fear of loss can automatically distance me from the beloved. In terms of Mother Earth, I can even find it difficult to embrace my feeling of loving connection to the beautiful valley oaks who are my neighbors: those in the savanna south of our kitchen, with its purple needle grass and blue wild rye, and the ancient ceremonial circles of valley oaks where a new neighbor intends to plant a vineyard.

I have always wondered if complexes, although problematic when they eclipse our egos, are also organs for the soul's purpose. Too often these patterns of behavior are seen only as maladaptive, blocking or distorting our access to the larger energies of the archetype behind them. Even the word *complex* implies something wrong—something to be worked through so you are a whole individual.

Indologist Heinrich Zimmer defines the space between the complex and the archetype using the Hindu concept of "permanent scars that go from life to life." Jungian psychotherapist Roger J. Woolger carries this further in framing Freud's concept of repetition compulsion in terms of *samskara:*[15]

> We repeat the same old failure one life after another; we are repeatedly attracted to lovers and spouses who hurt and betray us, or we end up with bosses and especially parents who bully and tyrannize us; we contract diseases and undergo pains that other bodies have suffered before and so on. Depressing as this picture may appear to some, I can find no better one to encompass the extraordinary variety and uniqueness of each person's allotment of what Hamlet called "the heart-ache and the thousand natural shocks that flesh is heir to" in one lifetime.[16]

Are we born into circumstances that create the psychological ground upon which our souls have incarnated to resolve or to impact? Are these circumstances, in fact, seminal to our incarnation this time around? Is this the bedrock of my activism? Are our relationships, whether with Earth or a spouse, a laboratory of soul's purpose?

Whatever preserves and enhances this meadow in the natural cycles of its transformation is good; whatever opposes this meadow or negates it is not good.
Thomas Berry, *The Great Work: Our Way into the Future*[1]

View of the meadow that borders our ranc

CHAPTER 4

The Phone Message

THERE ARE TIMES THAT indelibly stain us, the split second that changes everything. I think of some of those times: the phone call at Uncle Rufus's house in Chicago when I was sixteen. My family had spent the night and was about to leave for O'Hare International Airport to meet Charoula, our foreign exchange student from Greece for the next year. We were elated with anticipation. I don't remember the phone ringing, but suddenly Uncle Rufus's voice was solemn as he called my father to the phone. My father's face froze as he listened. He hung up, looked at my mother. "Wayne's in the hospital," he said. "An aneurysm."

Uncle Wayne was my father's oldest brother, and they farmed together. He always wore overalls and was gruff with us kids, but he also had a pond where we swam on hot July evenings. We celebrated his August birthday with a family watermelon party at which we could eat all we wanted. Once my sister and I dug a "raccoon trap" in the fall stubble of my father's cornfield, a three foot by four foot hole, about three feet deep. In the bottom, we placed marshmallows and then disguised the hole with dried cornstalks. The only thing we ever "caught" was the front tire of Uncle Wayne's tractor as he was spring plowing, and then we really caught it!

When Uncle Wayne helped my father at our farm, he joined us for dinner, which Midwesterners call the noontime meal. Many the time they argued loudly at the table over how and when to cultivate, my mother finally telling them both that there would be no apple pie if they didn't stop. My uncle was fiercely protective of my father who was fourteen years his junior. Once when we were eating dinner an attorney arrived to question my father over the recent hush-hush suicide of a distant family member. My father had evidently found the body, but we kids had only guessed this from overhearing whispered fragments of conversation. When the attorney persisted to insult my father, Uncle Wayne picked him up by his collar and threw him down the back steps of our house. "You ripped my shirt," the attorney yelled. Uncle Wayne threw a five-dollar bill at him. "Buy another," he yelled. "Get out of here!"

Uncle Wayne died within a week of the call to my Uncle Rufus's house. His strong, imposing figure would no longer sit at the far end of our table opposite my father, bellowing his opinions.

Another of those times: when I left for college in 1966. As Mom, Dad, and I backed out of the driveway, my sister Judy, two years younger than I, stood at the fence, tightly grasping white pickets in each hand. She was a brilliant, lean kid, a tomboy ready to protect every animal and always volunteering to help my dad in the field. When she became a teenager, my mother tried to get me to make her wear makeup, which I resisted. Judy and I were companions through almost everything, the constant in my life during my mother's hospital stays, the birth of two siblings, our beloved grandmother Peabody's death. We devised pranks together, letting the sheep out when we were bored while spending an afternoon with our grandmother Damery, who was visiting on the back porch with her own sisters. Grandma was grateful when we "found" the sheep and offered to corral them. We rode our bikes the half mile to Grandma Damery's house every day, at least twice a day in the summer, endured the hot job of cutting weeds out of beans together, fought fiercely. Judy will readily show you the scars on her arm from my fingernails. But I love her dearly. Although we now live 2000 miles apart, when we are together we immediately fall into the familiarity of sisterhood. Our relationship is the patterning of every friendship I have with my dearly loved woman friends. The day I left for college, though, I knew our childhood was over. Although I was ready to leave my parents, I was not ready to leave Judy.

Life is full of these moments. We often live under an illusion of constancy and are always surprised—often shocked!—at change. It is a child's fantasy that life is secure and constant. Healthy psychological development is predicated on the early weaving of this fantasy, as psychoanalyst Louise Kaplan writes:

> Human life begins in illusion … created by a down-to-earth mother's devotion to her ordinary baby. In her ordinary way of holding him, a mother gives her baby the impression of a world that will hold him together and make sense of the unformed excitements and appetites raging inside him. The baby then has the illusion that his appetites are congruent with the new world he has just entered.[17]

The gossamer fabric of this illusion, and then the rhythmic tearing of it in corrective, maturing moments in which we are not immediately held, allows for psychological separation from the mother and the development of what psychologists call "object constancy." The mother may disappoint by not being there immediately, but she returns, is still alive. Object constancy, internalized, forms a core in us, a rock on which we stand when we discover the broader truth: that life is fluid and volatile, energetic and ever-changing. Like dolphins leaping in salty seas, we too swim through grief of separation from that which birthed us, over and over, and hopefully, like dolphins, with some joy of living. And although I am jumping a little ahead of myself, collectively we are in a time when we can no longer assume we live in Eden, where everything is here for our own good. Climate change has made sure of that! We are having a maturing moment.

It is one of those maturing moments that I want to tell you about, because it is finally what put me on the course of writing this book. I have no illusion that I know how it is going to turn out; I tell you that in advance. I have had to give that up—the illusion of a stasis of living in Eden, which I had for a while. But that moment of reckoning began, again, with a phone call, this time a message on our home phone.

It was a mid-February afternoon in 2010, and it had been raining, one of the last rainy years before the long drought. I saw the flashing red message light and pushed the button to listen, with little preparation for what I was about to hear. Our neighbor's voice (whom I will call William) had left the message. William was a charming, brooding poet and an attorney who owned the oak savanna next door. He was active on a number of social causes. Attractive but worn, he had a history of boom-and-bust wealth. The economic downturn of 2008 had strongly impacted him.

We met William at a party given by his friend and our neighbor some fifteen years before, just as Donald was designing our home. We had had a close call with another possible buyer of the next-door property by a man who called himself an "environmental attorney." As it turned out, he was for the other side: how to skirt environmental law. When we gave him permission to use our wagon trail to bring in a drilling rig to drill for water, he drilled on our property line between two huge valley oaks within feet of the proposed location of our home. Thankfully, he found no water. We decided to purchase the five acres beside us and to find a buyer for the rest. That turned out to be William.

That February day, I had to play the message twice: the first time I only half listened and could not take in the severity of what William was saying. He was selling his 26 acres to his neighbors. "I am selling my ranch to the Sinclairs next door, and I want to bring them over to introduce you to them,"[18] the message said. They wanted to plant a vineyard, like so many who come to Napa.

Perhaps to you, dear reader, this all sounds romantic or benign, and to some, it would be. The land south of our home is an oak savanna that slopes into the center and is studded with ancient valley oak trees and their offspring. Donald and I watch that oak savanna daily. Wild turkeys mate in its stretches, the males parading their fans of fine tail feathers. Bobcats and coyotes slink along its edges and sometimes into the cup of its center in the early morning and early evening hours. Barn owls hunt at twilight, floating soundlessly like deadly white ghosts. Occasionally we are awakened by great horned owls hooting anguished mating calls.

Time stops when you walk into the savanna. It could be a moment or an hour; it doesn't matter. You simply step into another zone. Two groupings of trees grow on knolls at either end: one, a circle of oaks where my oldest son, Jesse, and his wife, Lisa, were married two years before this phone message; the other a site where ancient valley oaks grafted together, almost certainly a ceremonial dance spot for the Wappo First People who lived here for centuries. That savanna drew Donald and me to build our home on its edge, its energy changing me. My experience of its power could not have been greater than if I had stepped before God. The oak savanna is what Carl Jung would describe as a carrier of the Self, an experience that returns me to wholeness—and we did not own all of it.

You cannot own enough land to save the Earth. I tell myself that, perhaps to justify why we didn't buy it all when we could. I would like to blame William for not offering it to us before he sold it to the couple on the other side of his property. Anger is the easy part. After all, we did recruit him to buy the land in the first place, realizing how important our next-door neighbor would be.

William also loved the oak savanna. Shortly after his escrow closed, he presented us with a beautiful calligraphy of a Wendell Berry poem, "The Sycamore."[19] The oaks in the savanna mirrored this poem: they had witnessed the transition of the land being tended and held sacred by the Wappos, to being deeded to Salvador Vallejo by the King of Spain, then owned by a family of ranchers. Barbed wire was embedded in some of the bark. "It bears the gnarls of its history / healed over. . . . It has gathered all accidents into its purpose. / It has become the intention and radiance of its dark fate. / It is a fact, sublime, mystical and unassailable."[20]

Together, William, Donald, and I recorded an easement protecting these oaks on both of our properties, including the forest and meadow conditions in which they grew. We thought this would ensure the continuance of the savanna into the future—that it would "stand in its place . . . native and maker."[21] A vineyard would destroy not only the wildlife corridor of the savanna and its native grasses and trees, but also the ancient peace of the natural world going about its business in such an uncalculated way, a peace I hold sacred.

When I listened to that February 2010 message, I felt one of the iron cannonballs found in our creek had been hurled at me. How do we recover when we have been hit by such force? It is a question that I contemplate a great deal these days. Shock is protective, allowing us time to assimilate events outside our matrix of reality. I wanted to deny William's call, to roll back the calendar to a week before, an hour before, wrapping myself in the memory of first walking the trail along the ridge with Donald and seeing the oak savanna rolling and green. Early in our relationship, Donald invited me to the ranch to walk the steep wagon trail to the ridge. It was late fall, 1992. The autumn rains had sprouted grasses of three to four inches. We had just come to the trail that descends onto the deer trail to the upper pond when I saw the savanna's rolling grassy humps and ancient giants. I almost dropped to my knees. It was like running into someone you always knew but hadn't seen in a very long time.

But on that February 2010 afternoon, the ensuing vertigo of chaos won out and disorientation and fragmentation set in. Sometimes I wonder what I hated most: the change that was announcing itself in that phone message or the experience of fragmentation. Either way, nothing has been the same since.

My first pelican dream came four years after this fateful phone message, reflecting the angst of the task this book undertakes. I love pelicans! They are mythic to me. In fact, the pelican-headed Egyptian goddess Henet was associated with death and the afterlife, a protective symbol against snakes, or injury from the rising of spiritual energy, the kundalini.[22] As a landlocked child, I had never seen a pelican. When I arrived in California in 1971 as a young adult and observed a pod of them fishing as they flew along the Limantour Spit shoreline of Point Reyes National Seashore, I was awed, thinking I had come upon the rarest of sightings. In truth, they were listed as an Endangered Species in 1970, their decline

In alchemy, the pelican is the allegorical container in which the transformation occurs.

(Exaltatio V. Essentiae. Sapientia veterum philosophorum, sive doctrina eorumdem de summa et universali medicina, 40, 18th century. Manuscript with paintings, 58 folios, 16.9 × 10.6 cm. BnF, Arsenal, MSS 974, folio 39 © National Library of France.)

due to the pesticide DDT's softening of their eggshells. After DDT was banned in the early 1970s, their populations recovered until, by 2009, they were taken off the endangered list.

I often think of the pelican as a Jungian bird; the term *pelican* is an allegory used by medieval alchemists for the vessel in which the transformation occurs—but more on this later. In my dream, being served a brown pelican on a plate repulsed me. I didn't want to eat something so alive.

But eating is also incorporation, digesting something, in this case, something extremely hard to take in. Pelicans were endangered because of human activity, as our Earth is now. The threat to the oak savanna is a microcosm of what is happening worldwide.

A spiritual exercise used by many esoteric disciplines is to build up an image in great detail in your mind and then, when the image is vibrantly clear, to shatter it. You then wait to receive what comes next. Goethe, and Rudolf Steiner after him, say that this exercise purifies you of beliefs about what you are seeing, cleaning the slate, so you are open to genuine communication with whatever Being is before you.

This happened the day of the phone message. My illusion of Eden did not simply disappear. It shattered, sending shards deep into my soul, ripping into my heart. It would be my task to heal from this wounding and to prepare myself to face the reality of what would come forward next.

Writing about my struggle to understand the impending destruction of the savanna oaks and the oak circle is a microcosm mirroring the great changes occurring on our Earth. It chronicles my quest for a more conscious activism, one that involves a very different awareness, one no longer merged with Eden, hopefully one more mature and balanced.

CHAPTER 5

I Meet Oak

Trees are interstitial beings, connecting the atmosphere and terrestrial realms. They are rooted in the ground, but made of thin air, conjuring the sky, the atmosphere, and the sun to earthly form.

Lynda V. Mapes, *Witness Tree: Seasons of Change with a Century-Old Oak*[23]

I STARTED FIRST GRADE just after turning six. Our rural community had no public kindergarten, so I wasn't used to being away from my mother. My class was one of the first waves of the baby boomers, and in anticipation, after the Second World War, the school board moved two one-room schoolhouses from the surrounding countryside into town to accommodate us. We sat facing the blackboard, which extended the length of the west wall. To our right was the entry and a small, messy anteroom serving as a library and teacher's office. The south wall was lined with large double-hung windows opening onto the ball field—and a young red oak tree. Throughout that first fall I would watch its leaves dance, its dappled shade on my desk as the sun moved across the midday sky. That tree was my introduction to oak.

I remember the day my mother was supposed to pick me up after school. I hated riding the bus and its hour-long journey home, so the prospect of my mother getting me was a relief. Shortly before the afternoon recess, my teacher informed me that my mother had called and said to take the bus to my grandmother's. I remember crying. When a couple of girls asked why, I lied, telling them my aunt had died, not wanting to disclose the real reason. In fact, unbeknownst to me, my beloved maternal grandfather had suddenly sickened and would die within the week. My mother and maternal grandmother, of course, were bereft. My happy life darkened with loss.

On top of this, I was struggling with how to join with other kids. I knew no one in my class, and they all seemed to know each other. I was also frightened of doing anything wrong because punishments were harsh; children were paddled in front of the classroom for small misdeeds or sent to the principal for bigger infractions. Rumor had it that the principal had an electric paddle with nails in it, and I believed these rumors and took no chances.

At this time I began visiting the tree outside my classroom window. My sister and I knew box elders, having one in our yard that sported a baby swing when we were younger and, as we grew, became a great climbing tree. We spent many hours straddling its branches like horses. My grandmother Damery had giant sugar maples in her yard too big to climb, which provided great expanses of shade. But I had never been around oaks. That first fall away from home, I spent recesses collecting acorns, studying their fat shining bodies and the perfectly fitting hats. Steve, a middle schooler from our rural church, sometimes teased me as I sat playing with acorns under the tree that became my best friend.

My interest in oaks grew throughout my school years. I learned to recognize oak's various expressions: red oak, yes; but also burr oak, with its huge shaggy caps; and pin oak, with pointy tips on its lobed leaves. In high school biology we pressed leaves between pages of books until they were flat and dry, and then we pasted them to sheets of paper, printing the identification of the leaf and the location collected just below it. I loved finding the less frequent chestnut oak with its oblong serrated leaf.

All Midwestern oaks are deciduous. When I learned about evergreen oaks, I longed to see one, but it was not until I moved to California that I discovered evergreen coastal live oak and interior live oak, both with their thick unlobed, spikey leaves. Our ranch is resplendent with both.

The native stands of oak trees where I grew up still flourished along the creeks and the rivers, places unfriendly to farming. In the autumn we would take drives to view the fall colors: yellows, oranges, and reds. Winter revealed the oaks' structures, strong and tall. Even in the harshness of Midwestern winters, the oak stood, ever present, there long before any of the rest of us. Oak fossils date back to the Eocene Epoch, 45 million years before humans.[24] They are important denizens of our past, and their acorns carry our future.

Most of the Illinois land around my family's farm was flat and had been cleared. Few trees remained. Some were planted as wind breaks or along fencerows, including Osage orange, whose hard wood was perfect for decay-resistant fence posts, but along the creeks and rivers, the oaks thrived. Mosquito Creek meandered south and west of our farm. The creek was bounded by a glade with lush riparian habitat, and a little above that, a spacious meadow of oak savanna was populated with magnificent specimens of white oak. The land near the creek was undulating, often flooding during spring rains. With its stretches of grasslands punctuated by enormous white oaks that reached to the heavens, often spanning wider than they were tall, this was the most beautiful of all spots. White oaks live to ancient ages; some of the remaining Mosquito Creek white oaks are estimated to be 300 to 500 years old.

Along the edge of this glade and woodlands my father collected morel mushrooms for my grandmother in late April or May, after things warmed up. The oak savanna followed the creek west to an area where settlers picnicked. Across from the house of my great-great

The 500-year-old white oak in Hall Cemetery under which several of my ancestors are buried. My sister calls it Prairie Queen. It has been designated as the largest oak in Macon County, Illinois. (Photograph: Judy Damery Parrish)

grandparents, James and Louise Waltz, was Hall Cemetery. Within the cemetery stands the largest white oak in Macon County. My sister Judy, now a plant ecologist, takes her college students there to stand in awe at the white oak's two-and-a-half-feet thick horizontal branches stretching far into the cemetery. She and I could never climb the tree: climbing it requires equipment. Judy calls the tree the Prairie Queen.

The Celts believed the ancestors lived in the roots of oaks. I suspect this to be true. For 170 years this oak has been nourished on those laid to rest under and near it. I cannot look at the oak without thinking of James and Louisa Waltz; their daughter Matilda and her husband, Thomas Pope, and their twelve-year-old daughter Della, who died of the flu in 1898, a few days before Matilda. What remains of them now resides within the root structure of that *family tree*!

Just east of the cemetery lay the timberland of a farm leased by my uncle and his son. The oak savanna above the glade afforded a meadow for cattle grazing. To Judy and me, this oak woodland, this oak savanna was a magnet. We loved to ride our bicycles to the farm. We would carefully unlatch and relatch the gate of the barnyard, checking to make sure a bull was not with the cows, and, leaving our bicycles at the fence, cross the barnyard to the far gate into the hilly meadow and oak savanna. We loved exploring the rolling savanna, so different from the flat fields farmed around our home. In the savanna, grasses gave way to oaks and oaks to riparian flora, including wild false indigo and wild senna, both attractive to bees. Jewelweed bloomed along the creek in the fall, drawing hundreds of ruby-throated hummingbirds and bees. Here the creek flowed year-round, minnows flashing above the rocky bottom, muskrats diving into the singing waters.

One day Judy and I took our younger brother, Mark, who had just gotten his new blue bike, to this beloved spot. Our cousin who lived in the farmhouse was not home, and we did not have permission from him or our parents to be there—not that this stopped us: the place was just too magical to resist. Again, leaving our bicycles at the gate, we crept through the barnyard to the far end and into the wild area. What really happened next is confused in our memories, but my brother got hit in the face with a branch and it broke his nose and blackened both of his eyes. Given that we were not supposed to be there anyway, given that we had so profoundly betrayed the trust given us for the care of our little brother, we all agreed on a story: we were playing baseball with a branch and accidentally hit Mark in the face. I am not sure where we proposed this fiction took place, but we somehow avoided most of the fallout, perhaps because Mark's condition warranted all the attention. And sadly, for long-forgotten reasons, we never returned to our magical savanna.

Years later when Mark was in high school, my father said to him, "Don't be afraid to take chances." Citing regrets from his own life, he told Mark a story about the farm with its glades and ancient oaks. My uncles and cousin had wanted my father to go in with them in purchasing the land, but my father, being overly cautious, had hesitated, and they lost the chance. As it turned out, the man who bought the farm cut all the oaks and graded the land into terraces so he could farm right up to the creek's edge. I will never know what my father or uncles would have done with the land—farmers too often are no friends of oaks—but I like to think they would have preserved it as it was, a cornucopia of native life, including oaks.

CHAPTER 6

A (Very) Brief History of the Environmental Movement

Obligations have no meaning without conscience, and the problem we face is the extension of the social science from people to land.

Aldo Leopold, *A Sand County Almanac*[25]

MY EARLIEST MEMORY CONCERNING fear for the environment is of Fourth of July during a dry spell on my childhood farm. We did not irrigate Illinois fields because it almost always rained at the right times. Even if it was a little dry for two or three weeks, we knew it would rain soon. The rich black prairie topsoils are thick and hold moisture, so plants survive.

Nevertheless, we were interested in rainfall totals when it did rain. Everyone had a rain gauge. When you met someone in town after a storm, you always exchanged rainfall totals. Farms south of town could vary by two or three inches from ours, three miles north. I still have a rain gauge that I religiously monitor, even checking it in the middle of a stormy night with a flashlight to make sure it doesn't overflow. I have recorded daily rainfall totals for the twenty-seven years I have lived on our ranch.

Water is life, and you know it when you are a farmer. If you don't irrigate, you depend on the frequency of rain to be dry enough to plow and plant, then moist enough to sprout and grow the seeds. Some years a crop has to be replanted in low places that get flooded out in late May. And if the rain doesn't come, and your corn and beans don't shoot up, well, that is your income for the year. Farming is a risk that puts you in humble touch with the weather and the earth.

That Fourth of July I stood in the forty acres north of our home in corn that didn't reach my knees, praying for rain. *Knee high by the Fourth of July*—but it wasn't. These days with chemical fertilizers and GMO (genetically modified organism) seed, the corn can be higher

than your shoulders by July, but in those days, the corn wasn't on steroids. My mother told me rain always comes, but this did not assuage my anxiety that year. My fear for my mother's health and my grandmother's death the year before, almost certainly amplified my angst.

My father seemed oblivious: "It rains when it rains," he would say. "Nothin' we can do about it." Seasoned farmers appear to have this attitude. Stoicism was our drug in those days. Underlined in my childhood Bible are the Matthew 6 verses that support this stance. *Do not be anxious about your life... Look at the birds of the air; they neither sow nor reap nor gather into barns, and yet your heavenly Father feeds them.... which of you by being anxious can add one cubit to his span of life?*[26] Those passages, and unprocessed anxiety about the helplessness of it all, made small farmers vulnerable to industrial and chemical predators' greed. They applied this same docile attitude in the face of corporate giants, as if they were gods—corporations that owned the seeds, despoiled our water and soils, and lied about the impact on the environment.

The birds of the air. In 1962, at about the same time as that Fourth of July, Rachel Carson's book *Silent Spring* was published, addressing the demise of the environment and birds through the use of pesticides and DDT.[27] After the Second World War, farmers were encouraged to use the excess ammonium hydroxide left from weapons production as a superior source of nitrogen. Almost all farmers, my father included, took up this militarized farming. The results were impressive. DDT was used to control pests, including mosquitos. Small planes swooped over our crops as we stood in the yard watching them rain poisons on the fields and, yes, on us too. The consequences of this on humans and the greater environment, when known, were not publicized. In my family, all of us kids have autoimmune conditions.

Specializing in aquatic biology, Rachel Carson had studied the impact of synthetic chemicals on bird populations, including the brown pelican. Her book, highly contested by the chemical industry, brought the consequences of the overuse of pesticides before the general public. This contributed to the forming of the Environmental Defense Fund in 1967 and was instrumental in the banning of DDT as well as in the formation of the Environmental Protection Agency by the Nixon Administration in 1970.[28]

Until that time, the USDA regulated pesticide use, which Carson called a *conflict of interest.* When agriculture is viewed primarily as a commercial enterprise, not as a partnership with the earth, its interests are often in opposition to those of wildlife and the general environment, as we are discovering in the Napa Valley. An early advocate of balance, Carson was influenced by biodynamic pioneer Ehrenfried E. Pfeiffer, who performed a wealth of research on the impact of DDT overuse, and by the teachings of Rudolf Steiner's biodynamic agriculture, an influence not realized until recently.[29] Although Carson did not advocate for the banning of DDT, she did stress the need for the prudent use of it. Not only was it having a detrimental and cumulative impact on the environment, but also

OPPOSITE: *Lily browsing in oak savanna*

it was producing resistance in the very pests it was targeting. By overusing pesticides, we inadvertently strengthened the pests.

Carl Jung labeled this process as *enantiodromia*—a word from ancient Greek *enantio*, "opposite," and *dromos*, "running course." When things reach an extreme, over the course of time they turn into their opposite. "This characteristic phenomenon practically always occurs when an extreme, one-sided tendency dominates conscious life; in time an equally powerful counterposition is built up which first inhibits the conscious performance and

Farm tractor spraying pesticides and insecticides herbicides over green vineyard field. Napa Valley, Napa County, California, USA. April 5th, 2020

(Adobe stock photo)

subsequently breaks through the conscious control."[30] This is true with the psyche when we are too one-sided and it occurs in nature, all to bring balance. Jung deemed this process important in individuation: the maturing into the wholeness of ourselves.

Carson's passionate work as a scientist spurred grassroots environmental action. In fact, the middle of the last century brought a groundswell of public awareness about humans' impact on Earth. Just a couple of months before I was born, Aldo Leopold, forester and arguably father of modern ecology, died of a heart attack while fighting a fire on a neighbor's land. *A Sand County Almanac* was published posthumously later that fall. "We abuse land because we regard it as a commodity belonging to us," Leopold wrote in the Foreword. "When we see land as a community to which we belong, we may begin to use it with love and respect."[31]

The concept of a community of organisms was further developed in the late 1960s by British scientist James Lovelock, who coined the term *Gaia*. He postulated that "the organic and inorganic components of Planet Earth have evolved together as a single living, self-regulating system. It suggests that this living system has automatically controlled global temperature, atmospheric content, ocean salinity, and other factors, that maintains its own habitability."[32] Lovelock added a precautionary note:

> Every evolutionary step in a component of the biosphere has the capacity to change the environment.... It seems very unlikely that anything we do will threaten Gaia. But if we succeed in altering the environment significantly, as may happen with the atmospheric concentration of carbon dioxide, then a new adaptation may take place. It may not be to our advantage.[33]

Microbiologist Lynn Margulis extended this paradigm to cell development. Evolution of the nuclei in cells was not just survival of the fittest, but also involved cooperation and symbiosis: "Partnerships between cells once foreign and even enemies to each are at the very roots of our being. They are the basis of the continually outward expansion of life on Earth."[34]

Cultural historian and priest Thomas Berry called the task of becoming responsible citizens of our Earth, "the great work."

> Responsible people no longer think of the world simply as a collection of natural resources. We have begun to realize that the Earth is an awesome mystery, ultimately as fragile as we ourselves are fragile. But our responsibility to the Earth is not simply to preserve it, it is to be present to the Earth in its next sequence of transformations.[35]

David C. Korten's *The Great Turning: From Empire to Earth Community* furthered this in discussing the political shifts necessary in moving from a system based on corporate consolidation of power to an earth-based egalitarian community.[36] UC Berkeley Cognitive Science and Linguistics Professor George Lakoff embedded the polarities of conservative and progressive ideologies and our attitudes toward environment and each other in early childhood experiences and neuroscience.[37]

Of course, there are the great environmental writers of the nineteenth and early twentieth centuries—Ralph Waldo Emerson, Henry David Thoreau, and John Muir—whose writings remind us that all could be lost. Muir, known as Father of the National Parks for his activism in getting Yosemite and Sequoia National Parks preserved, wrote volumes of essays that married religious passion with scientific observation. I did not take my sons to church, but from the time they were toddlers, we made a yearly pilgrimage each August to the high country of Yosemite. In the evenings while my sons poked coals in the campfire, I read aloud Muir's essays. Such passion! Such vitality! One of our favorites was his account of climbing a carefully selected Douglas spruce during a December windstorm.

Being accustomed to climb trees in making botanical studies, I experienced no difficulty in reaching the top of this one, and never before did I enjoy so noble an exhilaration of motion. The slender tops fairly flapped and swished in the passionate torrent, bending and swirling backward and forward, round and round, tracing indescribable combinations of vertical and horizontal curves, while I clung with muscles firm braced, like a bobo-link on a reed.... I kept my lofty perch for hours, frequently closing my eyes to enjoy the music by itself, or to feast quietly on the delicious fragrance that was streaming past.[38]

I might add that the reason Donald planted Chardonnay grapes was that the vineyard across the road from us was one of the vineyards that supplied Chateau Montelena with Chardonnay grapes, whose 1973 vintage won the 1976 French blind tasting.[39] The grower, John Muir Hanna, was John Muir's grandson. Muir's great-grandson Bill Hanna and his great-great-grandson Michael John Hanna now farm that ranch.

In 2010, the same year I received the February phone message about the oak savanna, Bill McKibben published *Eaarth: Making a Life on a Tough New Planet*. Our Earth is no longer the Earth we once knew, and now we have to learn to live on a kind of new planet, he explained. The global temperature rise in 2010 was already one-degree Fahrenheit, and weather abnormalities were occurring. "The greatest danger we face, climate change, is no accident," McKibben wrote.

> It's not a function of bad technology, it's a function of a bad business model: of the fact that Exxon Mobil and BP and Peabody Coal are allowed to use the atmosphere, free of charge, as an open sewer for the inevitable waste from their products. They'll fight to the end to defend that business model, for it produces greater profits than any industry has ever known.... to fight back, we need a different currency, our bodies and our spirit and our creativity. That's what a movement looks like.[40]

In this very brief history, I cannot leave out the ecopsychologists who teach that this Great Turning is a psychological and spiritual task as well. Buddhist Joanna Macy emphasizes the importance of experiencing our grief and anger about the changes to our Earth in the transformation of ourselves and our attitudes toward each other and our planet: "The question 'How could the Great Turning happen through me?' invites a different story to flow through us. This type of power happens through our choices, through what we say and do and are."[41]

The phone message of that February 2010 afternoon woke me from my Edenic stupor and moved me toward an activism stoked by a fierce love of Earth and Oak, an activism that has taken center stage.

CHAPTER 7

Letter Writing

EVER SINCE I COULD print, writing has been my way of approaching the world. I was eleven years old when I wrote my first letter to the president of the United States, Dwight D. Eisenhower. Although I do not remember the exact content, I know it involved achieving world peace. Even then, in my belly, I knew this letter was an outlet for the unbearable anxiety that my young self could not articulate about my family's survival. I remember my parent's curiosity when I received a hand-typed envelope addressed to me from the White House, postmarked June 3, 1960, which I still have stowed away in a cigar box. A white embossed card reads,

> I deeply appreciate your support of our country's efforts to bring about an honorable and lasting peace. With faith and confidence, our continued and combined efforts, together with those of our allies, must succeed. Thank you for your thoughtfulness. **DWIGHT D. EISENHOWER**

When questioned about what would have instigated such a letter, I lied, telling my mother I wrote about Eisenhower's playing golf. I was embarrassed by my fear about her survival and wanted to protect her from my worry about the implications of my toddler brother's regular monthly visits to Barnes's Hospital, about the innuendos in what was said and the gaps in what was not said. In answer to my report that Grandma Peabody had said she was better, that the swelling of her ankles had gone down, my mother had offered a disquieting response. "Well, what Grandma thinks is all that matters." Within a month Grandma Peabody died.

When I write this now, I feel the overload. I learned not to rely on anyone because it could be too much for them and they might die. Handling my feelings by myself was a way of protecting my parents, and particularly my mother. This included writing to the president of the United States about a way to achieve world peace!

Do *letters to the editor* really make a difference? I don't know. Maybe sometimes. But writing them brings me into a larger collective conversation, conversations that are also important as we find our way through this extraordinary time in which multinational business interests eclipse those of human rights and the rights of ecological systems, as changes to our climate and Earth accelerate. I include an edited series of letters I wrote, mostly to the local Napa paper, *The Napa Valley Register,* as they chronicle my own maturing as an activist.

LETTER TO THE EDITOR
Napa Valley Register, March 13, 2013

Filmmakers document Napa history, its ancestors

Napa Valley Opera House was well-populated Tuesday evening, Feb. 19, 2013, for the premier showing of two locally produced films: "Awakening Healing Voices of Our Ancestors: A Destiny Reclaimed" and "The Sky Is the Roof."

Filmmaker Beth Nelson, Tewa and Cherokee, and Suscol Council Executive Director Charlie Toledo, Towa, documented history unknown to most of us—that of the demise of the Native American populations of the Napa Valley.

One of the areas most densely populated in North America with 30,000 to 40,000 people, Napa was "a cultivated paradise." With the arrival of General Vallejo in 1833, the native populations of Mayakmah, Mutistul, Mishewal, and Onastis quickly diminished through smallpox and "Indian campaigns," i.e., forced marches and battles.

The first film opens at the pow wow in Yountville, near the Veterans Home, on one of the last Indian war battlegrounds where many Indians were killed. In the background, one hears drumming and singing, watches family groups arriving, dancing, generally enjoying a day in the sun. Attendees are interviewed, and stories of the older times were told. One feels the heartfelt sentiment of celebration of life and family as well as grief for what was lost.

At intermission, Charlie explained that the pow wow will be held on this spot at the Veterans home for a total of 10 years to heal the land and the injury perpetrated there. She also explained that the first pow wow in recent times was held for 10 years on the grounds of the Napa Valley College, upon which the Spanish army had camped before beginning their onslaught war on the native populations. . . .

"The Sky Is the Roof" documented the severity of the water problem and how European invasion into the valley has created an imbalance that will result in a severe water shortage if changes are not made very soon. . . . Charlie's suggestions to the Flood Control Board of using native cottonwood, willow, and other natural flood control plantings were largely ignored.

This brings up the importance of reclaiming what knowledge is still available in these broken lineages of peoples whose ancestors lived here in balance with these forests, meadows, and rivers.

I am haunted by the clips of a mallard duck swimming alongside an orange plastic construction fence in the section of the river that we now call Oxbow, one of the most sacred areas to native peoples in the valley. The duck seems confused as it swims along the plastic fence, perhaps looking for a hole to climb onto land.

PATRICIA DAMERY
NAPA

CHAPTER 8

The History of Our Garden

Every man should have his own plot of land so that the instincts can come to life again.

C.G. Jung, quoted in: *The Earth Has a Soul*[42]

FOR MANY OF US on the West Coast, the year 1993 felt like our country was politically getting back on track. In Moscow, George H. W. Bush and Boris Yeltsin signed the second Strategic Arms Reduction Treaty in early January, followed by the inauguration of Bill Clinton as forty-second president of the United States, an election that Donald and I both celebrated. But although we were not really talking much about climate change in those days, the Great Blizzard of 1993 hit the Eastern United States in March, bringing record snowfall from Canada to Cuba, and over the next months, the Missouri and Mississippi Rivers flooded large portions of the Midwest. In the summer of 1993, the Missouri ripped out two-thirds of the graves in the small town of Hardin, Missouri, sending nine hundred caskets and burial vaults of generations of town residents down the river toward St. Louis.

That year, 1993, also brought the flowering of Donald's and my love, and that spring, we decided to plant the yard south of his 160-year-old farmhouse, built by one of the original white settlers in the Napa Valley, with a vegetable garden. The old house is on the east end of the long narrow parcel that extends a mile up the ridge. Between the old house and the creek that traces the northern boundary of the ranch grew the largest valley oak I had ever seen. In fact, like the oak outside my first-grade classroom, this was my first intimate experience with a valley oak. Its breadth was so great that it took four of us holding hands to encircle its trunk. Within its thick branches, ring-necked doves built nests and squirrels preformed their acrobatics. An enormous wild honeybee colony lived within it, sending off swarms two or three times each spring. The tree was so large that Donald would say no one ever noticed it. However, its presence made clear that the garden would need to be south of the tree's range of shade, which was a good deal of the yard.

I was surprised to find myself excited when we plowed the deep clay-loam soil across the sunny side of the house. Gardens are work, and I had plenty to do without a garden too! Although a generation apart, Donald and I both grew up on small farms in Illinois. Donald's family was German; mine, Irish and English. The Irish were more lackadaisical in their habits; the Germans, more structured and neater. Nevertheless, we all knew the importance of growing food, an art lost to most of the people I know today. When I was growing up, almost all families had gardens, perhaps a holdover from the Victory Gardens of the Second World War. My mother and we kids planted our garden on a long Saturday in late April or early May after my father had plowed and disked the soil. My mother used

California buttercup

a hoe spade to make inch-deep V-shaped trenches in which we kids placed onion sets 4 inches apart. In the next rows, we planted peas and beans, then tiny lettuce and carrot seeds. Later, when all danger of frost was past, we spent another Saturday transplanting tomato, pepper, and cabbage starts, seeded several rows of sweet corn and, always, a row of red, gold, and orange zinnias and purple coneflowers for my mother's vases. Beginning in June, we picked bushels of peas; then, into July, beans, tomatoes, and corn. My mother, my two sisters, one or both of my grandmothers, and I would clean and prepare the vegetables for freezing or canning.

Our first summer, Donald and I planted twelve hills of zucchini and twelve tomato plants. We planted that many because tomatoes came in six-packs, and the starts were small. We also naively figured we might as well plant all the zucchini seeds rather than let them go to waste. Ah, the fate of most seeds, to not sprout! The resistance to that fate is the driving force of our world!

We were thrilled when the first zucchini reached five inches. We ate it as if it were the rarest of vegetables, well aware that every molecule in it came from the air and the soil in the alchemical laboratory of our yard. We savored its stored sunlight. I bought saltines and eggs, and we were thrilled to have fried golden blossoms, like my mother served when the pumpkins were blooming—and then, two weeks later, we were eating zucchini every meal. In another couple of weeks two-foot wonders lay like fat armadillos up and down the length of the garden.

However, we didn't have to worry too long about excess vegetables; the gophers soon discovered what we were up to. We would be eating a sautéed dish of zucchini on our porch, basking in the delight of our garden, when an entire bean plant would disappear underground, leaving only a hole the size of a golf ball. We consoled ourselves with the thought that we had enough to share. But gophers do not share. The yard was soon barren earth, riddled with telltale holes. The next year we planted deer-resistant, drought-tolerant landscaping that gophers don't like.

When we built our house up on the ridge, we thought of planting a vegetable garden again, but this time in the form of a potager. In a potager, you plant a small plot outside the kitchen door so you have just enough to keep you going on vegetables year-round, which is possible in our Mediterranean climate. In the winter that means a lot of greens and in the summer, yellows and reds, all fresh, all organic.

To plan for gophers, we dug a two-foot trench around the square of the garden and buried gopher wire. The path in the garden is that of a labyrinth. You enter through a gate of waist-high rue with its stringent musky scent. Here you begin a long journey that takes you through many twists and turns. After the rue, you brush foxglove and hummingbird sage, sticky white sage and yarrow, before proceeding past tomatoes and peppers to (turning the corner) milkweed and scarlet sage, delicate valerian and chamomile. The path then passes a bed of potatoes (turning the corner again) before entering a transitional forest of prickly purple verbena, which chooses its own space in the garden each year. Evening primrose gifted to us by a native plant guy also makes this choice, although I definitely have to pull a significant number of starts as this native behaves like an invasive. The onions and leeks pick their location as well. In short, I allow the garden to reseed itself. I have found that the best policy is to allow whatever chooses to grow, to choose where to grow as well.

From time-to-time Donald complains about the number of flowers and comments that this does not look like his German grandmother's garden. He explains that she did not grow flowers at all and that she used a board to draw out the line of the row in which she planted seed. He offers to do this with me in our garden. I refuse. Our garden is a community, I remind him, one that is always renewing itself.

I learned this from my grandmother, Gusta Louise Pope Damery. Petunias naturalized in her main vegetable garden (she had three), offering their strong pungent scent when you accidentally bruised the fragile sticky blossoms while picking peas or weeding beans. My sister and I were allowed to pick bouquets of volunteer bluebells in her shade garden behind the volunteer white peach tree and under the silver maple each spring, where we also hunted asparagus, a delicacy before anything else was producing. The serpent-headed stalks pushed up between vines and violets and were some work to locate. Our grandmother instructed us to never pick the tall airy stalks, so the asparagus could reseed. In these ways, she initiated me into a tangled, imaginative way to garden.

Although I understand this method is not for everyone, gardening in this way has trained me in learning to balance a receptive attitude of what the land wants (and what wants to grow here) with my more assertive intention of what I want (more veggies and fewer rodents, so-called weeds, and raiding birds). It is truly a laboratory for me to learn to listen to soils and water, sunlight and seasons. There we get the nourishment we need.

Planners, please preserve watersheds

A letter to the County planning commissioners: My husband, Donald Harms, and I live on Dry Creek Road. We own a certified biodynamic organic ranch, growing grapes, lavender and other aromatics, and some fruit. Most of our ranch is forested and rugged.

We share a property line with our neighbors, which has a tree easement protecting a portion of one of the few remaining oak savannas in our Napa Valley. This consists not only of huge old Valley Oaks but native grasses and plants and many animals. To them, this looks like a good place for vines; to us, we see a vital part of an ecology that helps sustain a healthy watershed.

There are so many issues to address, and I will continue to be in contact with you and the Board of Supervisors. But today, I want to voice my sincere wish that as we all move forward in 2015, that our county government in its many facets will work with citizen groups, several that have worked long and hard, some that are just now forming, to develop guidelines that protect the agricultural preserve but also the watersheds.

Watersheds are like mothers. When mothers are healthy and functioning properly, the children flourish. The mother for the most part is invisible, taken for granted. That was always my wish as a mother: that my sons could take me for granted! But when the mother is sick or depleted, she's noticed. The children suffer.

In the case of watersheds, if we ignore the importance of our watersheds, if we don't maintain the conditions that provide healthy watersheds, and restore those that have been depleted, our water is at risk. Water is our lifeblood. It is what unites us. It is the commons, belonging to no one person, but to all of us.

In my husband's and my own situation, if we look at that oak savanna and see open space for vines . . . if the water is sucked up for new vines and expansion of a winery, we are depleting an important part of a watershed. And believe me, in this drought, our trees are suffering. Way too many are dying or are sick, stressed by lack of water.

Oak savannas and woodlands and all the plants and animals that are part of those communities are a vital part of our watersheds. The Native Americans maintained these hillsides for centuries, but a lot of that knowledge has been lost with them. These watersheds need study and protection and, yes, in many cases, restoration, certainly not further degradation and exploitation for farming. In an Ag Preserve and Ag Watershed, some things should be protected, and if they are not, we will all suffer the consequences. Water unites us; water reminds us that we are of one piece.

PATRICIA DAMERY
NAPA

Steep Madrone and Oak Forest

Animal Trails

rock Pile

Mysterious Wild Area

Wild Grapevine

Seasonal Creek

Pioneer Farm House

Bog Candles

Coastal Oak That Saved Casey's Life

Monterey Pine

Property Line

Driveway

Driveway

Piece of blue Tarp From Tornado

Pioneer Cemetery

Old Roadbed This way

Steep Oak Savannah

Fallen Cedar of Lebanon

Old Stock pond

Our Home

Vines

Our Home Land Map

my Studio

Wild Turkey Hangout

Crate

"Goodwill" Gate

N

W   E

S

Old Ceremonial Grounds

Dense UnKept Forest

Shared Irrigation Pond

Road

The storied map of our ranch, an enclosed garden, of sorts

CHAPTER 9

The Enclosed Garden

THIS INCREASINGLY CONSCIOUS COMMUNION with the Holy Ghost—the life force—was carried to another level in late 1999 when Donald and I were confronted with the impending loss of a grape crop. Several acres of pinot noir grapes were not ripening in our vineyard on Mt. Veeder, and the winemaker informed us that he would not be taking them that year, which represented a substantial financial loss. A friend told me he knew of a man who could help us ripen the grapes, and at this point, we were open to anything. In the space of two weeks and ten biodynamic sprays, this man, whom I have called B.B. (Bruja Bill), ripened the grapes in what would have taken six weeks. The crop was saved. This is how and why we learned the discipline of biodynamic farming.

Biodynamics is rooted in the philosophy and approach of Wolfgang von Goethe and Rudolf Steiner after him. The living spirits of the plant, animal, and land are addressed through work with various "preparations" made from animal and plant material in ways

"In a paradise garden blooms the rose within the Gril, an image of Eden restored within the human soul." (Printer's mark, 1655, Europe. Courtesy of ARAS)

that enhance the life force, the subtle energy, of the substance. Of course, this also works on the farmer or, as Steiner said, the quintessential—consciousness. biodynamics, practiced correctly, brings consciousness to the farmer and to the land.

Donald stirring biodynamic preparation 501, horned silica, as the sun rises.
The preparation is sprayed above foliage to bring in solar forces.

In biodynamics, the whole farm is viewed as a living organism. As Demeter-certified farmers, we are mandated to develop the individuality of our farm or ranch, while at the same time remembering our place in the local ecosystem, an embodied sense of Mother Earth. In this way, in my heart, our ranch became what Jung has described as the *hortus conclusus*, the enclosed garden.

The enclosed garden was depicted in medieval paintings and tapestries as the Virgin Mary sitting, sometimes with her baby, almost always with other women, in a courtyard. Sometimes a white fountain is in the center. Often there is a unicorn, symbolic of that tamed-by-love rhinoceros—representing, as Jung wrote, the wrathful God of the Old Testament. "Even as late as the seventeen century the learned Jesuit, Nicolas Caussin, declared that the unicorn was a fitting symbol for the God of the Old Testament, because in his wrath he reduced the world to confusion like an angry rhinoceros (unicorn), until, overcome by the love of a pure virgin, he was changed in her lap into a God of Love."[43] Jung called this transformational space a feminine temenos in which the babe of the new consciousness is born, a consciousness of the "spiritualized earth"[44]—of the light of nature[45] that unites us all in matter.

The process of biodynamics, which I have written about extensively in other places,[46] weds one energetically to the land and the plants that you are cultivating. It develops awareness of the flow and transformation of energy within living systems. B.B., the consultant Donald and I hired to teach us biodynamics, spent over a year with us, showing us the use of the applications and reading Rudolf Steiner's *Agriculture*. He explained the very foreign, esoteric principles and orientation of biodynamic farming; it has taken me years to understand some of Steiner's enigmatic philosophy. Take this statement:

> There is a big difference between nitrogen and nitrogen, between dead nitrogen that is found in the air we breathe, and another kind of nitrogen. I am sure you wouldn't deny that there is a difference between a human corpse and a person who is alive and walking around. One of them is dead and the other is alive and ensouled. The same applies to nitrogen and other substances.[47]

Steiner says that if nitrogen was alive in the air we breathe, we would always be unconscious. "But the nitrogen in the soil, the nitrogen which must enter the soil with the manure, must be formed under the influence of the entire heavens; this nitrogen must be alive."[48]

Biodynamic farming necessitates relating to energy in ourselves and in the universe, and one way we do this is in the stirring and application of the preparations. When, as Rudolf Steiner directed, we stir the preparations into "sun-soaked water for a full German hour," we include as many of us as possible who live and/or work on the ranch. These days Wesley and Sabien join in, standing on concrete blocks around the sixty-gallon oak barrel, the stirring tripod set over it. *Start at the far reaches of the barrel in circular strokes, get it going fast, I direct them, and then move toward the center.* In this way, my grandsons learn to make the vortex that swirls to the bottom of the barrel. Then we reverse direction. In stirring this way, we throw the mixture into chaos, that state in which Steiner says we are most open to the divine. As we stir, we imagine everything and everyone on the ranch thriving.

Then we spray. For earth preparations, we spray on the ground in the late afternoon; for solar preparations, into the air above the plants before noon. In these ways, we bring the balance of wholeness to our ranch and to ourselves. When we first started practicing biodynamic agriculture, our grape harvest doubled, bringing it up to where it should have been all along. The capacity of the soil to hold water increased dramatically. Until we leased our vineyard this last year, we were almost able to dry farm.

It is truly a paradigm shift for many of us. But Steiner also warned that once we relate to land in this way, once we work with the nature spirit energies, it is a great betrayal to return to old extractive farming methods that deal only with the "corpse" of a plant or the soil, not the living substance.

This is all important in understanding what the phone call announcing the arrival of the new neighbors meant to me. It provides the foundation for my activism. Even that February day I knew what this experience of relating to the divinity of the ranch and the savanna would mean. Perhaps that scared me more than the specter of death.

One morning shortly after we moved into our new home on the ridge, I was showering and looked out our bathroom window onto the oak savanna just south of our home to see a coyote watching me from 10 feet away. He just sat there. I heard later that coyotes are shy and curious. Often their acts of witness are misinterpreted as impending aggression. That morning I am sure the coyote wondered, *What on earth?* We had, after all, moved into territory that had been his for millennia.

Coyote is such a trickster! In Native American mythology, he creates the world through his conjuring, including stealing the sun and moon. You never know which side he is on. Navajo myth says he was there at the beginning with First Man and First Woman. He brought life-giving fire to humans, but he also brought death. Without death, this myth says, there would be too many humans, no room for corn.[49] Coyote plays with mortality, bringing the polarities that afford creation: good and evil, light and dark, life and death. His enigmatic gaze that morning sent shivers of recognition up my spine. Even in the fullness of the sun on the savanna as I showered in our just-built home, I knew there might well come a day when I would be alone on the mountain, or an afternoon when a fire would take the ravine—or now, after that February phone message, a day the sacred oak savanna would be clear-cut for "a great cab." I won't keep listing these, not because I deny they may happen; I am well aware, Coyote, these possibilities are there in the shadows of potentiality. It is just that too often I have avoided the fullness of the present in my fear of its loss.

The Temptation of Adam and Eve

(After Jean d'Ypres (French, ca. 1480-1510). *Le Premier Volume de la bible en francoiz historice ce nouvelle-ment imprimée*, ca. 1501. [Harris Brisbane Dick Fund. 1924 [24.16.1]. The Metrpolitan Museum of Art, New York, NY, U.S.A. Image copyright The Metropolitan Museum of Art. Image source: Art Resource, NY.)

CHAPTER 10

Rattlesnake

BEFORE THE LAND ALONG our far northwestern boundary was permitted for vineyard estates and a winery, before the meadow and forest were cleared for the development, we had not seen a rattlesnake on our property. An old-timer just to the south and down the hill from us said that he had known of only one rattlesnake sighted within a mile radius of us in the last one hundred years.

I knew the meadow that stretched north along the ridge from the time our first goats ran away, goats we had acquired from a man near Donald's architectural office. Like coyotes, these goats were shy of humans and required some effort to catch, but we were promised that if we got collars and leashes, they would be following us around like dogs within the week. The goats had other ideas, however. Shortly after arriving at our ranch, Hornsby knocked down Casey, eleven at the time, and ran over his head, leaving a hoof print on his eye. Both goats got loose and crawled under our house, and Donald had to pull their fat black bodies out by their short hind legs. Their curved horns hooked and pulled out the house wiring, which was stapled underneath the flooring. This was the first time I ever saw Donald really angry.

But for reasons I still cannot articulate, I loved these goats. I worked to befriend the little devils, even when Tarquin showed no remorse when he missed the dog and butted me instead. Being on the same end of the trickster spectrum as coyote, neither goat had inclination for domestication. In bringing these horned pygmies into our hearts, we were opening ourselves to the unexpected joys and mishaps of that which cannot be tamed.

Then one afternoon I returned home to find both goats gone. Unbelievably bereft, I looked everywhere. I contacted our neighbor Clarence, who owned the land along the northwestern ridge, and he drove me over its vast reaches in his pickup. Although I didn't find the goats, I did see a beautiful, pristine piece of property, even though cattle had been run on it for years. We never did find Hornsby and Tarquin.

Clarence died a few years later and his children inherited his land. Two of them sold their part to a man who foresaw an opportunity for vineyard estates and a winery. Forget that it stressed the neighbors' water, particularly the spring-water source of one of Clarence's daughters, which totally dried up. After all, to quote a Napa County Supervisor, *Napa is changing. Progress should not be stopped.* The implication: progress is inevitable and to consider stopping it is delusion.

Once I heard Greg Sarris, Chief of the Graton Pueblo, say that "wild" is what happened when white man arrived. Before then, as Charlie Toledo told me, the West was a carefully tended landscape so different from anything Western Europeans knew, that the invaders had no idea what they were seeing. In the case of the far western boundary of our ranch, "white man" arrived in the incarnation of a wealthy, enterprising owner. And the same thing was happening with increasing frequency all over the county. The incursion of buyers were not small winemakers or farmers, but individuals and corporations as large as IBM who could afford the escalating price of Napa County land. The issue of balance was not an issue. The buyers ignored the facts on and in the ground: that hillside water is precious and scarce; that hillside aquifers are unique and unpredictable and often do not replenish in winter rains; that the oak woodlands and forests, home to robust populations of native species, are essential to replenish the aquifers. They paid no attention to the kinds of agreements that farmers make with each other so we all can live together, agreements that also protect the integrity of the land—agreements made about sharing water and driveways and infused with neighborly trust. In the case of this project on the westernmost boundary of our ranch, when earth movement began, a rattlesnake den was disturbed and all hell broke loose. With the arrival of this *white man,* our ranch became *wild* with venomous reptiles.

The first rattlesnake was found on the path between our home and Donald's Jeep. Donald and Casey killed it, Casey dangerously holding down the fighting snake with a hoe while Donald hacked at it with a machete. It was about three inches thick. We were sickened by this killing but frightened by the snake's proximity to our home.

The second appeared right after my oldest son Jesse's wedding, which, with our neighbor William's permission, was held in the tree circle in the savanna. My sisters' and brother's families were enjoying a leisurely meal the day after on the outside patio by the dining room. We were in the luxuriousness of a long supper conversation when an alarming rattle shook the air.

Why is it we instinctively know what that sound is? Even the goats jump twenty feet when they hear it. This particular evening a rattlesnake was hunting its dinner hiding in a pile of rocks that separated the barbecue area from the savanna, only three feet from our table! Chairs fell backward. The tenor of the evening changed to panic. I am ashamed to say, again, we killed the snake. We couldn't let it continue to hunt in the rock pile by our barbecue area.

But the most shocking snake appearance was the day that I was talking on the phone to my friend Jimalee as I was waiting for the organic certifier to arrive for the annual review of our ranch. The day was extremely hot, the thermometer reaching over 100°F. Fortunately,

I had all the French doors closed, trying to keep our home in the 70°F range. To my disbelief, at the very moment I saw the certifier walking up the gravel path to our west door, I witnessed the largest rattlesnake I had ever seen—as thick as my forearm and long as I am tall—crawling up the glass of our door, trying to escape the heat of the western afternoon sun.

"A rattlesnake!" I shrieked. I dropped the phone and rushed to try to detour the certifier, who was heading for the door. The snake slid along the south side of the house, carving a trough that remained for some time, daily reminding us of the snake's short-lived visit. With the certifier safely ensconced into the house, I called Donald and Ramon, our vineyard worker at the time, who were at the other end of the ranch. When Ramon walked around the side of the house, the snake leaped from behind a flowerpot, clubbing his thigh with its heavy body but not biting. Again, we regretfully killed this giant but not before it fought for its life. So traumatized by the brutal ending of the snake, the organic certifier spent the night. Charlie Toledo shamed me again for this killing. I ask myself: what's the alternative? It is an important question to contemplate, and there is no simple answer. Certainly, the arrival of the Serpent in rattlesnake guise was announcing my own eviction from a sense of the benign, safe abundance of Eden, to which I return.

LETTER TO THE EDITOR

Napa Valley Register, November 25, 2014

Protect our watersheds from wanton development

A quote arrived in my email box this week, and it could not be at a more appropriate time: "Snowflakes, leaves, humans, plants, raindrops, stars, molecules, microscopic entities all come in communities. The singular cannot in reality exist" (Paula Gunn Allen).

Saturday morning, my husband and I spent three-and-a-half hours at a Napa County Board of Supervisors', hearing on water rights. A new winery and vineyard next to our property had been permitted and now their neighbor's residential natural springs have gone dry, purportedly for the first time in the approximately 170 years the family has lived on the property. They were appealing the permitting of the winery's vineyard operations.[50]

My husband and I knew the previous owner.[51] He did not plant vineyards but ran cattle. He had an old rancher attitude, keeping his meadows free of encroaching forest by girding oaks, a practice of killing them by cutting completely around the trunk of the tree into its growing cambium layer, that, frankly, horrified me. But he was generous with his time. Once, he drove me all over his meadows in his pickup truck when I lost two goats.

When the previous owner died some years ago, the land was divided, and some family members sold their shares to people who wanted to build vineyards as well as an event winery. Here is where the trouble began, at least the trouble that brought them to the Board of Supervisors' hearing. Due to over-pumping of wells and springs and drought, two of three springs have gone dry and the third has toxic levels of boron and arsenic.

The family still living on their piece of the oak woodland property is often without water, and the winery wants to expand. Planning gave them a permit to do so. However, the State of California puts domestic use above that for irrigation. California Water Code Section 106 states: "It is hereby declared to be the established policy of this State that the use of water for domestic purposes is the highest use of water and that the next highest use is for irrigation."

Although the Board of Supervisors did not see their way to limiting the winery's permit, it did put into place a system of independent annual monitoring to the Planning Department of the vineyard's and winery's water usage as well as of neighbors' water supplies, by a county-appointed independent hydrologist. Should their water usage exceed the estimates and neighbors suffer, the winery/vineyard will have to curtail some of its scope.

But a much more serious issue was addressed by Tony Climons, who had helped create the General Plan for Napa County forty years ago: the incursion of vineyards and wineries into the mountain forests—and watersheds. If we degrade our watersheds, we degrade our water supplies, our agriculture, and our environment.

Citizen groups are gaining momentum in bringing this issue to the foreground. We farmers need to think carefully about the water on our farms and ranches, doing everything we can do to maintain the watersheds that connect us all. "The singular cannot in reality exist."[52]

PATRICIA DAMERY
NAPA

CHAPTER 11

Paradise, the Serpent, and Lilith

MOST ACCOUNTS OF THE Garden of Eden creation story leave out the details about the Serpent.

The Old Testament tells how the Serpent tempted Eve to eat the fruit from the forbidden tree, The Tree of the Knowledge of Good and Evil. The kind of fruit varies in the different versions. Some say an apple; some, a pomegranate; some say it was a grape that the Serpent offered. You know the story: The Serpent appears, tells Eve it is okay to eat the forbidden fruit; she'll just become wiser, like a god. Eve succumbs and then feeds the fruit to Adam. God finds out and throws them both out of paradise, cursing Adam to labor for his living and Eve to labor in childbirth. The Serpent is relegated to crawling on its belly. Many medieval paintings depict the Serpent with a woman's head.

Jewish folklore from the medieval period elaborates. The tempting Serpent is named Lilith, who is said to be Adam's first wife. Adam cohabited with her until he was given a soul, the in-between of spirit and matter that we incarnate to develop. At that point, it is said that Lilith *flew off*. In this story, she is always out there, ready to cause trouble with her anger and her sexuality.

But Lilith is also described as the undifferentiated "soul of all the beasts of the field and 'every living creature that creepth.'"[53] As such, she can talk with plants and animals. Being the instinctual level of our being, she refuses to be suppressed. When we ignore this level, we pay a high price in the health of our bodies and of our planet.

I have learned a great deal about Lilith from my goats. In the last few years, after I found myself continually captivated by photos of Swiss alpine goats, we acquired three with their long crescent horns. I was drawn to their stunning beauty and power, perhaps a little naively so, I might add. Each day I walk with them, as many as nine of them, as few as four, and they have taught me the ways of the land. But they are dangerous. To walk with them, you need to develop mindfulness, a present-in-the-moment quality, paying attention to where you are, where they are, what else might be present. Twice I have been flattened

The Fall of Man

The Fall of Man. The tempting serpent is Lilith, who is said to be Adam's first wife. She is also described as the "soul of all the beasts of the field and every living creature that creepth."

(Limbourg Brothers [Herman, Pol, Jean] [fl.1399–1416 CE]. Expulsion of Adam and Eve from Paradise. Illuminated manuscript page from the Très Riches Heures du Duc de Berry. 1416. 29 × 21 cm. Ms. 65, fol. 25 verso. Photo: René-Gabriel Ojéda. © RMN-Grand Palais / Art Resource, NY) by a 150-pound goat joyfully gambling down a narrow trail because I was lost in thought. It is like a Zen master's whack.

The herd has needs, and it is your responsibility to be sensitive to those needs: the need to stay together, to be protected from predators, to find food, and last, but certainly not least, to have fun. Trying to dominate a goat is like trying to dominate Lilith—deep Nature! The goats will fight you and figure out how to win. It is where they get their bad name—like Lilith! *She who refuses to be subordinated!* I think of the Earth today—and climate change. We will not subordinate Nature in her Lilith aspect. No, if we continue to try, she with her windy tresses and fiery breath, will seek revenge.

CHAPTER 12

More Intrusions into Paradise

ABOUT THE SAME TIME we were inundated with the rattlesnakes, I discovered a 4-foot pyramid-shaped pile of sticks and branches in the understory of a canopy of coastal live oak near the ridge. I had never seen anything like it. Obviously, something had built this structure, although there was no indication to my uneducated eye as to what. Every day I passed the pyramid of sticks as I walked the trail, tracing the line where forest met the meadow and oak savanna. Each time I examined the area around the structure. Sometimes it appeared a coyote or some other animal had been digging into the side, but the identity of the animal creating this structure remained a mystery to me—until one day Jimalee's biologist daughter, Sarah, who specializes in oak woodlands, identified it: this was a wood-rat structure, the home of what is more commonly known as *pack rats*.

I was fascinated and thought it a rare find until I discovered six such structures under the blackberry bushes along our driveway. The structures were about twenty feet apart, and again, there was no evidence of the rats, at least not in daylight hours when I could actually see them. Over time, I learned these structures can be up to eighty years old.

My most shocking encounter happened much later. I was driving my new Prius to San Francisco when several warning lights came on all at once. I pulled to the side and checked the owner's manual, which said to get to the nearest dealer as soon as possible. I was flabbergasted to learn that the wiring had been chewed to the tune of $12,000.

Rodents love the Prius's wiring. We have no garage, and I wasn't going to get rid of my car. I was going to have to learn to live with this predator of electrical wiring. My first efforts involved keeping the hood open so the warm engine did not provide a haven for a cold rat. One winter evening after forgetting to do so, I rushed out, lifted the hood, only to discover a wood rat sitting on the motor rubbing her paws together to warm up! Yes, I admit that I reluctantly set traps under the car and in it as well as on the motor and that I caught several rats. I still carry electric traps on the floor of the car. Occasionally one dies in the dashboard. Wesley and Sabien call my car the P-U-Prius.

A friend told me that Irish Spring soap repels rodents. The wood rats snacked on it. The soap had gnaw-marks all around the edges, and green soap crumbs were scattered all over the floor mats. The smell of the soap almost fumigated *me*. I sprayed pepper spray under the car, under the hood, and even on the floor mats (don't try the latter), and this worked some.

But I also began to find odd objects in my car: a black plastic tube with loops along the side that had no apparent function, feathers, pens that were not mine. One day I opened the glove compartment to find the odd plastic tube (yes, I had not thrown it out) and its loops were woven with a feather. Later I learned these wood rats—pack rats!—share a human desire to decorate their nests. Was my car now synonymous to them with their nest?

I continue to suffer higher car-maintenance bills due to having the air filter changed frequently and regular rodent cleaning of the engine ($300, if no damage). But I also feel better knowing that wood rats are a keystone species. Their presence reflects a healthy ecosystem. They are a food source for a variety of animals, including barn owls and great horned owls, hawks, coyotes, bobcats, mountain lions, gopher snakes, and rattlesnakes. They are nocturnal, so we seldom see them, as they sleep about twenty hours a day. But it is said that if at night you shine a light into the canopy of an oak or madrone over their nests, you will see the shining red eyes of pack rats harvesting.

Such intrusions are corrective. Who else is living here and how do we accommodate them if not become good neighbors? We are part of a web of life. Our Western European attitude of controlling the natural world to extract the most profit puts us on a collision course with nature. As Robinson Jeffers laments in his poem "Science," "Like a maniac with self love and inward conflicts . . . / Now he's bred knives on nature turns them also inward: they have thirsty points though."[54]

Thinking we are above nature and then not learning her ways is where we get into trouble. Take coyotes. People fear coyotes. Ranchers misguidedly kill coyotes, thinking they are a threat to cattle. But a single coyote will feast on 1800 rodents a year—including pack rats. Coyotes live in family packs in which only the alpha male and female breed. You want a stable coyote pack on your ranch. Yes, coyotes are curious and will watch you from afar. Studies show they seldom hurt humans or eat pets or kill larger game.[55] Only when the pack is destabilized by the death of an alpha do the others seek new territory and get into killing larger game. In getting to know coyotes' habits, we can learn to live in a more balanced way with their presence. Coyotes are an important part of many ecosystems and certainly ours in the Napa Valley.

In biodynamic agriculture, we are mandated to keep at least 10 percent of our ranch wild. This is how we preserve "harmony between the made and the given worlds."[56] The wild lands provide habitat for native pollinators, birds, and other animals, and allow for a natural biodiversity. All of this is part of a natural law; the more complex an ecosystem, the healthier it is. The more life there is, the more life that can be supported. Recent practices of monocropping and intensive livestock management have simplified ecosystems, often to the point of sterilization.

And then there's fire. One of the most dangerous ways of managing our environment in the West has been to exclude fire, something Donald and I are learning the hard way. Our first up close and personal experience began with a yurt.

In 2008 my oldest son, Jesse, and his wife, Lisa, built a yurt from a kit on our property during a period in which they were deciding if they would take over the farming of the ranch. They picked up the kit from a manufacturer in Oregon in late winter on their way back from living on Lopez Island, pulling its many pieces by a trailer down Interstate 5 to our ranch. We all watched as they assembled the kit over the next few days: first building the round wooden platform, then stretching the lattice wood around the perimeter and adding the domed roof. This was all covered by thick tarp material. We loved the yurt. It allowed an intimacy with the elements in its simplicity and beauty: the crickets at night, the winds, the beauty of wood within and the oak woodlands without. But it had its faults: the tarp hardly insulated! At night, the yurt was freezing, and twelve hours later it was too hot to occupy. Over these months it also became clear Jesse and Lisa would neither be living in the yurt, nor taking over the farming. They moved into town, and we used the yurt for meetings and as a kind of guest room.

In the spring of 2009 Donald and I traveled to North Carolina to celebrate his brother Richard's eightieth birthday. We were sipping martinis in Richard's living room. I remember Richard standing by the fireplace, tall, tanned, and smiling, when I noticed the red message light on my cellphone. Faintly disturbed, as in those days almost no one had my cellphone number, I slipped away and punched in my code.

There was not one message, but several. First the panicked voice of Ramon who was managing everything in our absence. "There is a fire!" he exclaimed and hung up. Then there was a second call and a third, each more panicked and beseeching. By the time I got to the message from Jesse, I too was in a panic. Jesse was evidently just walking up the path to the yurt site as he left his message—"Mom, there has been a fire . . . it burned the yurt . . . Oh no, it's burned all the way to the house!"—and hung up.

I returned to the festive gathering and blurted out, "There was a fire, and it has burned all the way to the house!"

The room fell silent. "Call Jesse." Donald had assumed his take-charge mode. I dialed Jesse's cell number, was relieved when he answered and learned the fire was out. He said not much had been damaged, although it looked bad. Trees scorched, grass blackened everywhere, piles of brush burned to ash, all disturbingly close our home.

The yurt was gone. Sometime earlier Jesse had been refinishing the wooden deck outside the entrance and had left an oily rag on the deck while he took a lunch break in town. The rag spontaneously combusted. When he returned to apply the second coat, he discovered firetrucks choking the driveway and men rolling up hoses. Two helicopters had delivered thirty firefighters into the meadow who hurriedly dug a firebreak surrounding the consuming grassfire. Part of the garden fence was melted, some of the lavender had burned, but the house, the goat barn, and the goats were okay, largely due to Ramon's quick action to water down the ground.

This was our first personal experience with fire in California. Its exclusion has created an extremely dangerous situation. Not only has the underbrush built up when smaller fires have not been allowed to burn, so fires are hotter and more destructive, but also diseased debris, including acorns, have accumulated. As a result, an increasing number of our trees are infected with oak root, crown rot, and, since the mid-1990s, Sudden Oak Death fungal infections.

The fire burned clean the grass but did very little damage to the oak trees

On the other hand, we discovered that our cleared one hundred-foot defensible space around the house gave firefighters the space to defend it. Although the leaves on the oaks were browned by the flames, the trees pushed new leaves and survived. We spent a summer with a scorched earth look around the house, but in the fall, when the first two inches of rains came, the savanna was once again the color of a fairy's coat. We also learned, if we are going to live in balance with our fire-dependent environment, we'd better forgo light-weight wooden yurts. Yurts are structures for the desert conditions of the Steppes, not forest and oak woodlands. Learning to live with all our relations is at once a meditation and a practical necessity.

Consider "direct marketing" in more substantive ways.

When did agriculture become so entangled with tourism? This question is foundational in the land-use issues that are spreading as fast as wildfire in Napa, Sonoma, Mendocino, and Lake counties.

In Napa County, after 2010 and the Winery Definition Ordinance, direct marketing has officially become "an agricultural activity." Now tasting rooms, food pairings, and commercial kitchens, events with hundreds of visitors, all are supported in the lands protected under the Ag Preserve and Ag Watershed zoning ordinances of 1968. We are left with the unintended consequences of impingement on the environment, increased traffic on roads not meant for this level of service, decreased air quality, and the weakening of the fabric of our community.

But long before 2010, agriculture was finding ways to get people onto farms and buying product, all a subset of what is also called *ecotourism.*

My husband, Donald, and I are personally involved with this. Our aromatics and lavender are estate-grown and -distilled. Early on, we began the ritual of an annual open house to introduce people to our products as well as to educate about the way we practice biodynamic agriculture.

We held the open house in mid-June when the lavender was in full bloom. At first, the open house was lightly attended, but after a couple of years and several articles in the local paper, magazines, and a notice in *The New York Times,* we suddenly had more people than we could possibly handle. Donald spent all day helping people park, trying to keep them off the road and its dangerous curve. Judith Larner spoke on the native plants of our area of the ranch; Charlie Toledo spoke on First People's care of the land before white people arrived; and Ami Mautner of Napa Valley Apothecary spoke on how to make cosmetics from lavender. We gave tours on how we farm biodynamically, and we sold products. People were hungry for a less glitzy experience than that of the large wineries. (This was definitely less glitzy! People had to walk a quarter mile up a dusty, rutty vineyard road to get to the site beside our main lavender field and use a porta potty.) I hope it also stimulated an awareness of the earth under their own home.

But at some point, a tipping point happened; the tourism element was like a tidal wave. More and more were not local people, but tourists in search of an "authentic experience." Suddenly our ranch and our home were viewed as a public place—also an unintended consequence. People still show up unannounced most summer weekends, still walk the quarter mile past the "Do not enter sign, we are not open." We find them in the lavender, photographing. When we ask them to leave, say we are not open to visitors, they take their time. One year a Chinese website posted in Chinese that we were open all day every day, which caused havoc for us.

Yes, visitation increases sales. It did for us. But visitation also severely impacts the neighborhood with traffic and noise. Although our neighbors tolerated this one-day annual event, I am fairly certain that if we did it regularly and more often, they would complain. As we get more and more tourists, and more and more wineries and small farms direct marketing their products through events (event centers) and tasting rooms, traffic and noise become real problems for those of us living in Ag-zoned and residential lands.

Agriculture is about a relationship with the earth. Yes, the farmer—or grower—or distiller—or winemaker—needs to make a profit, but should that profit be on the back of the neighbors, of nature, of the social fabric in which a community evolves into a tourist economy?

I believe there can be balance. What if we had a system like Farm Trails (Wine Trails?) with designated times in the year when small wineries/farms tucked into the Ag Preserve and Ag Watershed zones are open for visitation? Many counties support such direct marketing of farm produce and value-added products, customers being given a map marked with participating farms that are selling their produce. Direct marketing would still have an onsite venue, but would more heavily depend on other methods: skilled use of internet marketing, wine-tasting shops downtown, which stimulate other businesses (two birds with one stone!), and the creative cultivating of relationships built through the "events" happening three or four times a year—at most!

I have heard it said that the "myth" of the small winemaker is a hijacking of the term by the wine industry to push their own corporate agendas. But there really are a number of us growers (and we don't all grow only grapes!), distillers, and winemakers who are legitimate small businesses and need to market our products. There are ways to do it without further damaging our environment.

Perhaps this idea of direct marketing needs to be considered in a much more substantive way that considers the realities of the commons and returns agriculture's prime aim to stewardship of the earth.

PATRICIA DAMERY
NAPA

CHAPTER 13

Goatsong

When did things start unraveling? I tire myself thinking about all the *what ifs?* It's a mistake to think you can live forever in Eden, which, of course, has the germ of its demise from the beginning in that tree with its forbidden fruit. At some point, you are going to succumb. The Serpent tried to warn Eve about Eden. "Paradise is not all that God makes it out to be," she hissed. "Eat this and find out!" In eating the fruit of knowledge of the opposites, Eve got a chance to grow in consciousness.

In this creation story, the eating of the fruit is the beginning of a possible transformation, the creation of the stone of soul. Jung spoke of the transcendent function, that which can appear when we consciously entertain all aspects of ourselves without projecting what we don't want to claim. Only then a third possibility comes, something entirely new and often beyond our wildest imaginations. In the Jewish esoteric text of the Kabbalah, this fruit-eating is synonymous with "the great task of *beirurim*, sifting through the mixture of good and evil in the world to extract and liberate the sparks of holiness trapped therein."[57] In this system, evilness depends on holiness to draw down the divine life force, but when separated from holiness through this alchemical sorting process, the life force is cut off from evil, causing it to disappear. Then the Shekinah, the feminine face of God, can return to Earth.

The Shekinah is a concept that you must experience to understand. I reveled in Her presence those first years on our ranch. I heard Her song in the creek after heavy rains or in the cobbled ditches along the driveway after downpours. I saw Her hair glistening in the dew of the bunch grasses of the savanna, felt Her breath of sweet west wind when the rising sun flamed the western mountains. In classic Jewish thought, the Shekinah refers to a kind of indwelling of spirit. And once you know Her, Her visitation can only be described as Grace: you can never forget Her. It is said that in Her presence the connection to the divine—and Mother Earth—is more perceivable. Her absence is a tomb. Knowing Shekinah at all is where the trouble begins!

She has other names. She has been likened to the gnostic Sophia, that feminine spark "caught in the dark embrace of matter." In the Song of Songs, she is the Shulamite, whom

Jung describes as "the feminine personification of the *prima materia* in the *nigredo* state."[58] Her beauty can only be released through various alchemical operations.

For me, one of Her most meaningful presentations was announced in a big dream just as I began my personal analysis in 1978, followed by a synchronistic blackening of my skin in a sulfur pool. I have written about this in other places.[59] But this blackening, this descent into matter, was given a name in my dream, a name I had never heard before: *manitou*. Manitou is a term of the Algonquin-speaking peoples and those linguistically connected to them and defies translation. It is tempting to equate *manitou* with Great Spirit, yet Great Spirit implies a duality and a Western European concept of the divine: Great Spirit and His creations. In fact, manitou may best be described as animating spirit that is All.

Early Europeans visiting the continent noticed the placement of stones that resembled a human torso. These stones were called *manitou stones* and revealed a harmony of sky and Earth through many astronomical alignments. Early missionaries observed that the Indians directly addressed Earth, River, Lake, dangerous Rocks, and Sky, believing that all of these are animate. Humans were responsible for living in harmony with the natural world, not dominating it. Two scientists who studied the manitou stones of New England, Byron Dix and James Mavor, suggest another meaning of manitou:

> We perceive manitou as the spiritual quality possessed by every part or aspect of nature, animate or inanimate. Things relate to each other by means of this quality, which may be good or evil, temporary or permanent, fixed or changing. Manitou includes aspects of the natural world that are sensed but not understood.[60]

When I try to make sense of my anguish over the potential planting of the savanna, I remember that this savanna, this ranch, and, especially, my love for Donald were my awakening to the indwelling of Spirit in Matter. I wrote a poem for Donald early on in our relationship, a poem entitled "Prayer":

Sometimes it's like prayer. Sometimes
I feel the energy swarm about us, and I feel
that orange red heat of intent,
that total immersion in the Other.
Sometimes there is not enough skin to touch
to express the broadness of the energy. It's like
Ah! Yes! My partner in flesh and in energy,
is it you, or are you God? Each movement
bears that quest, that search for the limits of carnality
and finds them in the rolling thunder, the tumbling tornado
of flesh and legs and arms and Yes! Yes! The rain

that comes then, the fertilizing rain that races across the plains in curtains
silver curtains skimming back, rippled by the winds,
or has the wind come! and now the earth lies dampened?
They say God is spirit, that disembodied attribute,
But I say God's not that easy to define.
I have felt the cells in my body long for the Other,
burst into flame.
I have felt the egg nuclei
sprout wings and fly up,
a flock heading out to meet the winds
dancing across the world.

Our lovemaking flamed us both. We lived in an ecstatic sense of spirit during our early years, infused it into every concrete block of our home. During the time of construction, our two pygmy goats, Boris and Natalie, walked with us along the three-quarter-mile dirt road to the house site. Their tinkling Swiss goat bells summoned Pan with every step. The construction workers loved the goats' visits, rubbing Boris's head roughly, which incited Boris to stand on his hind legs and dance toward them for a great head butt. I tried to discourage this, because once they get into the habit, goats like to butt everyone. Once when the men were plastering the walls, which went on for five months!—Boris returned from visiting his construction buddies with his entire head covered in wet white plaster. He had rubbed his head in what they had just finished. I wiped him clean and got both goats out of there.

One afternoon when I was putting away journals after looking up snake dreams to discuss with a consultant, I found a black plastic tonette from fourth-grade music class in the top of the old trunk in the storage locker. The goats were nearby, waiting to take the walk up the mountain. Raising the tonette to my lips a most beautiful melody emerged: a goatsong. The minute Natalie heard it, she stopped her exploration of the storage locker, walked closer, and stood, listening intently. The song was a Soul Song, melodic, a little sad, but strong. I had never heard it before, yet it was not unfamiliar. It was as if it had been growing in that tonette all those years and was just now emerging. I felt such relief to play it. Then Boris came closer. Neither could do anything but listen. Pan was with us.

The song continued to develop. Walking to the pioneer cemetery in the center of our property and vineyard, I discovered which notes wanted to be played and how. The goats followed, eating sweet peas and listening, eating minor's lettuce and listening, eating tender shoots of new grass and listening to these enigmatic notes.

Donald came home and I played the song for him. The goats listened. He said it must be in their collective memory, that sound of the flute that shepherds played as they watched their flocks. We walked to the top of the ridge. I played the song on the mountaintop in case Hornsby and Tarquin might hear, the goats who had run off the year before. After I put the goats in their barn and loaded their feeder with alfalfa hay, I played the song again. Natalie stopped her ravishing of the hay to watch and listen, hay hanging from her mouth.

Then at 3:30 A.M. I awoke to the sound of the tonette in the yard and Elsie's vicious barking. I sat up confused and alarmed. Was someone mocking the goatsong? And who might be playing the tonette? Donald was already up. He let Elsie outside. I opened the bedroom door to the outside to listen more carefully.

The tonette was actually a coyote. She was quite near and howled over and over, her voice warbling. Had she overheard the tonette and thought it a Coyote Song? Or do shepherds play their flutes not so much to ward off boredom as predators? Had I warned the coyotes that these are my goats? And was this coyote's answer?

It was as if those tonette notes vibrated the web of creation and we were all energized. Having grown up immersed in nature, I had experienced Spirit before. The mysterious oak savanna and verdant glade of the creek had ensured that. But the ranch and Donald's and my relationship afforded a daily baptism in the sacred waters of that animating spirit. The cells in my body reverberated with the increased energies. Beauty transforms one's soul; beauty, apprehended, *grows* one's soul.

Goatsong. Yes, we lived it, and we still do, but now with broader Shekinah overtones. A colleague named it for me during our visit after I found the snake dreams and the tonette: *goatsong,* the original tragedy. From the Greek word for "tragedy," *tragōidia: tragos*, meaning "goat," and *oida,* meaning "song." Goatsong is the mysterious combination of humility and that essential ability to climb above, like a goat or a song! Later this same principle would be underscored in a second pelican dream. To know the *goatsong* of tragedy is to be reborn.

Goats browsing on a morning goat walk

CHAPTER 14

When an Old Friend Dies[61]

WHEN THE GREAT VALLEY oak by the little farmhouse fell, Donald and I did not hear or feel the thud. There was only the phone message from Ramon, time-stamped at 2 A.M.: *Everything is okay, but a big tree has fallen. I turned off the water supply and the tree smashed a car, but the house is okay.*

I had just made morning tea, only as an afterthought checking the answering machine for the flashing light of a message. Suddenly I was awake! Hurriedly I woke Donald, and we drove the ¾-mile gravel driveway down the mountain, hoping it was not the giant valley oak that stood by the old farmhouse, which Ramon and his family occupied before Casey and Melissa and the boys.

The tree was the oldest living thing around, at least 250 years old. It grew here in the Napa Valley when the First People camped along the seasonal creek that defines our north property line; its acorns, a staple. Then some of the first white settlers in the valley built the farmhouse and a small shed beside it, the proximity of the shed a factor in the weakening of the tree's roots. Some of its branches were trunk-sized. Beneath the tree, we tearfully buried Donald's mean old cat, Peabody, the cat he had found nearby as a stray kitten. Small wild plum trees sprouted out of the tree's cavities, a clue that the life of this beautiful presence was nearing its end. In the words of Wendell Berry, *There is no year it has flourished in / that has not harmed it. There is a hollow in it / that is its death. . . . It has become the intention and radiance of its dark fate.*[62]

As we rounded the bend in the driveway down to the house, our fears were confirmed: Our beloved valley oak lay oddly horizontal, its leafy bows, once stretching to the heavens in that graceful way of valley oaks, shattered into myriads of pieces the size of a man's forearm. Huge amounts of debris now blocked the driveway and beyond for a couple hundred feet. The tree miraculously harmed very little in its *Fall,* save the fence, the two youthful valley oaks it injured on the way down—probably its progeny—and the car. Those hollows that had been homes to bees, squirrels, and raccoons were much deeper and wider than we had imagined. Years before, a tree specialist had told us that if the tree fell, it would not hit the house, but we had not wanted to think about the fact it almost certainly *would* fall: most trees die this way if they are not killed. Surveying the hollows of the fallen giant, it was clear that its time had come.

Like the tree, Donald and I felt shattered. For days after, the ranch reverberated with the stunning loss as the giant lay slowly dying, some of its roots still in the ground. This tree was one of the few remaining old valley oaks in the Oak Knoll area. In the last century or so, 95 percent of the valley oaks in Napa Valley have been cleared, first for orchards and more recently for vineyards. If we are all interconnected, what is the repercussion when an elder, so old and huge, dies? Donald called this a *millennium event.*

Interested in death, Wesley, then aged three-and-a-half and awed by the corpse of this giant, asked, "Grandma, did it live out its natural life?"

"Yes," I replied, perhaps fudging a little. That shed was certainly a factor.

"Will it have a circle of little trees growing around it?"

"No." I explained how valley oaks spread their acorns, helped out by birds and squirrels. "Its baby trees are already all around," I added.

But while Wesley seemed to be satisfied by this, Donald and I were not. We loved this tree. Nothing will ever replace it in our hearts. Things *pass,* including the valley oak, and yes, the new valley oaks grow nearby. In the world before now, the tree's death would be sad, but it would have been enough that it reproduced. As Goethe said, nothing is static; everything changes: seed, sprout, tree, seed—and so on. Death is part of a natural cycle and the tree's eternalness, or that which Goethe termed *Ur,* or archetypal plant. Its *Ur*-ness lives on as seed, sprout, tree, seed—hopefully.

But things are different now. This tree was one of the remaining 5 percent of Napa's valley oaks. Humans are their greatest enemy. And I cannot separate its death from this period of environmental shift. What is the natural cycle, and what is not? So much of what is killed or dying off in this age is not a natural progression of life. In this time called the Sixth Extinction Cycle, we are increasingly aware of changes many of us never imagined would occur in our lifetimes. Species disappear at alarming rates; storms pound our coasts, or elude them altogether, while polar vortexes freeze our interiors. We can no longer take for granted the seasons and the cycles, that rain will come when it should in the amount we know to be normal, that storms will be within recognizable limits, and that wildfires will not devour everything in their paths each summer and autumn. Plants and animals and, yes, humans too, are dying long before they live out their natural lives, as Wesley puts it. We all know, if we quit denying it, that at best, this is how it will be for a long while.

Climatologist and alchemist Dennis Klocek calls climate the "soul of the earth," the *anima mundi.*[63] Climate involves that sheath of gasses regulating life, a sheath sensitive to changes in the environment on Earth as well as to radiation from the sun and that of other stars and to the positions of planets. This sheath is the nursemaid of life on Earth, uniquely composed of three classes of gasses: oxidizing, neutral, and reducing. Like all stars, when the sun was young, it put out less energy, and the reducing gasses on Earth (ammonia/

For days we cleaned up the broken tree.

Small wild plum trees sprouted out of the tree's cavities, a clue that the life of this beautiful presence was nearing its end.

methane) predominated, absorbing more of the sun's energy. This was critical to keep the planet from freezing so life could begin. But as the sun aged and started putting out 30 to 50 percent more energy, the balance shifted, the protective sheath necessarily absorbing less solar energy so life would not burn up. Oxidizing gasses (oxygen and carbon dioxide) predominated, and oxygen became the dominant gas supporting life.[64]

This sheath, the physical representation of the *anima mundi,* the Soul of the Earth, is undergoing a great period of transformation, and so are we. We are inseparable from it. Our behavior has increased the carbon dioxide and methane, which, when out of balance, hold in heat, oddly imitating conditions early on when the sun was cooler. A new cycle is beginning: Earth is warming, the polar caps melting at six times the rate we expected. There have been catastrophic changes before, but this time we humans have brought it on. If we are to have any mediating effect on what is occurring, if humans are to continue to live on Earth, we are going to have to change beyond our wildest imaginations, a change that necessarily involves a shift in consciousness. As Albert Einstein stated in an interview in 1946, "A new type of thinking is essential if mankind is to survive and move to higher levels."[65]

Trees, and particularly old trees, are essential to returning some balance to our atmosphere. Ninety percent of the solid material in the trunk, branches, and roots of a tree comes from the elements plucked out of the air through photosynthesis. One of those elements is carbon. Through photosynthesis, trees use the sun's energy to sequester carbon from the atmosphere within the trunk and branches, roots and leaves of the tree while, at the same time, releasing oxygen that is so important for life on earth. Then we breath that oxygen during respiration, which is the reverse process of photosynthesis, taking in oxygen and exhaling carbon dioxide. Every moment of every day we take part in a holy communion with trees, joining them in rhythmic opposition.

But back to our old tree. Klocek calls the hollows in the trunk of a tree like those of our old valley oak, the *Saturn gesture*. Saturn was an old god and, in that ancient world, the gate through which the cosmos incarnated. Impending incarnation is experienced as chaos. The Saturn gesture is present in a plant that has strong verticality, like our old friend valley oak, while at the same time developing these hollow spaces, like the horizontal rings of Saturn.[66]

Klocek describes a practice in Europe between the time of Rudolf Steiner's death in 1925 and the Second World War in which peasants built composts in the hollows of trees. These composts were then used to bring the forces and energies of the outer planets and cosmos to the seed in an attempt to influence the fruiting. The records were lost in the war, as were many of the bombed fields and forests, but anecdotal evidence suggests effectiveness.[67]

To this end, Donald and I collect a large hollow section of trunk from our old friend. In this we layer goat and llama manure, straw and lavender trimmings, and infuse the mixture with the biodynamic preparations that sensitize the soil to the cosmos and make its minerals more available to the plants it nourishes. It is yet another of the valley oak's parting gifts: this hollow of the Saturn gesture, gateway to the cosmos. Over the next months, the mystery of the hollow will seep into this *prima materia* to become rich compost.[68] We will then stir it into *sun-soaked* water to fertilize the earth of our ranch, and, perhaps, energetically, us as well, preparing us all for what is to come.

CHAPTER 15

Wholeness and Lavender

If there are scents that return us to wholeness, one of those for Donald and for me is that of lavender. Not just any lavender, either. In fact, until we started growing lavender, I wasn't particularly fond of its scent. But when the lavender mounds around our home start blooming and the bees arrive, turning the fields into gigantic buzzing hives of activity, when the scent wafts through our open bedroom windows at night as we drift on pillows of sleep, and the still reveals the concentrated essence that drops me into the present, I realize how enchanted I am with this plant.

We happened into growing lavender. Some of our grapevines were not thriving, and our viticulturist had just taken a workshop by a propagator of lavender, so he suggested we diversify. Marketing lavender was not as easy as he was told it would be, providing hair-raising challenges the first couple of years when the 3500 plants bloomed. We sold fresh and dried flowers and took the excess to a local distillery. But it wasn't until we purchased a small fifteen-gallon still and started distilling the lavender in small batches ourselves that we discovered the five places we planted lavender on the ranch produced five distinct scents of lavender essential oil. Lavender has a *terroir* that reflects the environment in which it grows.

There is a scene in *Wind in the Willows* when Mole, who has been away for a while, smells home. Author Kenneth Grahame writes:

We others, who have long lost the more subtle of the physical senses have not even proper terms to express an animal's inter-communications with his surroundings . . . have only the word "smell." . . . It was one of these mysterious fairy calls from out the void that suddenly reached Mole in the darkness, making him tingle through and through with its very familiar appeal. . . . A moment, and he had caught it again; and with it this time came recollection in fullest flood . . . Home![69]

This is the "fairy call." I experience it when I smell our oil. It returns me to home. Our oil comes from where we live. The plant shares the same sun, the same water, and is rooted in the same earth we live on. It is grown biodynamically, an individuating process for a plant and a farmer. We enter a dialogue with lavender, which supports conditions that help the plant thrive. When a plant is grown in this way, it is a well-organized plant that fits in with the whole. Fractional crystallization shows crystals that are beautiful and symmetrical. Wholeness is present.

Both Carl Jung (analytical psychology) and Rudolf Steiner (anthroposophy and biodynamic agriculture) addressed wholeness. Although contemporaries, they never met. And

Photograph: Lowell Downey)

although they had little good to say about the other, they shared a common philosophical ancestor, Wolfgang von Goethe. (Rumor has it that Jung may have shared more than a philosophical lineage as his grandfather may have been an illegitimate offspring of Goethe's.[70]) Both men studied Goethe's book-length poem *Faust* as teenagers, Jung at the suggestion of his mother and Steiner encouraged by a teacher who was editing *Faust* at the time. Goethe's work presents an alternative approach to the natural world and the psyche from the mechanistic way that has developed since Descartes. It reflects an approach that perceives the whole as *a living substance,* whether that be the human psyche or the flower growing along the roadside. Goethe developed techniques to communicate with *the living substance* of a plant, techniques that quiet the mind and require the use of imagination and receptiveness.

In his autobiography *Memories, Dreams, Reflections,* Jung describes early experiences walking in the Jura Mountains of Switzerland near his home.

> Plants interested me . . . but not in the scientific sense. I was attracted to them for a reason I could not understand, with a strong feeling that they ought not to be pulled up and dried. They were living beings which had meaning only so long as they were growing and flowering—a hidden, secret meaning, one of God's thoughts. They were to be regarded with awe and contemplated with philosophical wonderment.[71]

Rudolf Steiner, too, bemoaned the desacralization of the natural world in our industrial, scientific age.

> In the course of the materialistic age of ours, we've lost the knowledge of what it takes to continue to care for the natural world. The most important things are no longer known. Because of certain healthy instincts, things are continued, but these instincts are gradually disappearing; the traditions are vanishing.[72]

Biodynamic agriculture was his attempt to bring back work with healthy instincts.

The common ground of these men's philosophies is a receptive attitude to the *living substance*. Growing lavender biodynamically offers us this challenge. Every stage of the growing process is in concert with what else is going on. We carefully plant lavender directly into the earth around our home, not plowing, so as not to disturb the soil structure of land that has never been plowed. As a result, the plants have grown more slowly than those in the vineyard, yet they produce great oil. We still harvest these plants for distillation, and they are now twenty years old.

In one of the five areas, we planted a labyrinth, a universal pattern said to be that of the minotaur. Using a string and stakes, we swung arcs that we traced with chalk lines. Donald is a wizard in bringing substance into form. He doesn't think twice about building an imaginative booth for trade shows, easy to assemble and airy as scent. He used these skills that day as we laid out the labyrinth, finally snaking irrigation tech line along the chalk lines and planting lavender every three feet by an emitter. There is an energetic center in the labyrinth—the heart of it—in which we planted medicinal plants, including a large white sage plant propagated by his oldest daughter, Adamine. Early summer it sends up great spires of tiny white flowers. The morning after we laid out the pattern, I returned to find a snakeskin in this most energetic area upon which you do not walk.

Being on a steep hillside, the labyrinth path is difficult. When you walk that path, you have to pay attention. People often bring a rock or carry one from the sweat lodge from the days when Lakota medicine woman Pansy Hawkwing led sweats here. On the way in, you hold in your heart a problematic issue until reaching the labyrinth's center. Coming out is a reversal; you return to the world, hopefully with a larger perspective on the problem, leaving the rock alongside the path. I consider the oil that we distill from the labyrinth to be liquid prayer. It is never sold, only gifted, and especially to those who have walked the labyrinth that year.

Does our wholeness depend on developing the quietness meditation affords, a quietness that sensitizes us to subtle energies of ourselves and of the earth? Carl Jung said healing happens when one is put in right relationship to the archetypes—the patterns of wholeness. All true healing systems incorporate putting the patient back in touch with wholeness.

My spiritual teacher, Norma T., taught that our job here on Earth is to make ourselves as energetically big as possible. Many of us drawn to Jung and analytical psychology are drawn to this expansion that comes when we listen to the unconscious through dreams or imaginings and incorporate what is missing into our conscious acceptance of our whole selves. We *are* larger when the energies of the Self are accessible. Dis-ease results from suppression of unacceptable qualities or feelings, or from too much criticism from self or other; expansion happens when we are joyful, grateful, and loving life.

Alchemists describe the alchemical operation of *multiplicatio* as "an extension of the one to the many." The student learns by transmission, or resonance, from the higher resonances of the Self stimulated by the teacher's own personal work. My most important learnings have come in this way from spiritually developed teachers. Although these unique teachers, including Norma T., were ahead of me, I never felt lesser than. Rather, I knew just a little more in their presence than I could have on my own. My growing edge expanded. But I might also add that I get this same kind of expansion from walking the steep, dusty trails of our ranch or meandering through a glisteningly moist redwood forest or listening to the rhythmic breath of the sea as the tongue of a wave licks the sand smooth and hard and then recedes, over and over. I felt it as a child exploring the creek's glade. I feel it in the oak savanna. The Earth in her great energetic self is also a great healer.

One blue moon in 2012 a group of us walked our hillside labyrinth, offering our prayers, until the orange moon rose over the eastern ridge. Afterward Charlie Toledo and I lay on our backs within the circle of valley oaks where Jesse and Lisa were married, the earth warming our backs, as we exchanged stories of spirals and watched dancing stars through oaks nodding overhead. "For 60,000 years people have lived here," Charlie said. I imagine them also feeling the sun's heat in the earth on their backs and her light reflected in that which rises at twilight. Wholeness.

CHAPTER 16

Dementia and Distillation

DEMENTIA IS A LONG slow death, one that allows everyone plenty of room for denial. At first you explain the little forgetfulnesses away. As we age, many of us forget a name, or can't retrieve a word immediately, or occasionally forget what we were going to do when we walk from one room to another. We reassure each other: we all do this. But sometimes the little things happen more often and become bigger; agreements made, forgotten; and any attempt to remind the other, met with anger and distrust. Slowly you realize that you can no longer talk through disagreements. You have to avoid them. Gaps in memory are bridged by stories you do not recognize, stories that make the world make sense again—to your spouse. Bits and pieces of memory are collected and glued together, like the song of the mockingbird. Everything is there, only in new order. Assumptions become reduced to what they really are: *assumptions*. Everything is up for grabs.

Donald regularly searches for the cause of his cognitive impairment, which was finally diagnosed in the fall of 2016 as Alzheimer's disease and vascular dementia. None of his relatives were known to have Alzheimer's. He has had a sleep disorder most of his adult life, awakening in the early hours each night; lack of good sleep can cause dementia. Did that arc of our bedroom's vaulted ceiling that he generated in the wee hours twenty-five years ago take its toll on his brain? What about his fall in 2006 from the flatbed truck? Our neighbor Dave called that morning, telling me Donald had fallen 4 feet onto his head while they were loading fruit bins. I rushed to the site. Copious amounts of blood gushed through the once-blue bandana Donald was holding to the top of his head. He wouldn't let me call an ambulance, so I drove him the fifteen minutes to the local emergency room. As I drove up, several nurses and emergency room technicians who had been leaning against the hospital entrance smoking, rushed to our car, one having grabbed a neck brace, which they immediately strapped Donald into. As they struggled to get Donald's tall body, stiff from the neck brace, out of our Subaru Forester, they scolded me for not calling an ambulance. "He didn't want me to," I told them. "You let someone with a head injury make that decision?" they countered.

He is used to being in charge. He planned and built a number of the parks in the East Bay Regional Park system, including Point Isabelle and Point Pinole, and designed emergency rooms, maternity wards, and updated special equipment rooms in several Bay Area hospitals. He knows how to get things done. I am used to deferring to this quality, as it certainly isn't my skill. In building our home, I brainstormed with him, but he did the work. He mapped out our driveway when I said I wanted to build our home on the mountain, not on Dry Creek Road, as he originally planned. He followed the old wagon trail three-quarters of a mile up the mountain before turning into a forested area and blazing the last five hundred feet to the house site with a machete, hacking through thick stands of poison oak and invasive Himalayan blackberries without cutting one tree. Donald not only had vision but also the ability to bring vision into form. He suffered no fools in the process, although he would deny this about himself.

A friend commented that Donald doesn't have the personality for dementia, but who among us does? After being rightfully scolded that day in the emergency room, I consoled myself with the fact that I had refused to take him to St. Helena Hospital forty minutes north, an emergency room he designed and insisted I take him to. But this was all only a hint of things to come: having to make decisions he disagreed with, for his own good. For our own good. In dementia, not only memory goes, but also judgment as well.

It took many layers of stitches to repair the skin on Donald's head, but nothing could repair what was happening in his brain. Statistics say if we live to be seniors, a third of us will die with some kind of dementia.[73] Dementia affects everyone; a pebble cast into a pond sends ripples to the shores. I seek the bedrock that holds firm through the earthquake of Donald's brain, which no longer perceives and processes information in ways it always had.

But once you accept the neurological changes, you are on new ground, and it gets easier. It's another kind of distillation. To survive with any semblance of sanity, you must distill away the impurities of assumptions and habits you have always had with each other and learn to live more often in the eternal Present. Old routines are boiled off, new ones developed, and then boiled off again as the disease progresses: Donald's driving himself to his downtown office to manage our commercial property, which he had done since 2000 when he retired from his architectural office; my own private practice as an analytical psychotherapist—all of this has to be reevaluated on a regular basis. Is he still capable of making decisions about a lease with a tenant? Can he manage the bank accounts? Should he be driving at all if he gets lost in downtown Napa and falls asleep at stop signs? And concurrent with that: how much can I actually do if I have to take over the many tasks he used to do?

Chemist and philosopher Primo Levi wrote, "Distillation is a slow, philosophic, and silent occupation which keeps you busy but gives you time to think of other things. . . . When you set about distilling, you acquire the consciousness of repeating a ritual consecrated by the

OPPOSITE: *Wintering valley oaks*

centuries, almost a religious act, in which from the imperfect material you obtain the essence, the *usia,* the spirit . . . purity is attained, an ambiguous and fascinating condition . . . ."[74]

When we first consulted Ray Dolby Brain Health Center in San Francisco in 2013, I was told that our marriage, as we had known it, was over. I rejected this, wanting to believe that Donald would get better. More sleep, change of diet, exercise—all of these might cure his forgetfulness and his increasing mood changes. But he got worse, not better, and the diagnosis changed from mild cognitive impairment to Alzheimer's disease. As things stand now, there is no cure for Alzheimer's. There may be in the future, but it will probably be too late for Donald. I am told not to count on it. We are left with the question, what essence, what spirit, what dark gift of dementia, do we distill in the vessel of our marriage?

CHAPTER 17

Activism

I dreamed that I saw the Tree of Life
holding the Scales of Justice.
Justice itself would be determined by the Tree of Life,
the Owl nesting in its branches,
The Rain and River that water its roots.

Carolyn Raffensperger, *Women's Congress for Future Generations*[75]

IN NOVEMBER 2014, WHEN my friend and colleague Leah Shelleda encouraged me to join her in attending the Women's Congress for Future Generations in Minneapolis, Minnesota, I quickly signed on. I was growing into a state in which I would do anything for the oak savanna.

I arrived at the conference a few hours before Leah, finding our hotel and the Earl Brown Conference Center. For four days, we followed the labyrinthine-enclosed walkways protecting us from Minnesota's bitter cold, from our hotel to the rooms of the conference center to listen to women activists from a diversity of professions talk about their struggles to preserve our environment for our children, grandchildren, and our great-grandchildren, our seven generations. There was a decided urgency, a wealth of information, and, yes, a call to joy!

The conference was organized by Carolyn Raffensperger and Ann Manning, executive director and associate director of the Science and Environmental Health Network, respectively.[76]

Carolyn Raffensperger spoke that first evening with an in-your-face anger, as if channeling Lilith. Ann Manning was gentler but just as intense. In an earlier interview that fall conducted by Minnesota Women's Press, Raffensperger was asked why she organized the Congress:

We have had a congress mostly defined by men for a long time. How well has that worked to protect the environment? How well has that worked to protect living wages, health, mental health? . . . One emerging idea is that not only do we have individual rights—religion, free speech, to carry a gun—but there are rights of community, rights that we share—the rights to the commons, to healthy rivers. . . . There is a sense that we'll gamble with the Earth. . . . And guess who will bear the brunt of the gamble when it goes bad? The public, the Earth and future generations. One of the things that we are saying is that we will not accept [corporations'] bad bets.[77]

In this same interview, Ann Manning was asked about the goals and desired outcomes for the Congress:

We see ourselves as a part of the bigger movement and we are beginning a new tributary to the movement. One of the key goals of the 2014 Women's Congress is to see how the constellation of environmental problems is connected to our current economic structures. We can change this by making those connections more visible to people. We want to shift the worldview from isolation and separation to the interconnectedness of all things.[78]

Manning introduced the evening speakers, who were conservation biologists. "Conservation biology is a biology of hope," she said. "Having something to do brings hope, and these people have ideas." University of Minnesota conservation biologist Karen Oberhauser, a lovely, quiet-spoken woman with long dark hair, opened with a discussion on monarch butterflies, which she called "flagship species." Flagship species are different from keystone species in that they are noted as a species in trouble with the purpose of stirring people's passions for protection.

I am becoming more and more concerned with the impacts that humans have on monarchs and other organisms, and with the precarious balance between human needs and the needs of the species with which we share the planet. I'm convinced that learning as much as we can about our fellow earth-inhabitants and then sharing the amazing things that we discover will tip the balance in a direction that will be better for all of us.[79]

Monarchs are a butterfly most of us know from childhood. In my mind's eye, I can see their large, fluttery orange-and-black wings in my grandmother's gardens, visiting red zinnias and blue cornflowers, lovely hollyhock and sage. Monarchs capture our imaginations not only because of their beauty but also because of their migratory feat: they travel three thousand miles a year, from Mexico to Canada and back. And a big part of this migration is afforded by the presence of their only host plant, milkweed, upon which the female lays her eggs.

Milkweed: As a teenager, I walked soybean fields in Illinois, cutting out anything that wasn't beans—and particularly milkweed, a plant that bled sticky white sap when you cut it. During the Second World War, Donald collected the white fluff from milkweed pods to stuff lifejackets for soldiers.

However, in the mid-1970s farmers used Roundup (glyphosate) to control weeds in fields so teenagers no longer needed to walk the beans. These same fields had provided 50 percent of the milkweed needed by monarchs along their migratory path from Mexico to Canada. As a result, populations of monarchs are seriously declining.

On to birds: Kristin Hall of Audubon Minnesota explained that half the birds in the United States are at risk due to temperature and precipitation changes and changing seasons. Threatened birds include the bald eagle, burrowing owl, Baltimore oriole, and Allen's hummingbird. In the last 400 years, nine species of birds have become extinct. In the next one hundred years, 314 North American species are threatened. She spoke of creating safe havens for birds.

And the bees: Rebecca Masterman of the Bee Squad reported that since 2006, one-third of our honeybee colonies die each winter due to poor nutrition, pathogens, pesticides, and parasites. One of the most important things we can do is plant for the pollinators and then make sure we don't spray what we plant!

That first evening we were given a list of things to do: plant monarch stations in our yards and gardens; stop using herbicides, including glyphosate; learn the story of what we put in our bodies—grow our own food, learn to cook it, and eat what is locally grown. Having *something to do* contributes to hope, and there is a lot we can do every day.

The momentum built as we four hundred women and a few men openly talked about our feelings of what was happening to our Earth. We were a diverse group, all ages and genders. We sat at round tables throughout the cavernous dark room, effigies of four super-life-sized goddesses along the sides, representing the four elements—earth, water, air, and fire, respectively. Earthy Rhea, the ancient Titan goddess, sat, enormous and covered in moss and bouquets of chrysanthemums, against one wall. An Indonesian goddess, draped in blue-and-green silk and wearing an orange-and-gold-striped robe, held a blue bowl in another corner. An African goddess dressed in green and purple held her bowl, birds about her head. The fourth goddess was circled with flowers. Anger, pain, and discouragement faded to resolve. Something must be done, and it must be done now. "We are the first generation to fully experience climate change, and we are the last generation who can do something significant about it."[80]

In the next days, speaker after speaker confronted us with the task through their own work. Attorney Carol Raffensperger advocated for the precautionary principle. "If an action is suspected to be harmful to the environment or the public, and in the absence of scientific proof, the burden of proof that it is not harmful is on those taking the action." In this case, this would involve considering the result of an action on our seven generations, a concept of stewardship that considers living in a way that benefits seven generations into the future.[81]

Will it harm them? Raffensperger explained that the basis of government as we know it is economic growth, not a public trusteeship of the commonwealth and common health for future generations. The concept of private property rights is one Western Europeans brought with them to this country and is often in direct opposition to the rights that hold people together with the land. We can see this at all levels of our government: local, state, and federal. Too often, the intention is not to protect and promote human rights, but business interests. Injustice is almost always economic.

Biologist Sandra Steingraber, a tall, strong woman just in from New York state after being arrested for civil disobedience in successfully protesting fracking, discussed the science of climate change. She would return to spend Thanksgiving in jail. She told of her teenage daughter's grief when she learned her mother would not be at the Thanksgiving table. "I have to do this," Steingraber told her. "My job is to protect you."

Also a cancer survivor, Steingraber discussed two ways our climate has been destabilized: the use of fossil fuels and resulting heat-trapping gases carbon dioxide and methane, and the "toxic trespass" of toxic chemicals into living systems, including our bodies. Her book *Raising Elijah: Protecting Our Children in an Age of Environmental Crisis* tells the story of her research into her son's illnesses caused by common toxic building materials.[82] Ever since reading *Raising Elijah,* I have insisted we replace and dispose of every possible piece of treated lumber on our property. This lumber, "pressure treated" with chromated copper arsenate, was used originally for telephone poles and mine shafts and then, during the 1980s as wood became more expensive, for playgrounds and decking. In 1988 the EPA deemed it toxic enough to require a warning label, a requirement the timber industry objected to. The government complied, requiring only a tear-off information sheet at the place of sale. Although this form of arsenic is no longer used, arsenic is known to cause bladder cancer. It continues to leach into our waterways, our soils, and into our skin if we touch the wood without gloves.[83]

Speaker and Nebraska native Mary Pipher, clinical psychologist and author of the book *The Green Boat: Reviving Ourselves in Our Capsized Culture,* used the term "willful ignorance" to describe the most dangerous defense the human race can adopt.[84] Willful ignorance occurs, she explained, when we are caught between facing something too dreadful to acknowledge yet too dreadful to ignore. "We cannot solve a problem we cannot face," she asserted, and she continued to lace the hard facts of climate change and the political corruption supporting its denial, with funny anecdotal stories, including influencing state legislators with apple pies (and not in the face, either!).

"We have a disordered relationship with the web of life," she said. "We never get into the zone to work on issues." She told of her own activism in forming a group in Nebraska to oppose the Keystone XL tar sands pipeline through their state, and particularly through the ecologically vulnerable Sandhills, actions that successfully tied up the passage of the pipeline through the state for a few more years.

"Never ever allow yourself to get caught up in either/or," she advised. "Move to a both/and." She discussed how her group found common ground among people who have been manipulated to be polarized around issues that should not be politicized. We all want clean water. We do not want to be poisoned into perpetuity by spills or dumping of toxic chemicals. And many of us love the place we live. By not allowing ourselves to be divided by corporate interests and corruption, we can find common ground to make positive change.

The phrase "moral imagination"—coined two-and-a-half centuries ago by Irish statesman Edmund Burke—threaded itself through the conference like a theme song. Moral imagination allows us to judge the right or wrong of an action without the driving force of benefit to ourselves. It means considering our part in the whole of things, using our hearts to make decisions.

On Saturday afternoon Joanna Macy, scholar of Buddhism, systems theory, and deep ecology, spoke. In her eighties and recovering from a flu, she appeared by video. "As we age," she said, "we have a wider, freer relationship with time. The experience of time in our culture is speedier than any other time in history. Industrial culture presses on us, making it hard to be present in our world. Our attention has been hijacked."

Continuing, she explained how, in order to produce the fuels and goods necessary for the growth of our economy, we are using up what goes to future generations. "The consequences of our actions last forever," she said, and she listed three main arenas: nuclear power and contamination; GMOs (genetically modified organisms), which we can't undo; and fracking. The toxic chemicals used in fracking and put into underground water cannot be removed. Eight million gallons of water require forty thousand gallons of chemicals added, and you can't remove those chemicals.

Macy continued to quote disturbing statistics about abuses of water. In nuclear power, "two-and-a-half-billion gallons of water a day are pumped back into the ocean. This water which has been used to cool the nuclear reactors is 20° warmer than ocean waters and is now contaminated with 'allowable' radiation." We also treat water as if its quantity is endless. "In Los Angeles, 25 percent of the potable water leaks away." Macy reminded us, "Historically it's women who've been the stewards of water," and she cited the Global Women's Water Initiative, a grassroots organization of women that began in Kenya and promoted sanitation and hygiene.

"These technologies change our relationship to the past and to the future. They have taken past and future and bent them into a circle of time, the present we are in—the pickle we are in." She spoke of her ancestors and her relationship with them. "Go ahead, you are the one that's alive now," they tell her. "And I work for them and they hold me, help me see that my life is just a grain in time. Ancestors and Future Beings."

Her face was soft and hopeful, even in the pain of which she spoke. "It is like the ancestors are witnessing us and can help, but only through our hands. It is a great privilege to be alive when the future ones want so much. Be willing, even glad! to be living in a time of so much uncertainty!"

I thought of Wesley and Sabien, aged four and two at that time. When my own sons were that age, I was demonstrating to stop the nuclear arms race. When I was pregnant with Casey and Jesse was but a year old, I wondered to myself, *What am I doing having children in such an age?* And then it came: they are my vote life continues, and now these grandchildren are that vote as well. I felt my ancestors close as Macy talked of hers. Yes, my parents voted life go on, as their parents before them, and I am that result! With my *hands,* I must help.

But on returning home, we were confronted with a heart-stopping development. For the first time, Sally Sinclair (again, not her real name) presented us with "their plans." Unbeknownst to us, in early 2013, 2.5 acres of the savanna was permitted for vines, some of which was in the tree easement and butted up against our property line. They were now applying for an acre and a half more, including more in the tree easement, plus permitting of an expanded winery (they were bringing in three other labels, although the number keeps changing upward) and an event center, with daily visitors and large events. When I expressed dismay, Sally informed me that if I said anything against the winery, and unless Donald supported their expansion, she would not negotiate on the tree easement.

Where is *moral imagination* now that I need it? It is so easy to become self-righteous under these kinds of circumstances. In my Irish family, self-righteousness was a fighting tool. My uncle Wayne was a prime example! Yet self-righteousness obliterates the possibility of moral imagination, which requires at once a kind of sympathy for the other and the freedom of intuition to seek solutions that may have no personal gain.

This was also a pep rally for my inner Lilith—*she who refuses to be suppressed!* I knew that I had to be a voice for the sovereignty of the savanna, that I could not use any part of it as a bargaining chip. Donald cautioned me that we had to be sensitive to the Sinclairs' needs, that that is part of negotiation. It became clear, though, as Donald and I met with the Sinclairs that they were cutting no bargains and fully planned to get their way. "This is a great spot for a great cab!" Sam Sinclair stated.

It is also a pristine, rare oak savanna, one of the few remaining in the Napa Valley. In 1800 there were about forty-five thousand mature valley oaks in our county.[85] These days there are about one thousand. It was clear that our neighbors were restrained only by the extent of the law that they couldn't get around. Nature needs an attorney when you are dealing with a mentality that sees nature only as a resource for one's own profit or pleasure—or a *great cab.* The fight had begun.

Let's hear it for the NIMBYs!

Many of us are reluctant to be characterized as NIMBYs when we object to projects in our "backyards" such as event center wineries or vineyard incursions into our hillsides and watersheds. Such a designation often implies a narcissism.

The American Dictionary defines *NIMBY (Not-In-My-Back-Yard)* as "a person who objects to the siting of something perceived as unpleasant or potentially dangerous in their own neighborhood, such as a landfill or hazardous waste facility, especially while raising no such objections to similar developments elsewhere." Many definitions include that this objection is to a project that is also for the common good.

We protect what we love. Many of us love this valley we call home. A project next door that we perceive as harmful in some way to us or to our environment sparks this love. Often our individual situations reflect much larger issues in our county, in our country, and in our world. It wakens us to the way things may be out of balance, and in the case of land-use issues in our valley, to the ignorance that would further degrade our hillsides and watersheds, our air and community fabric, whether that ignorance be our own or of those whose ambitions seek profit, regardless of impact.

These projects often pushed by developers and financial interests can hardly be called "in service of the common good."

Thank goodness for NIMBYs! But our love of homeland and our life here—our sense of place—must extend to a larger vision of where we are going. Napa Vision 2050 is a growing movement in Napa County in which a dozen-plus local citizen groups are gathering out of love of this land and our lives here. We are in serious need of changes in our policies around the environment and water, climate action, and economic pressures that have defined our commerce without substantive regard of those who implement it: our farm and hospitality workers.

This is a movement that needs all of us—residents, growers, wineries, laborers, and local governing officials—to join in truly acting for the common good.

PATRICIA DAMERY

NAPA

CHAPTER 18

From NIMBY to the Grand Coalition
and Napa Vision 2050

Our second and last meeting with the Sinclairs took place on our joint property line at high noon on a Sunday in early December 2014. The Sinclairs arrived in their Mule, a small off-road vehicle, after Mass, driving through the grassy bowl of the savanna, Sally in a mink vest and Sam, Napa casual, with an open collar shirt and tan slacks.

Donald and I had sought to discuss the easement from the beginning, but both Sam and Sally had avoided this discussion. Sally said they needed to get the land surveyed first; Sam kept deferring for vacations and being out of town. Honestly, I think we were all a little relieved to put off a discussion of difficult issues with each other. But this Sunday it quickly became obvious that Sally had no intention of abiding by what we understood to be the terms of the tree easement. At the point on the property line where we stood, the easement extended 160 feet into their property. "What do you want?" she kept asking. "We want you to abide by the agreement," we said, which reads, *"The general intent and purpose of the foregoing restrictive covenants is to reasonably maintain the native forest and meadow conditions within the Tree Easement Area for the protection and enhancement of the value and amenity of the Benefited Property and for scenic enjoyment of its owners."*

Sally, being an attorney herself, argued why this did not matter, a reason that, not being an attorney, I did not understand. "How about twenty feet pull back?" she countered. Donald and I considered whether we could live with one hundred feet. We offered the possibility of purchasing a quarter acre. "Sam doesn't want to sell off any land," she said.

It became clear that Donald and I needed legal representation in understanding our rights—and Nature's rights. This was not going to be a friendly agreement between neighbors. We interviewed several attorneys and learned we needed specialized assistance from an attorney who understood the complexities of contracts and easements.

At the same time, the Sinclairs contacted surrounding neighbors, presumably assuming that if they delivered poinsettias, cookies, and wine for Christmas, the neighbors would support their project. Everyone I knew was appalled at the scope of their dream. At present their six acres of grapes were crushed offsite. Now they wanted to build both a state-of-the-art building as well as one of the largest caves in Napa County and increase production from the currently permitted 30,000 gallons to 50,000 gallons. These 50,000 gallons would include a custom crush for three other labels that their winemaker would bring with him. At present, they had no permitted visitation. Now they were asking for 256 guests a week, plus two wine and food pairings a month of 30 people, 10 events a year of 100 people, one 200-person event and one 300-person event a year, plus participation in the Wine Auction. All of this right next door to us.

Our hillside is pristine, with drapes of usnea lichen hanging from the ancient valley oaks

Young trees are critically important to the savanna's survival

in the meadows. Acorn and pileated woodpeckers, bluebirds, and ring-necked doves live in the forest and oak savanna around us, along with bobcats and coyotes, mountain lions, and, of course, the wood rats. As Suzanne Gilmore from California Department of Fish and Wildlife stated, our ridge is a hotbed of biodiversity. Not only did the Sinclairs intend to plant the savanna, now they also wanted to entertain visitors next door until 10 PM on weeknights and midnight on weekends, all on our quiet mountainside.

The neighbors called a meeting. Our Napa County agricultural lands are supposedly protected by the highly touted zoning of the *Ag Preserve,* or the valley lands, and the *Ag Watershed,* the hillsides. Most of our neighborhood is in the Ag Watershed, a designation that considers thin topsoils and unpredictable, limited groundwater. The Ag Watershed also contains flora and fauna important to the health of the watersheds.

Twenty of us filled a neighbor's barn. Ginna Beharry, a tall, attractive, and articulate woman with short blonde hair, listed our concerns on a large piece of newsprint: the industrialization of agricultural land with the advent of this event center; the long, narrow flagpole-like one-lane driveway access from Dry Creek Road, which came within thirty feet of our neighbor Jeff's just-built home; increased traffic and safety issues on the s-curve by the proposed Dry Creek Road entrance; the requested visitor and special events numbers; the known lack of groundwater in our locality, and the potential to further impact residential wells.

An elderly couple leaned into each other as they listened, looking bewildered. They had raised their children here when kids could ride their horses all over these hillsides, a time when neighbors often did the farming themselves. Four families of neighbors arrived in the 1990s after retiring from places south and east, planted grapes and studied winemaking. They were former social workers, realtors, physicists, attorneys, and economists. We were an educated, lively group who loved our neighborhood. A number of us were members of the Napa Valley Grapegrowers and/or the Farm Bureau. We objected to this potentially disastrous commercialization of what we had voted to protect for agriculture.

We addressed our concerns in a letter to the Sinclairs. At the top of the list were water, traffic, and noise. We also informed them that the neighborhood group, which we named the Dry Creek Road Alliance (DCRA), had formed and was meeting regularly to review and research the expansion proposal.

Several of us in DCRA began attending Planning Commission and Board of Supervisor meetings and writing *Napa Valley Register* Letters to the Editor. The Sinclairs project was not an isolated case. Numerous citizen groups had organized to ask our county governing officials to protect our watersheds, roads, and community from wanton development. One of the larger projects in process with the Planning Department, the Walt Ranch Project, initially intended to cut 28,000 trees on over 500 acres of oak woodlands for vineyard estates. *Defenders of the East Napa Watershed* organized to protect these pristine acres. Many feared that this project, as proposed by Craig and Katherine Hall of Hall Winery, would threaten the water supply of the adjacent community of Circle Oaks, as well as negatively impact the Milliken watershed and reservoir, a source of water for the City of Napa.

Through a string of emails from local water activists, I was introduced to Dan Mufson. A retired executive in the pharmaceutical business, Dan was a hub of information about who was doing what. His clear thinking and leadership skills organized the coalescing of forces in what would come to be called Napa Vision 2050.

I first met Dan in Peet's Coffee one Sunday morning in early January 2015. "You can recognize me with my yellow baseball cap," Dan said. And sure enough, he was there in his yellow cap, perched on a stool and ready to go! That morning we talked about the projects that brought us into what was becoming a larger movement—for me, the tree easement and the Sinclairs' larger project; for Dan, the Walt Ranch Project and the Defenders of the East Napa Watershed. We aired our anger and despair at feeling bullied by winery and vineyard applicants' aspirations. We still thought it possible to influence our local government through the Planning Commission and the Board of Supervisors. We contemplated how to change laws and made plans for more meetings.

In an email to a number of us, Dan stated we may have reached a critical mass. "Sparks of great conversationalists' insight from up and down the county are becoming more frequent and focused." The fact that the planning commissioners and staff were speaking of a "new normal" gave us heart. In an early Planning Commission meeting, the recently hired director of Planning, Building and Environmental Services, David Morrison, his long hair pulled back in a ponytail, joked that he had only recently learned the difference between Chardonnay and Cabernet. He then stated that he would hold a meeting with the Board of Supervisors and Planning Commission in early 2015 to discuss and sharpen the rules and regulations to allow more objective project approval. Morrison cited two recent examples where there was great outcry but no clear guidance to staff.

Dan warned that we needed to be ready with our input. The Napa Valley Vintners and the Winegrowers, two of the industry groups, would be there in force with their lobbyists and attorneys. (We would soon discover how true this statement was.) The planting out of the valley floor by Mondavi and Caymus, Beringer and Charles Krug, all families whose wines made the Napa Valley famous, were forcing vineyards and wineries onto the fragile hillsides of the zoned Ag Watershed Open Space lands. Land prices escalated. Donald bought our ranch in 1982 for $200,000. Now it is worth at least twenty times that. International corporations such as Australian-owned Treasury Wine Estates, Constellation Wines, and E.&J. Gallo, are buying up small family-owned wineries as the owners age. Then there are the wealthy who can afford to pour unlimited amounts of cash into their "dream" of a Napa Valley vineyard. Too often the needs of the land are off their radar.

The small winemakers and growers of days old, such as Warren Winiarski, knew that growing healthy vines was the first step. They understood the importance of protecting the ecology of the area. Winiarski, whose Cabernet won the Paris blind tasting in 1976, stated in a 2008 interview with the *San Francisco Chronicle,* "Particularly in Napa, with the explosive growth, it's more important than ever to be fanatical about the land and the use of land."[86] And in 2015, shortly before his death, the late vintner Volker Eisele (see Chapter 44 for more on Eisele), understanding the ongoing threats to the environment, stated:

> There are more very wealthy people and corporations coming into the valley, and they are not interested in the environment. They are only interested in the expansion of their vineyard properties, and the only place left [for them to go] is in the ag watershed. So watch out. Trees are going to start coming down.[87]

While the General Plan of Napa County defines agriculture to be the *highest and best use of land,* intended or unintended consequences were commercializing our beautiful wild hillsides and making our valley what some called a "tourist Disneyland." Now environmental considerations were forcing all of us to reconsider. Preserving and restoring the health of the watersheds, critical to the water supply and ecological health of the valley, may have to trump agriculture as *highest and best use of land,* a revolutionary idea in a county in which foreign investors and corporations clean up on the Napa brand, willing to use every tactic to interrupt and corrupt the definition of agriculture.

Key issues continue to be the guiding stars in our work. Since 2010, the Winery Definition Ordinance (WDO) has allowed direct marketing as an accessory use of agriculture in our Ag Preserve and Ag Watershed lands. The unintended consequence is commercialization of residential and agricultural neighborhoods. Our fragile Ag Watershed lands have been opened to activities and development never allowed before, all in the name of "direct marketing."

Witness Sinclair Winery! But Sinclair is only one of many. Driving up the dead-end road of Soda Canyon, I am saddened at the pillaging of a pristine remote environment for wineries, vineyards, and caves—all in the name of agriculture. Mountain Peak Winery is six miles back on a road that becomes ever more narrow, perhaps the largest project to date in the zoned Ag Watershed Open Space. Off this same road, The Caves of Soda Canyon dug a portal in a cave that opened into a lookout over the valley without a permit. They were fined and given a year to reapply to use the portal, just a slap on the wrist. Our governing officials justify clearing forests, oak woodlands, and chaparral for vineyards, agriculture being "the highest and best use of land." For eight years, on our ranch's western border, the Woolls Winery project has reverberated with the grinding and growling of bulldozers and earthmoving equipment ravaging Clarence's land.

How do we protect the fragile Ag Watershed lands? How do we establish a mandatory oak woodlands and forest management program to replace the voluntary one in place since 2008? And what about enforcement of existing regulations? Forty percent of self-audited wineries are out of compliance with their permits. What does that portend for the remaining wineries? What do we do about these transgressions?

The more I learned, the more upset I got. Violation after violation was forgiven, first by the Planning Commission and, when appealed by contesting neighbors and concerned citizens, by the Board of Supervisors. The cost of business included a small fine and then forgiveness. In fact, after two years, The Caves of Soda Canyon reapplied for a permit to use their illegally constructed portal and were rewarded with not only a permit to do so, but also a doubling of their gallonage from 30,000 to 60,000. Planning Commission Chair Jeri Gill commented on the approval, "This is something I'm completely comfortable with."[88]

At home, I felt heartsick at the possibility of the savanna's soils being ripped for vineyards and then sprayed with herbicides and fungicides. Being immune compromised, I worried for my own health. I meditated. I couldn't separate my hate for what our neighbors were doing from my feelings about them. In our last meeting with the Sinclairs, Sally aggressively pointed out in a gotcha style that we had broken the terms of the easement ourselves in planting a garden outside our kitchen door, something we had done early on, long before the Sinclairs bought the property. I met this with contempt while also trying to talk myself out of a self-righteous steam. We all have dirty hands in this sullying of our planet. Westerners have used more resources, done more polluting than anyone else on Earth. I reminded myself that the savanna was a microcosm of the issues in the county, the country, the world. Forester Aldo Leopold said many years ago that we cannot heal the planet if we don't heal our relationships with each other, and that concurrently, we cannot heal our relationships with each other if we don't heal our relationship with the planet.[89] But I was hardly in the healing mode.

On Tuesday afternoon, January 20, 2015, The Grand Coalition to Save the Napa County filled a rented room at the Napa Marriott. We were expecting twenty people, fifty arrived, crowding the square assemblage of tables two deep. Various citizen groups were represented, including newly organized nonprofits such as Defenders of the East Napa Watersheds and Protect Rural Napa. Several of these groups had hired experts and attorneys to address the burgeoning number of wineries creeping onto the hillsides and the lack of code enforcement. Many in the room had worked tirelessly through the years to preserve the natural environment. Jim Wilson, a tall, handsome man in his late fifties and a retired waste management executive of Anheuser-Busch, discussed his plan to author a watershed initiative to protect the Napa River watershed by tightening deforestation. He and Mike Hackett would spend hundreds of hours within the year tabling in front of Whole Foods in Napa to get the Water, Forest and Oak Woodland Protection Initiative on the ballot. Many in the room advocated for clear standards to keep the Ag Preserve for agriculture, not allowing the commercialization of Ag land with "event centers" and hundreds of visitors at all hours of the day and night. Many in the room were retired from successful careers in various professions and now were donating those honed skills to the benefit of the common good. The *highest and best use* of elders!

As we sat around the table, representatives from each group gave a brief account of their interests and actions. The Yountville Hill group discussed the increase in traffic this Disneyland-like project would generate on Route 29 if permitted. Ginna represented our neighborhood group, DCRA, and explained the Sinclairs' proposal. Seasoned land-use advocates, including Ginny Sims, a past member of the Board of Supervisors in the late 1960s and the first woman ever to serve in that capacity, imparted their wisdom: *"We must be fact based. Do not presume the other side, whichever side that is, is the enemy!"*

The high energy in the room coalesced into a steering committee composed of a member from each group with the purpose of forming a mission statement and creating a doable agenda—the beginnings of *Napa Vision 2050*. We agreed on the importance of attending Board of Supervisors and Planning Commission meetings as often as possible and picketing projects that degraded the environment. We would make ourselves known as citizens of Napa County who stand for preserving the natural beauty and health of our ecosystems.

I remember Ginny Simm's caution that day, probably sensing the anger in the room. "Find common ground. Do not make enemies here. The other side is not your enemy."

There is common ground, and we all share it—common ground that is becoming more obvious under the pressure of severe drought and climate change: that of the watersheds and water, of our atmosphere and warming planet. But would we be able to agree on *common ground*? We discovered this was a tall order.

Ancient coastal live oaks

CHAPTER 19

Sleepwalking into Extinction

IN EARLY 2015 I received an email announcement about a documentary on the Russian River watershed: *The Russian River: All Rivers*. Having raised my two sons on that river, I was curious and suggested I meet my sons in Petaluma for the screening. The email flier said it was free.

The day of the screening I checked the flier only to discover the need for a reservation. By then it was fully booked. I called my sons with the sad news. Casey, then living in Petaluma, decided to walk to the theater anyway, which was near his home, to check on tickets. He called me immediately: the theater had moved the screening to a larger theater to accommodate the crowd; there would be room. I had exactly one hour to get from my office in Napa for the 7 P.M. showing.

It had rained all day, something gratifying as we were in a third year of drought. Because of the flooded roads between Napa and Petaluma, the main route at Schellville was closed. As I detoured, passing just south of Sonoma, ponding water erased the right edge of the lane. The irony! We were in drought, and I was dodging flooded roadways, racing to arrive on time to a documentary on watersheds. Was this holding the opposites, or is this what climate change looks like?

The filmmakers were making opening comments as Casey and I felt our way through the darkened theater to our seats. Even with the last-minute change of venue, the theater was almost full. I recognized some of faces as those of local water and fish activists interviewed in the film.

Once seated, I felt a growing excitement. Many years ago, my sons' father and I had bought a cabin on a hill above the Russian River, seduced by the grandeur of the redwoods and the vista of the river below. We were younger then than my sons are now, and this was our first house. Summer afternoons we descended the steps of the public easement passing by our kitchen door to the highway and then on to the river. Like salmon, we swam the mile upstream to town and a local bar, luxuriating in the warm ease of the waters.

We married on the deck below the house, splurging on our favorite bluegrass band. We

Jesse jumping into the
Russivan River
(Photoraph: Elisa Baker)

Casey and Jesse
(behind) wading in
the Russian River

(Photograph:
Elisa Baker)

purchased a book on remodeling and dismantled a wall, only to discover the cabin's single wall construction was not covered in the do-it-yourself directions. A little knowledge is a dangerous thing! A carpenter friend informed us that we had removed a weight-bearing wall, which he helped us repair in the months before Jesse's birth. Both he and Casey were born while we lived in that house, and both consider the redwood forest and the Russian River community, home.

The film opened with an aerial view of the Russian River. Like Mole's smelling home in *Wind in the Willows,* the familiar sinuous curves of the river brought the heart-rendering remembrance of home. Until Napa and our ranch, this is the land I loved the most. Summer mornings a thick, white fog caterpillar wormed its way up the river until the sun fought it off. Evenings it often returned.

This is the home where we watched winter storms from the window seat spanning the south side of the living room, overlooking the woods where the boys played as if they were coyote pups. This is where we watched the river rise.

And then the sentimentality faded. The film confronted us with hard facts, that the Russian River is being exploited by several industries and has been for a long time. Vineyards invaded the riparian corridors and use river water free of charge, and often illegally, for irrigation and frost protection, greatly impacting water flows. Syar Industries, Inc., an asphalt contractor, has taken gravel from the river for years, again free of charge, a practice that has destroyed salmon-spawning grounds. Santa Rosa dumps treated effluent in the river. The Coho, chinook, and steelhead, once abundant, are all listed under the Endangered Species Act. By 1997 the Coho were almost extinct. Wine is made at the expense of these endangered species. Although only a little over two hours, the story's intensity made it feel like an eternity: it was simply too much to bear.

I remembered my own stories, the ones sentimentality obscures: the late spring afternoon in the mid-1980s when I took my young sons swimming at the quiet beach that used to be Ginger's Resort. We sat in the shallow water and played. Later we learned that Santa Rosa had another "accidental" spill of sewage and we were sitting in it. It was during this time that a masked local businessman, affectionately known as Manure Man, took his tractor and manure spreader to Santa Rosa and spread manure around the courthouse, stating, "If it's good enough for Guerneville, it is good enough for Santa Rosa!"

These sewage spills upstream contaminated residents' wells for days after. The *Press Democrat* printed a picture of a Santa Rosa city official drinking a glass of treated effluent, demonstrating the safety of the treated water from the sewage treatment plant, a picture we scoffed at. These were war days: a battle of those downstream from those upstream. It was really a coming-into-consciousness of how much we impact each other. What is that old saying? We all live downstream?

Watching the documentary on our Russian River that evening in the darkened theater, I scribbled notes in a small notebook, phrases that I return to over and over:

Watersheds should dictate land-use.
Watersheds purify water.
We are abusing water.
Flood planes are important.
We are sleepwalking into extinction.

"We are sleepwalking into extinction"—a quote from Canadian author and water activist Maude Barlow. In her no-nonsense way, she looks directly into the camera as she asserts this, her hair bobbed and business like. It is a hard-hitting line. Sitting beside Casey, father of my young grandsons, Wesley and Sabien, I felt stunned and fearful for my progeny. We are in a fight for the continuance of life on Earth as we know it. It is that dire.

Barlow spoke of the dangers of how we treat water. In a radio interview with Amy Goodman of *Democracy Now!,* Barlow discusses the hydrological dangers of moving large quantities of water from one country to another. The United States exports one-third of our water. "The hydrologic cycle has been dramatically and deeply affected by our abuse and displacement of water, and we have to stop," Barlow says. "Our abuse, pollution, misplacement, displacement and just mismanagement of water is actually one of the causes of climate change." Barlow said that if we continue as we are, we will run out of water.

> My concern was that this government, in particular, the United States, but many governments, are putting all their water eggs in the basket of cleaning up dirty water, instead of conservation, instead of protecting water at its source.... The way they're coming at it now is to clean up water after it's been polluted. And there's huge amounts of money to be made. And my concern is, who's going to control that? Who's going to own the water itself?[90]

The film reported that the water being sold is part of the commons and the public trust doctrine. As such, it can't be abused or owned. Legally, we have the right to use water, but not own it. Half of our water comes from groundwater. If water is removed to another country, it is not there to complete the hydrological cycle. It does not naturally return to replenish groundwater.

By contrast, the European Union requires river basin scale management, much like water activist Charlie Toledo asserts we must do here in California. This means that water is not moved from one end of the state to another to supply farmlands or cities in deserts. It means you take care of your watersheds so groundwater is replenished and that you recognize the relationship between surface runoff and groundwater, something effectively ignored by our county officials. That you live within your water budget.

When you make *balance* a priority, you take a step toward seeing Nature as a being in her own right with needs of her own. Everything changes. We need moral imagination to find this balance. Nature is no longer there to exploit for our own pleasures or gain. We are humbled when we recognize that we, too, are Nature. Sioux scholar Vine Deloria, Jr., quotes William Powers in differentiating the Lakota cosmology from Westerners, a philosophy at the core of finding this balance. "For whites, humans were the last to inhabit the earth, and are therefore a crowning glory of all that preceded them. For the Lakota, humans were the last, and that makes them newest, youngest, and most ignorant."[91] In the case of water, our task then is to consciously work with those ecological organs of a watershed that maintain ground and surface water and to live in balance with the water supply of an area.

This requires profound changes. Until the 1976 French blind tasting, 85 percent of grapes in the Napa Valley were dry farmed. Then extractive economics set in. Instead of 400 vines per acre, growers now plant 2500 vines per acre and irrigate those vines from surface runoff held in ponds, from wells tapping groundwater, and in Sonoma County, with water pumped directly from the Russian River. Water levels in wells have dropped; wells have gone dry. Many more wells have been drilled. The Sinclairs alone are utilizing and have drilled a total of eight wells on their two parcels—not counting dry holes—in an attempt to document that there is enough water for their project.

And then there is the escalated use of agricultural chemicals. In 2015 in Napa County, the use of glyphosate, the active ingredient in Roundup used to control weeds, ballooned to 53,809 pounds.[92] Glyphosate and other agricultural chemicals have been measured in rainwater, groundwater, our rivers, and the water coming into our homes and into our bodies. An endocrine disrupter that affects wildlife as well as humans, glyphosate causes digestive disturbances because it also kills gut bacteria. Residues are found in almost all our processed foods, in breast milk, and in almost all wine. Since the increased use of agricultural chemicals to boost production and profit, wine-growing regions in Italy, France, and, yes, Napa County, have much higher cancer rates, particularly bladder and brain cancers. In fact, according to the Lucille Packard Foundation, Napa County has the third highest diagnosis rate of childhood cancer[93] and the second highest incidence of all cancers[94] in the state of California. When these statistics were brought before the Board of Supervisors to be studied, Napa County's public health officer Dr. Karon Relucio worked with the Department of Public Health to issue a report that blamed the high incidence of cancer among Hispanics on their poverty. There was neither action by the Board of Supervisors to create a task force to understand what these statistics might mean, nor consideration of why low-income Hispanic-populated areas in the county, and those areas closest to Napa's Syar Industries, Inc. quarry, have the highest cancer mortality rates.[95] Why did the supervisors not insist this statistic be intensively studied as to causes and remedies?

One does not have to look far to understand why. The grip of prevailing industries, in Napa's case, the wine industry, hospitality industry, and Syar Industries, Inc., prevents rigorous exploration of upsetting facts by governing officials, officials they have effectively bought through campaign contributions. This results in governmental complacency that stops any attempt to use moral imagination in finding solutions that attend to the health of our environment, our community, our water—and especially those most vulnerable, our children.

In a recent address to a group of Silicon Valley business people, *New York Times* commentator David Brooks stated that only a well-governed people has the luxury of not caring about politics. He also said that ignoring politics does not make it go away.[96] We need moral imagination, that ability to use intuition and sympathy, in building a healthy world for us all, because a world will not be healthy if it is not healthy for all.

My friend Leah tells me a story of moral imagination. When the cosmos was being churned and all the universal energies were mixed with good and evil, Shiva protected the Earth by swallowing the toxins and holding them in his throat, which turned it blue. In this way, he allowed the gods access to the nectar of immortality, which lay below a contaminated sea of milk.

Where is the blue-throated Shiva now? How do we sort through our self-interests, our fears and hatred, to avoid contamination of our hearts? What is that nectar of immortality so sought by the best of ourselves? How do we support the eternal life force of our planet? How do we stop ourselves from *sleepwalking into extinction?*

CHAPTER 20

March 10, 2015, and Anna's Passing

MARCH 10 IS A memorable date for me for many reasons. Each year I remember two big events occurring on March 10: my Welsh great-grandmother Rachel's birth in 1842, and exactly 140 years later, Casey's conception. I always celebrate this day in a quiet internal way, the way a woman *does* the conception of something very new, to be held privately for a period of time before its presence makes itself shown.

March 10, 2015, was no exception. In the early days of that year some of us still hoped that if we presented the Napa County Planning Department, the Planning Commission, and the Board of Supervisors with the right information, they would do the right thing to protect the commons. We attended Planning Commission meetings, met with the Planning Department project planners and with individual supervisors. We wrote Letters to the Editor and letters to the many governing officials involved with these various projects. As many as 40 percent of wineries self-reported that they had exceeded their permitted gallonage and visitation. Some code violations were as blatant as opening a cave without permits and filling in creeks. Such egregious violations were too often forgiven if the project was resubmitted after a period and met "the requirements."

There was an apparent conundrum: the county planners said that they were only enforcing the law and the guidelines set by the Board of Supervisors. Their job was to see if the applicant followed the rules. Whether a project *should* happen or its cumulative impact was not the issue, only if the applicant filled the requirements. The planners reported to the commissioners who almost always okayed the planners' recommendations. The commissioners claimed that they did not receive direction other than this from the supervisors. The supervisors stated that the commissioners had more power to make the "should" decisions than they were taking. No one appeared to be taking responsibility for making hard decisions, and it was costing the residents and citizens who questioned these decisions a great deal in legal and expert fees, time, and angst.

Because of this tension between the Planning Commission and Board of Supervisors, and the growing unrest of the community, David Morrison called for a joint hearing of the

Planning Commission and Board of Supervisors to hear public comment. We had high hopes in this man's approach. The *modus operandi* of *do what you want and then ask for forgiveness* was causing community outrage. Erosion control plans were not being supervised, and chaparral, oak woodlands, and conifer forests were being clear cut for vineyards in our delicate watersheds. Wineries complete with commercial kitchens and visitation on the scale to be called "event centers" were being permitted on dead-end, substandard roads. More and more tourists flocked to what was becoming an amusement park. Gridlock traffic choked our two main arteries during rush hour and beyond. Napa's economic success had drawn Big Money interests into the county. The focus was no longer on winemaking but on marketing wine, and not just wine but also the remote beauty of our hillsides and wildlands. Any consideration of the impact that any single project had on its local environment was ignored. Code enforcement, if done at all, seemed minimal, and fines only part of doing business. Big Money could afford to get its way.

March 10, 2015, was the date set for the joint hearing, which was held in the old Napa High School auditorium. Several board members of Napa Vision 2050—including Dan Mufson, now president of Napa Vision 2050; my neighbor Ginna, vice president; and Jim Wilson, secretary and future author of the watershed initiative—greeted upward of 460 people as they filed into the building. We staked out our seats in the darkened cavernous room, descending rows of theater seats facing a stage upon which the planning commissioners and Board of Supervisors sat at a long table. A podium stood on the right side below the stage.

I remember a *Napa Valley Register* reporter asking me about the Napa Vision 2050 button I was wearing. It was the first that he had heard of us. Later the Napa Valley Vintners would characterize us as "a bunch of retired gray hairs" in an attempt to discredit our voices. Gray-haired, maybe, and as Dan described us, "mostly in the 60–70 club," but we were also a powerful mix, bringing our well-honed skills into service for the community. Our skills and experience ranged from corporate and banking executives, to architects, engineers, and psychologists, to a retired state labor attorney and fellow goat lover Kathy Felch, an elfin pit bull. A number of us grew vines, and several had land, such as Donald and me, in the Ag Watersheds. But on this day people knew little about us.

Almost all of the seventy-five commenters that day spoke in defense of the environment and of the quality of life of the locals. People spoke of the need for affordable housing for those who work here. Forty percent of the low-wage vineyard, winery, and hospitality workers cannot afford to live in the valley; their commuting adds to the traffic. Many were concerned with traffic and housing and with the expansion of vineyards and event centers into the Ag Watershed Open Space lands, impacting our watersheds and water supplies. The impact of vineyard conversion at the rate of approximately two hundred acres of chaparral, oak woodlands, and forests a year,[97] all critically important in carbon sequestration and climate change, was just beginning to be addressed. One result of this daylong hearing was the formation of an ad hoc committee, the Agricultural Protection Advisory Committee

(APAC), a committee of seventeen members of the county to be appointed by the Board of Supervisors (BOS) to make recommendations to the BOS in addressing the various concerns on that day.

But on this March 10 day another event also occurred. The morning of the hearing, my dear pygmy goat Anna, who had been ill for a few days, worsened. Our vet recommended that we take her to Davis Veterinary School Hospital over an hour away under the best of driving conditions. I learned of this just as I was preparing to leave for Napa High School.

Anna was the last of our pygmy goat herd. I attended her birth, helping Anna and her twin brother, William Wallace, into the world. Each day for years she walked with me and the herd on the two-mile loop of our ranch, sliding down grassy hillsides on her belly whenever possible. Goats do only what's fun. That has been one of their lessons to me: seek the joy in life! She was twelve-and-a-half years old, an older goat, for sure, but I always hoped for much longer.

Although she was about the size of a large Welsh corgi, Anna had a big attitude. She butted the legs of our llama if he got too close while she was eating and had no trouble keeping her authority when the horned Swiss alpines joined the herd. Yet she was sweet to Wesley and Sabien, allowing them to pet her and feed her all kinds of treats. They adored her, and she came to the fence whenever she saw them.

So on that Tuesday, March 10 morning, I was presented with a dilemma: was I going to go to the hearing and read the statement that I had prepared, the one that I naively hoped would somehow save the savanna, or was I going to take Anna to Davis? I was torn. I knew Anna had to go, but I also knew I wanted to make this statement to *save* our land, which was almost magical thinking. And I made a decision that I regret: I asked our vineyard worker's wife, Blanca, a trained vet assistant, to take Anna. She agreed.

I am told that Anna was frightened, that even though she was not usually particularly friendly with Blanca, that she leaned on Blanca for comfort. Although our vet had promised there would be treatment for Anna at Davis, the Davis vet disagreed: Anna had a tumor that was probably malignant, and surgery could be in excess of $4000. There was no promise this would work.

I remember receiving various reports from the Davis vet during the hearing. Each time my phone vibrated, I strode up the aisle to the lobby and called. Each call was worse than the one before: the decision to have Blanca leave her there, the results of the sonogram, and the final decision.

I am sorry that I did not go with Anna, that I was not with her at the end, as I was at her birth. I felt the living entity of our land also needed me, but I am sorry that she spent her last hours alone and frightened with strangers. It was one of those impossible decisions we are increasingly having to make: sacrifices of what we love for what we love—with no promise of good coming of it. These were choices Adam and Eve never faced in that land of the easy harmony of abundance and eternity—but it all ended with that fruit—the grape.

Valley oak view of Goat Mountain

CHAPTER 21

Growing Potatoes and the Eviction

IS THERE ANY CONSOLATION for eviction from Eden? What price do we pay for a taste of the forbidden fruit? With what terrible choices are we cursed?

The story of Eden is a story of creation, creation of consciousness. Carl Jung said that the world only comes into being when man or woman discovers the world. "But he only discovers it when he sacrifices his containment in the primal mother, the original state of unconsciousness."[98] Our entitled attitude that the Earth is here for our own purposes is a childish notion. As Lakota scholar Vine Deloria stated, we are the "newest, youngest, and most ignorant" of creation, not its "crowning glory."[99] Will we stay merged in this primal, childish delusion and be made irrelevant—extinct—or can we make the necessary sacrifice of realizing we are only one part of the Earth? What maturity might we gain in the sacrifice of our privileged ignorance?

Jung was said to be an earthy man. He derived pleasure in growing his own potatoes. During the Second World War, he plowed up part of his yard to do so. "We keep forgetting that we are primates and that we have to make allowances for these preemptive layers in our psyche," he claimed. "The farmer is still closer to these layers. In tilling the earth he moves around with a very narrow radius, but he moves on his own land."[100]

I too take comfort in growing potatoes, an activity I love to do with Wesley and Sabien. Both show a great deal of skill and focus as we take a potato with "eyes" and carefully cut it into pieces, each with its own eye. We then roll the potato in wood ash to protect the cut edge from rotting before it sprouts. We allow it to dry overnight before planting. Both boys love to dig the trench in which we plant the potatoes. They attentively watch the spot for the appearance of tiny green leaves. The plants quickly grow to two or three feet, bloom, and then yellow, which tells us it is time to dig into the earth and find the egg-like tubers. We carefully loosen the soil around the dying plant with a fork, and then each boy carefully feels into the earth. Squeals of joy! Resting around the stem are potatoes the size of a child's fists. Digging potatoes always feels like a miracle.

But potatoes have another side, which makes me wonder if they too are a candidate for the forbidden fruit (or forbidden root!). As delicious as they are, they are also members of the *Solanaceae,* or nightshade family, a family of plants that includes several poisonous—and medicinal—plants. These include peppers, tomatoes, eggplants, and petunias, as well as belladonna, mandrake, and Jimson weed, which, before herbicides, used to grow in my father's cornfields.

The word *solanum* is derived from *sol,* sun. Even its name is paradoxical: that of the sun yet in the "nightshade" family. The potato is a *gamopetalous* plant, from the Greek *gam*—one that "marries" unusual aspects and often opposites. The eyes are underground, in the earth. The potato is not a root, but a stem—the sprout, a branch. If the potato is exposed to the sun, it turns green with poisonous alkaloid *solanin.* The light of day brings out the poison!

But as is so often the case, the poisonous aspect makes some of the members of the nightshade family medicinal. I have used a medicinally prepared belladonna successfully with my children and goats in controlling high fevers. The belladonna fever is characterized by a sudden onset and by heat that radiates several inches from the body—like the sun. Once I treated a sick pygmy goat kid with such a fever by taking her with us to a dinner party in a dog kennel. (Of course, her mother had to go with her.) She needed the remedy every hour. After three doses, her temperature was normal. Fortunately, our hostess (my sister-in-law) was gracious!

Anthroposophist and natural scientist Gerbert Grohmann states that the toxicity of the nightshades weakens the human ego so that soul life becomes confused, causing altered states.[101] However, used medicinally, a poison can have a stimulating effect on the autoimmune system, perhaps, in a Jungian frame, breaking up maladaptive ego patterns to allow contact with the healing energies of the wholeness of Self.

In growing potatoes, we learn something of this, although not on an intellectual level. Light turns the potato green and bitter, and this bitterness cautions us to not to eat the skin that has developed a green tinge. We are brought into communion with the Earth and our instincts as we partake of potato.

Rudolf Steiner claimed that the nightshade is a "higher" plant due to an "astrality," or a developed spiritual capacity, that other plants do not have. He says this places potatoes somewhere between plants and animals. In the nightshades, we are confronted with plants marrying many opposites. In the right dosage, the poisonous nightshades are medicine.

Perhaps in growing nightshade potatoes, we are being nourished in our eviction from the naiveté of oneness with paradise or, as Jung might say, from the unconscious union with the great primal mother.

CHAPTER 22

Earthquake: Lilith and the Soul of the World

MY SENIOR CONSULTANT IN my training to become a Jungian analyst told me that healing is not the result of insight, but rather of divine intervention. As an analyst you simply keep things going in circular motion until a critical mass is reached. Then lightning strikes, and the world shifts. Having a chemistry background, I have another analogy. An electron does not shift into a higher energy cloud in increments but waits until it accumulates a packet of energy. Then pow! It's in a higher energy orbit! This story is that way for me as well, a story of circling some elusive center until a serpent awakens, and it's a whole new era!

In the early hours of August 24, 2014, I awoke to the slam of an earthquake that rocked the house and then kept going, increasing in intensity, for a full forty-five seconds. It felt like forever. Outside the sky lit up, confusing my dream-drugged mind. Was this a thunderstorm, something that we seldom have in California—or had a bomb just dropped? In the flashing blue light (a rare earthquake phenomenon), I could see our home's masonry walls waving and shaking violently. It was as if we were on the tail end of a game of crack the whip! The shocking, sickening crash of glass echoed throughout the house as cabinets dumped their contents onto the ceramic tile floor. Shards of our plates and glasses, my great-grandmother's crystal fruit bowl and antique sherbet stems, skated over the floors until they hit pools of olive oil, wine, and vinegar. The violent shaking flipped Donald upside down in his reading chair, the chair now a tortoise shell protecting him from the books raining down from shelves. Wood stoves, the butcher block table, the couch and overstuffed chairs, the grand piano—all moved two feet west. Even the house! Eight-inch trenches traced the perimeters along the east and west sides. Later the USGS (United States Geological Survey) told us the house and the earth under it *jolted* east and west, over and over, all of one piece.

Many spiritual disciplines say our task as we get older is to prepare for the transition of death. I can tell you, earthquakes aid in this preparation. For those prolonged moments, you don't know how it is going to turn out. That early morning, as the shaking continued and seemed to increase in intensity, I grew frighteningly alarmed. If you live in one of the most seismically active areas on Earth, as we do in California, you get used to occasional earth movement, but when it continues, as it did that morning, you know this is a game changer.

Yet in this realization, I was also amazed to feel a solid part of me, a calm part, the same calm part I felt during the long, difficult labor of my first son's birth, or the time when I was driving our Jeep in San Francisco and choked on a jelly bean. Surprisingly, in these times, I feel the rock of myself. In that realization, all is okay, regardless of life or death.

Patricia, llama Hijo, and goats on morning walk on old wagon trail
(photo: Cristin McDonnell)

And then, as if snared, the writhing of the earth serpent stopped. My son Jesse and his wife, Lisa, had spent the night, and now we were calling to each other in the dark, fearful that there would be no answers. But we were all alive, unhurt, and now looking for shoes and flashlights. Then, gathering in the relative safety of the courtyard with its panoramic views of the valley, we watched fires light up below as the ground continued to grumble. With this scale of destruction, it was clear we were going to be relying on our own resources.

Within a few minutes, we received a call from Ramon. The little house on our property by the road skated west sixteen inches off its foundation, giving Ramon and his family a shocking ride, although the integrity of the house was intact and no one was hurt. Later that morning we would learn that the city of Napa was gravely impacted, many of the government buildings red tagged, including both post offices and at least one hundred homes.

Even without structural damage, many of the homes on the west side of town experienced the breakage of almost every glass and plate.

The USGS studied the path of this serpent, naming it the ancient South Napa Fault. They traced her path by buckled roads and split foundations of homes, including the three-inch-wide, several-hundred-foot-long shadowed dent in the ground between our bedroom and goat barn, which they said was the north end of this fault.

One evening that same week, Donald and I sat overlooking the savanna south of our home, golden in the late summer sunlight. The earthquake gash ran through the middle. We were immersed in the kind of beauty that drops you to your knees, and she, that serpent, basked in the last rays of sunlight, a little pleased with herself, I thought. I felt like one of those dog people whose beloved companion has just trashed the house. Clearly we are living on tremendous energy. And as the aftershocks rumbled and rolled, it was also clear that we had to learn how to be related to her.

Charlie Toledo told me the Earth was angry. Indian wars up and down the valley may also have been fought in the savanna. Is that part of the karma of the ranch, this fight on sacred land? Did this serpent-rousing announce the advent of old karmic battles? Is the Earth trying to shake us off, rid herself of our abuses?

In the weeks before the quake, I had done a series of blogs and presentations on Lilith, that woman-headed serpent of paradise. Now I began to wonder, was I picking up on Lilith energies which would soon visit? Her rage has given her a bad rap, which has formed a real bias against recognizing her important attributes. She is described as knowing the language of the "beasts of the field and every living creature that creepth."[102] Perhaps this is why spirit of place, the genius loci, has been depicted as a serpent. Were my writings about Lilith premonitions to her return, a small taste of this language?

What consciousness knows the language of the natural world, a language that I have come to think of as the serpent mind, a language understood for millennia? The Celts followed energy flows in the Earth, known as *serpent paths,* using rock formations to amplify or fix the energies. Early people in the Americas also knew how to sense and relate to these energies, as witnessed by earth mound formations in various parts of the country, including the Serpent Mound in southern Ohio. Some suggest that weather patterns were manipulated by working with these energies. My father accepted dousing as a tool to use in farming to find water. We lived on land that had been drained by burying clay tile pipes so the land could be farmed. At times, and particularly during spring flooding, the tiles got clogged and my father had to locate the tile to know where to dig.

This consciousness requires a clearing of the mind and thinking, a resonance of being at one with the Earth. It is a resonance that animals may well orient by—especially the serpent. Jungian analyst Barbara Hannah likens this consciousness to the snake and our reptile brain in that we are then able to react on "a much broader and consequently more creative basis" than one ruled by the newer parts of the brain.[103]

Is this the evolution that Lilith offers in her encouragement of betrayal of the old Eden order, the unconscious union with the divine? In this state of resonance, we have empathy, even seeds of moral imagination. Our ambitions to dominate release. We again know the animating Spirit because we are one with It.

The hope Lilith brings stems from this deep empathy for the other, including the Earth. Our Western European extractive attitudes have resulted in the environmental and social mess we are in. Our hearts have been left out of it. In eating the fruit of the knowledge of the opposites, in owning what we would rather project, we must reincorporate not only her anger and rage at injustices, her liveliness and vitality, but also her oneness with the souls of creation. When we befriend the land and are good citizens of the Earth, then maybe we have a chance of setting things right.

The cultivation and farming of tourists

One of the most environmentally and socially destructive trends in land use in the Napa Valley is the recent expansion of the definition of agriculture to include direct marketing.

In 1968, after much heated debate, the Board voted to protect our agricultural lands in the first ever Ag Preserve. Volker Eisele, past president of the Farm Bureau and Napa Valley Grapegrowers, continued to ensure expansion of the protections of our woodlands and cautioned against the eroding of these protections. Although other activities could be included as "accessory uses," the definition of agriculture remained "the growing of crops, trees, and livestock."

In 2010, the Board of Supervisors, pressured by the wine industry, included direct marketing as an "accessory use" to agriculture in our protected Ag Preserve and Ag Watershed lands. These "protected" lands are now open to such activities as "event centers" with commercial kitchens, visitation, and the selling of tickets for food and wine pairings—effectively including the cultivation and farming of tourists as an accessory use in these once-protected Ag lands.

The unintended consequences are severe: increased traffic choking our two main artery roadways, Highway 29 and the Silverado Trail; deforestation and destruction of oak woodlands on our hillsides for more vineyards and wineries; decreased groundwater due to watershed degradation and irrigation and winery use—which depletes neighboring wells—not to mention the increased number of second homes and proliferation of short-term rentals for tourism.

Our county no longer includes tourism as a revenue source, but it is becoming increasingly dependent on tourists—a tourism economy. New wineries and vineyard owners are often not farmers of crops, but entrepreneurs having no idea of or care for the local ecology and little or no experience in farming or grape growing. Many are most interested in the investment and lifestyle.

A study of the recent votes in APAC[104] reveals some of the problems. Seventeen committee members were appointed by the Board of Supervisors from various citizen groups: two from environmental groups, two from the community, two from municipalities, two from business, two from the wine industry, two from agriculture, and one from each of the five districts. The effective result weighed in favor of business, hospitality, and the wine industry. Community, environmental, and agriculture members (six of them) often voted for preservation of agricultural lands and watersheds; the other eleven members often voted to support the business of wineries and business economies.

Any vote passing had to have a supermajority, or twelve votes. Most of the time, votes did not pass, often dividing on the above lines. Recommendations by supermajority included avoiding the use of variances for achieving compliance with land-use regulations (all agreed), establishing guidelines for future winery use permits based on a recommendation of the director of planning (again, all agreed)—and accepting the 2010 working definition of agriculture—which includes the commercial activities of commercial kitchens, visitation, and events (12 to 4). The four dissenters, of course, were the representative of agriculture, the environment, and the community.

It is critically important that the informed public demand that this ill-thought-out provision of including marketing as an accessory use to agriculture be removed. The preservation of our agricultural and environmentally sensitive lands is key to making the Napa Valley the beautiful valley it is, but it is also an environment at risk.

Please contact our elected and appointed officials (Board of Supervisors and planning commissioners) who serve the larger public and the commons to ask them to correct this error.

PATRICIA DAMERY

NAPA

PART IV

THE RETURN

Oak fog
(Photograph:
Bill Hocker)

Leo and Moka on a morning walk on the ranch (Photograph: Cristin Mc Donnell)

CHAPTER 23

Paradise Revisited

IN THE BIBLE WE don't hear much about Seth, the third son of Adam and Eve. Jung, however, amplifies this Biblical story in recounting an old Jewish legend in which Seth was permitted to gaze into Paradise after the Fall. He saw the Tree of Paradise, but it had withered. There were still four streams flowing, "which watered the world," and in the branches of the wilted tree lay a baby. Jung commented that the "mother" had become pregnant.[105]

He discusses this legend again in a later writing, now identifying it as an old English legend.[106] Seth witnessed the tree having no bark or leaves, and a skinless snake was coiled around it—"the serpent by whom Eve had been persuaded to eat of the forbidden fruit." But when Seth looked again, he saw a "great change." The tree now had bark and leaves "and in its crown lay a little new-born babe wrapped in swaddling clothes, who wailed because of Adam's sin. This was Christ, the second Adam."[107]

In being willing to look back at the destruction caused by this "sin" of consciousness of good and evil—to take a second look—Seth witnessed a great change. The skinless serpent and the barkless tree were transformed; a newborn babe rested in the crown of the tree. Jung said transformation is possible only when we consciously suffer opposites:

> If the projected conflict is to be healed, it must return into the psyche of the individual, where it had its unconscious beginnings. He must celebrate a Last Supper with himself, and eat his own flesh and drink his own blood; which means that he must recognize and accept the other in himself. . . . Is this perhaps the meaning of Christ's teaching, that each must bear his own cross? For if you have to endure yourself, how will you be able to rend others also?[108]

In bearing our own cross, the cross symbolizing the intersection of the opposites, we provide the womb to bear the new babe. This is critical to the development of Jung's interpretation of Christ consciousness:

> On the level of the Son there is no answer to the question of good and evil; there is only an

incurable separation of the opposites.... It seems to me to be the Holy Spirit's task and charge to reconcile and reunite the opposites in the human individual through a special development of the human soul.[109]

But first, you must be willing to take a second look, to suffer the pain of the destruction of the old order. The great challenge of climate change is the necessity to stay open to Earth and her changes, even though it means grieving life on Earth as we have known it. We *need* the Earth. Earth reminds us that we are interconnected, a part of a larger whole. When we get too far from these deep instinctual layers, we become unbalanced, anxious, arrogant in our feeling of dominion. Anger and blame give way to a false sense of control and/or entitlement.

Paradoxically, activists and climate-change deniers alike can avoid the profound grief about the changes happening on Earth. *We had nothing to do with this; it's their fault and we are going to make them change it. Or, this isn't happening! It is all part of a normal swing, we are in paradise, so business as usual.*

It is time we grow up.

CHAPTER 24

Jung and the Board of Supervisors

On December 15, 2015, the Napa County Board of Supervisors' room was packed, standing room only, and the overflow rooms, overflowing. Police in uniform strutted back and forth in the hallways, guarding the doorways. I overheard a county official tell one of the police that their uniformed presence changed the feeling in the crowd.

I felt an edginess I didn't usually feel at these meetings. I wondered whether it was the nature of the group that day or if it came from a mass shooting in San Bernardino the week before. Were officials afraid that the discord in the room could lead to violence? At the beginning of the meeting, Chair Diane Dillon asked for a moment of silence for the county employees shot. She said that she had been co-chairing a meeting with a San Bernardino official in Los Angeles when the news of the shootings came. She had also been in London at the time of the Paris attacks two weeks before that.

Watching the televised meeting in the packed standing-room-only lobby of the county building, I too began to wonder for our safety. Fear is infectious! But what was to come bothered me more. The topic of the day was the Agricultural Protection Advisory Committee's (APAC) recommendations to the Board of Supervisors (BOS) on wineries and vineyards in the Valley, recommendations that grew out of ten meetings of seventeen representatives appointed by the BOS—representatives, I might add, weighted in the direction of the wine industry. Since the March 10, 2015, meeting at the Napa High School auditorium, in which over four hundred alarmed citizens gathered to comment on the overgrowth of the wine industry, it appeared that the Board of Supervisors was paying closer attention to these larger considerations in our Valley.

Although only a handful of disgruntled winery owners were present, most of the first four hours of public comment was taken up by workers from one or two wineries, many arriving an hour early to get "reserved" seats in the main room. Someone had placed green sheets on all the chairs of the main room and overflow rooms, with signs saying, "Support Napa County Ag." Although the culprit wasn't known, his or her intention of usurping "green"—and saving the seats—was. Any of us arriving at 9 A.M. had no place to sit unless we took one of these (and several did). This skewed the nature of the discussion and prevented any real addressing of the issues at hand. Vineyard workers needing translators and cashiers at a wine shop expressed anxieties about losing their jobs if the regulations were adopted. I wondered, did these people have any idea what was being presented to the BOS and why? These regulations would not impact their jobs at all.

Obviously, the wine industry was threatened. The recommendations had to do with enforcing the entitlements of permits, limiting variances, and limiting new wineries in Ag Watersheds. Another old-time vintner, Stuart Smith, was quoted in the paper, characterizing APAC recommendations as "a solution in search of a problem,"[110] a sentiment that would be repeated by those against regulation throughout the next years, including, four years later in 2019, Ryan Klobas, CEO of the Napa County Farm Bureau, and Supervisor Belia Ramos, "trying to fix a problem we don't have."[111] At the first morning break I was confronted in the hallway by a large husky man, owner of one of the older well-known St. Helena wineries. He noticed my Napa Vision 2050 badge. "You have cost me $500,000," he raged. "Plus penalties!"

"Plus penalties?" I asked. *Really!* "I don't think you can blame Napa Vision 2050 for your penalties!"

He said that the wine industry had made the valley, and I should only be grateful. (Does he mean we should continue to give them full rein?) A woman wrapped in fur standing nearby snickered in support of him. My Irish bloom of anger threatened. Where was Uncle Wayne when I needed him? Alas, we are in another time, in need of other solutions to conflict! I turned to her and questioned why she was snickering—sneering really. She waved me off.

But he and I did have a discussion, and the heat went down between us. When I left, the two of them stepped together in conversation. Suddenly feeling vulnerable, I pulled my scarf over my Napa Vision 2050 badge, the last time I wore it. Later an old-time St. Helena vintner, Chuck Wagner, was quoted in the *Napa Valley Register*: "Vintners built the wine industry. It wasn't built by county administrators, and it certainly wasn't built by the naysayers and Vision 2050."[112]

The space for the business at hand with the BOS got hijacked that day. It was an abuse of the democratic process. A few people wanted to use their power to protect their private interests by stopping discussion of the real issues. It was a filibuster of sorts, or the creation of a straw man, as Ginna suggested.

One can only hope we find the space within ourselves to listen to the other, even when we disagree. In my Irish family, we loved provoking each other and entering into ridiculous arguments meant to prove one right and the other wrong. It is so easy to expound and enter diatribes with likeminded people. It is something else to use language that doesn't provoke and to listen to thoughts that may inspire hard feelings. Remember, Jung stated that it is only when we can hold the opposite view along with our own conscious view, that we can reach resolution, resolution that may be that *new babe*. We need this kind of dialogue in our valley—not with the aim of any one group winning, but for an establishment of *common ground* where no one is bullied. Is the new Adam a consciousness with heart that nurtures the livelihood of all?

LETTER TO THE EDITOR

Napa Valley Register, November 29, 2015

Stop urbanizing our Ag lands

At a time like no other in the recorded history of climate change, I continue to be shocked and disgusted by our Napa County government's business-as-usual stance in regard to our environment.

Last March, our planet surpassed the tipping point of 350 ppm of carbon in the atmosphere, the upper limit considered safe, until the plants in the northern hemisphere started blooming; 97 percent of international climate scientists say this is due to human activity.

There are things we can still do to mitigate the damage to our climate, which in Napa County include protecting our oak woodlands, our forests, and our watersheds; the continued development of sustainable energy sources; and keeping fossil fuels in the ground. For Napa County, this involves stopping the urbanization of our Ag Preserve, Ag Watershed, and forest lands, planning our cities in ways that include availability to mass transit, and creating affordable housing for those working here.

But, sadly, after nine months of APAC meetings and discussions, economic considerations of the wealthy few continue to trump and define land-use decisions. Recently, the Planning Commission, in a vote of 3 to 2, overturned the Planning Department's recommendation to disallow a variance (and I am relieved the Planning Department made this recommendation) for Summers Winery. It is as if the discussions and recommendations of the APAC committee did not happen.

Maybe to some it is a small issue—a granted setback from the highway. OK, but add to this the retroactive permitting of a non-permitted winery.

This is yet another variance and yet another forgiveness in a long history of such practices in our county, practices that effectively urbanize our Ag Preserve and Ag Watersheds.

The practice of building without permits and then asking for forgiveness is taking the law into your own hands . . . and our Planning Commission and our Board of Supervisors are supporting it with their habit of forgiving after action is taken. But more seriously, in terms of the environment, it is death by a thousand cuts.

Each of us, regardless of our economic base, is faced with the conundrum of thinking of our personal interests in context of the common good, which, above all, includes the environment. This is especially true for our governing officials whose job is to champion the common good. One wonders: Do our planning commissioners and our Board of Supervisors understand that they are letting special interests bend the rules that were made to collectively protect the agricultural, social, and environmental fabric of our county? Do they realize these decisions effectively erode land-use decisions by the populace, rules made to protect our agricultural lands?

What do we, the citizens, do now? When the governing officials do not act for the common good, what is our recourse? It is time for serious thought, and then it is time for serious action. Please ask your district supervisor to reconsider the Planning Commissioner he or she has appointed in terms of their standing up for the rules in place and for the recommendations put forth by APAC. Don't let a few (and economic interests) redefine our protections.

PATRICIA DAMERY
NAPA

A hawk in the valley oak.

CHAPTER 25

Travel: Loving to Death the Places We Visit

I HAVE LOVED TO travel from as far back as I can remember.

Monday's child is fair of face,
Tuesday's child is full of grace,
Wednesday's child is full of woe,
Thursday's child has far to go . . .

This was one of my favorite poems as a child. I was born on a Thursday. My mother read this poem to me over and over. I loved our family trips. Each summer my mother insisted we travel, at that time something uncommon for many farm families. I was hungry for the sight of a body of water that you could not see across (and when I was nine, that was Lake Michigan) and a mountain (when I was eleven, the Great Smoky Mountains). As we stood at a turnout overlooking the Cumberland Gap, I was frightened at the sight of the mountains. *What if all that dirt, piled on top of itself, fell?*

My mother's family lived in the city. Her father was a successful commercial artist, designing all the Hi-Flier kites at the time, the Heath Bar label, and many beer bottle tops. Her family traveled whenever possible. Shortly after the First World War, and before my mother was born, my grandparents and their toddler son traveled by train from Central Illinois to the West Coast, including the Napa Valley. They also drove to the top of Pike's Peak in a Model T when the road was first accessible, and they thoroughly explored Appalachia with my then young mother. On the other hand, my father's family farmed. His mother left the state of Illinois twice, once to visit her grandmother in Ohio when she was in her late teens and once to Missouri when I was a young girl. Both times she became so homesick she never wanted to leave the state—and our Macon County—again.

I have an image of me as a two-year-old child standing between my city and country grandmothers, holding them both by their skirts. Probably I was being doted on. I remember saying, "Two Mee-maws!" It is a memory I carry to this day. I was a bridge between my mother and father, between the city and the country, between loving travel and loving homeland.

When I was twenty-one, my mother gave me a porcelain figurine of *Thursday's child* holding a backpack and a sign: "This child has far to go." It was not long after this that I packed my Volvo with every possession I owned and moved to California. I drove through the Rockies, the western edge of my world at that time, and on through the high country of Western Colorado, the white salt flats of Utah, into the blue plains of Nevada. By the time I reached the red clay soils of the Sierra and descended into the Sacramento Valley and the coastal range of Northern California, my soul was enchanted by the West. I knew I could never move back.

I continue to crave travel. It is as if my soul, as rooted as it is in the soil of our ranch, requires the larger perspective of where we are on the planet. I count visitations to places on the Earth I have never been like beads on a rosary: the first time we flew over the jagged peaks of the Pyrenees and on into Rome, the first time we flew over the North Pole and saw the midnight sun illuminating the snowy mountains of Greenland, the first time I saw the foggy green isle of Ireland from the air.

And yet I have to question this passion of mine to experience the totality of our planet. What is the impact of travel on our climate? High-altitude flying produces carbon emissions that profoundly impact our atmosphere. Train travel is much more planet friendly, producing about 1 percent of the carbon emissions of airline travel.

Tourism alters community. In the twenty-four years that I have lived here in Napa, the city has gone from being a sleepy community to being overrun by tourists. Many of its historic buildings were demolished by renewal efforts in the 1970s, including a mall that failed. In 2015, the mall was mostly replaced by the six-floor Archer Hotel, the tallest building so far in Napa. At the time of this writing, there are ten hotel developments in various stages of review by the city, and if all are approved, there will be 1200 more hotel rooms. There is great concern about the balance between the needs of residents and tourists. As City Council member Juliana Inman stated,

> If we're not balancing uses between retail and offices and hospitality and restaurants, then we are going to have a lopsided build-out; we'll have too much of a good thing. This is a much bigger question than hotels or no hotels. With any commercial development, you have to ask: What kinds of jobs are created? What kind of housing does it generate? How many employees are we talking about? And where are they going to live?[113]

Napa County is dependent on tourism dollars. The county's focus is now on drawing even more tourists and extracting as much money from them as possible. This phenomenon is occurring worldwide: globally, we are transitioning into a tourist economy—a trend that threatens the integrity of community, making it nearly impossible for the children of locals and for service providers to live in the community they serve. As venture capitalists move in and wealthy families buy up attractive land for second homes, inflating property values, the social and ecological health of the community suffers. It becomes less about community and more about profit. Even as traffic gridlocks the main arteries of Napa Valley, making a commute of twenty-five miles north on Route 29 into an hour-long trip, the population of the county is dropping. This is because more homes are second homes or vacation homes, and our workers commute from less expensive communities.

I am aware of my contribution to this tourist economy in my travels, whether that be in Ireland, Spain, San Francisco, or even in my home of Napa County. How, then, do we support healthy economies and social structures in such places that others also want to experience? What is it we are really searching for as tourists?

"I can't think of anything that excites a greater sense of childlike wonder than to be in a country where you are ignorant of almost everything," travel writer Bill Bryson says.[114] Is it the child within us who longs to explore the extraordinary? What illusion do we create to draw tourists to an area? Many say Napa County is becoming a Disneyland for the wealthy, with the average annual income for a visitor being $161,000.[115] Visiting wineries is expensive; tasting fees for a tasting experience at a winery top $40 and rising. And tourists come for the scenery as much as the wine, wanting an "authentic experience" of the land where the grapes are grown. In a recent Board of Supervisor appeal hearing for Raymond Vineyards, a winery bought in 2009 by Jean-Charles Boisset and known for its code violations and flashy entertainment, Supervisor Alfredo Pedroza rationalized his vote to deny the appeal of the approval by the Planning Commission: "This is not Disneyland," Pedroza asserted. "It's agriculture in the 21st century. . . . Napa is fortunate to have experiences that are not one-dimensional."[116]

What is the cost to our communities and to our environment of these multidimensional experiences whose monocrop is tourism? Author Tahir Shah describes tourists as "corrosive." "The very places they patronize are destroyed by their affection."[117] How do we balance our curiosity and affection for exploring our Earth, for so-called *authentic* experiences, with the health of the communities that we visit and the land under our feet?

In April 2016, Napa Vision 2050 offered a forum on Tourist-Driven Economies, funded and organized by one of our board members, architect George Caloyannidis, a generous, persistent advocate for the environment. The forum featured three panelists on tourism, growth and prosperity, and traffic and was held at the Silverado Country Club. The large room's windows overlooked the golf course, the room packed to capacity, including a number of our supervisors, commissioners, and city officials. Professor Samuel Mendlinger, a short, stout, balding man from Boston University, discussed communities that have successfully navigated the influx of tourists and those that have not. Tourism changes communities.

Social conflicts ensue, with the middle and working classes often in conflict with the wealthy and the tourists. Locals fear being pushed out of town. The question arises: who should control future development?

Mendlinger also spoke of the successes of Majorca, Spain, in which governing officials included the local population in making decisions. This process resulted in the development of tight zoning laws, green belts, and good environmental policies. Locals thrived along with tourism, and Majorca became an international center for research on tourism. All this is the result of democratic action by informed citizens, not just a small governing group—a point not lost on those of us sitting in the room that day.[118]

On the other hand, Mendlinger discussed communities that have failed to remain balanced. Each year in Petersburg, New York, poignantly, the site for Thornton Wilder's *Our Town,* half a million tourists eclipse the six thousand locals, who are now mostly elderly and wealthy. Young people can no longer afford to live there. We ignore the tourism cycle at our own peril: preservation of a town or a region that attracts tourists, whether it be for beauty, history, or winemaking, which then draws more wealthy tourists, which then leads to the building of second homes, and so on. Ignoring this pattern only accentuates it. If addressed by everyone, governing officials and locals alike, all might prosper.

Next, Eben Fodor, a lively, intelligent man with thick salt-and-pepper hair, stepped to the microphone. "Growth is presented as the solution to problems it has never solved," he began. "A lot of studies are done by both local governments and private developers that show the benefits. If you look at these studies, and do the analysis, you will find that growth brings substantial costs." Fodor's study of the top one hundred cities in the United States demonstrates that the faster a city's growth, the lower the income of its citizens. His studies demonstrate how local governments do not consider the fiscal impacts of development and tourism on infrastructure, which then end up costing the taxpayers. Developers and industry groups, often multinational corporations, are the ones who make out. "If we divert [the energy] for more and more growth to making communities better places, places that serve the existing residents, places that have great neighborhoods, places that have great downtowns, and places that provide great services, people will be getting a lot more value out of their government."[119]

Susan Handy, tall, blonde, lithe, an advocate of bicycles, and professor in the Department of Environmental Science and Policy at Davis, discussed research on how widening roads leads only to more traffic and more development. "It's all about land use," she said. In planning communities, we must consider appropriate locations for functions such as event centers or high-density housing. Land use defines transportation. We need to prioritize development areas that are less car dependent. "Instead of focusing on making driving easier, we need to make it easier not to drive." She added that we can accomplish this with dynamic ride-sharing programs, micro and macro transit, and walkable communities. Instead of focusing on level of service (ample free parking, and so on), we need to focus on level of livability. Instead of planning for mobility, we need to plan for accessibility.

The questions raised that April day are ones critically important not only to Napa County but also to our world. What are our values? How are these values reflected in our land-use decisions and development? According to these studies, development must come from the bottom up—democracy in action. But we need a vision of where we want to go, a vision that needs to come from the bottom up, and then, as informed citizens, we need to be involved in getting there.

As I left the forum that day, I passed individuals getting signatures on a petition to put a tree protection on the November 2016 ballot. We were naively full of hope.

CHAPTER 26

Light Serpent in the Savanna

IN EARLY 2015 DONALD and I began to document wildlife moving through the corridor of the savanna to show the importance of our Napa wildlife and keeping this space open and fence free. A friend suggested a trail camera that she uses to photograph wildlife on her property, and I ordered it from Amazon, installing it on a fence post facing the savanna. We got photos of black-tailed deer, their eyes glowing in the spark of the camera's flash, of coyotes, gray foxes, and bobcats. In April of that year I moved the camera to the post on our garden to get another angle and left for Mexico and the Southwest for three weeks. The grasses had grown, waving in the winds, and the camera captured some three thousand photos of tall European grasses moving in the savanna over a few days' time.

This was annoying to me at first, until I realized the value of three thousand pictures over several days. All were pretty much the same, except the shadow of a particular valley oak directly across the savanna from the camera, which moved like a sundial, right toward left, day in and day out. There was also a time stamp on each photo.

On the morning of April 27, something peculiar happened. At 8:46 A.M., the camera recorded the grass, but there was a vertical bar of light, almost like a light serpent, on the left-hand side. It was there again at 8:49 A.M. and 8:52 A.M., seemingly swaying and dancing on the left-hand side of the picture as I scrolled through the images. At 9:14 A.M., it grew brighter, golden with a line of blue along its right edge. At 9:20 A.M., the photo showed a pickup truck on the far side of the savanna by an old well, and the light serpent twisted and turned, back and forth: 9:25 A.M., 9:31 A.M. (very bright!), 9:38 A.M., 9:39 A.M., 9:41 A.M. Meanwhile across the savanna a man unloaded what appeared to be PVC pipe, working on the old well that had gone dry at least twice in the last years. This continued, the man working on the well, the truck visible, the light serpent bright and dancing back and forth, left then right, right then left in the scrolled images, until its last appearance at 11:34 A.M., shortly before the man left. This phenomenon has not been recorded in any photos since.

OPPOSITE: *Grafted valley oaks on knoll in oak savanna*

The identity of the light serpent must remain a mystery, yet its presence and the timing of it warmed my heart. I thought of that woman-headed serpent Lilith and her refusal to be suppressed, she, the soul of all the beasts of the field, of the coyotes and deer, the wild turkey who sits on her nest hidden in the grasses for twenty-eight days before her young hatch. And the vegetative world as well: of the savanna, of the oak woodlands and the native grasses that are still growing here. When I know they are present and healthy, I am whole again.

CHAPTER 27

Attorneys—
or No More Mr. and Ms. Nice Guy!

AFTER INTERVIEWING THREE ATTORNEYS who might represent Donald and me in defending the tree easement, we chose Kevin, who knew not only wine but also contractual law. Our neighbor Jeff, whose home was within thirty feet of the driveway servicing the proposed winery, had found Kevin because he understands the complexities of use easements. The driveway also involved a use easement, this one over a third neighbor Paul's land.

Kevin is a short, solid man, smart and to the point. When Donald and I met with him, we were impressed and hopeful. He said we needed to get an affidavit from our former neighbor William as to the intention of the easement the three of us had recorded so many years ago. Kevin asked to see the tree easement itself. We set up a time for a ranch visit and went home, relieved.

When Kevin first viewed the savanna and the site, he immediately remarked: "This is beautiful! It has to be saved." I was grateful that he saw the conditions on the ground and made his own judgement. We walked along the tree easement property line, showing him the extent of the easement. Donald, in his increasingly meandering way, also wanted to show Kevin the house and to recount the history of the title of the property. At $475 an hour I listened to Donald tell how the land was deeded to the Daly family by General Vallejo's brother, Salvador. Hardly a noble gesture! The fact that the king of Spain and Vallejo violently ripped it off from the Wappo a mere two hundred years ago has faded from collective memory.

Kevin photographed the savanna, the well, and the "structure" of the electrical panel that provides power to pump the water, comparing it all to the map he had of the easement. "This has to be done," he said. "You have a strong case."

Within an hour of Kevin's departure, Jeff emailed us. Having also just met with Kevin on site at his home, he said there was good news on the road easement. He explained Kevin's findings. The road easement that the Sinclairs planned to use for their proposed new winery, which was on a separate parcel, was attached to the residential parcel, William's former property. It can't be used by the parcel on which they plan to build the winery, even if they merged the two parcels. Paul, the owner of the property with the road easement, is in contact with his own attorney, who is sending a letter to the Planning Commission, who, in turn, will send the letter on to the County Counsel, who should agree. Planning will then send the Sinclairs a letter saying that they do not have right to use the road easement, and they must prove that they *do* have the right. The onus is thus on the Sinclairs. Planning will tell the Sinclairs that they can either build a road on their own property through a twenty-foot flagpole tag of land or use their Redwood Road access. Because they have only twenty feet to work with, they would have to build a bridge across a ravine, which would probably trigger environmental review. Jeff concluded that they would have to use Redwood Road. "Sinclairs can try to contest the ruling, but Kevin says the law is quite clear."

Synchronistically, this same week I received an email from Ann Manning of Future First and the Women's Congress for Future Generations.

> Thank you for your camaraderie over the winter to allow for the fallow time that is so necessary when doing this important work. One of the gifts of the Feminine in each of us is the reminder that we must honor the need for deep inner work or the fruit of our work will not mature and be full of flavor!

She continued, "May each of you find your place in the movement that is nothing less than an 'all hands on deck' moment. Together we are powerful beyond measure."

The "Feminine" has many faces. As Lilith, she *will not be subordinated* and will not accept the status quo. As Eve, she tastes the fruit of consciousness and offers it to the world. As Mother, she nurtures. As Kali, her belt of skulls rattling as she dances the seasons, she knows *for everything there is a season, and a time for every matter under heaven.*[120] Timing—including fallow time—is important to the Feminine.

"Fallow time" for "deep inner work"? I felt driven by the mania of the Sinclairs plans and the county's timetable. There was little time for rest in this schedule, but rest was important for a receptive attitude within and without. But perhaps with Kevin working for us, Donald and I could relax. I told Kevin I was relieved that he was on board.

He said, "I haven't done anything yet."

"Yes," I explained, "but I have spent so much time worrying about what needed to be done and when we should do it. Now we have you to determine that." That alone is worth the money!

But as we would soon find, relief is like an island in a sea, a temporary but important resting spot, even if a regression to that wish to return to the worry-free land of Eden.

I am reminded of the first anniversary meeting of Napa Vision 2050. The Napa Valley

College auditorium was almost full as various members presented updates on projects. The Water, Forest, and Oak Woodlands Protection Initiative petitions had just come out, and promoters Jim Wilson and Mike Hackett were collecting signatures. Donald and I were among the first signers that evening of what would become almost 6300 signatures on that flagship petition. There were updates on the Walt Ranch Project and on an application for a private heliport for a wealthy young man who did not want to drive the twenty minutes from the airport to his winery. Neighbors were outraged, concerned about the noise and the potential decline in property values should this heliport be permitted. At one point Dan, president of Napa Vision 2050 and master of ceremonies of the evening, lamented the lack of county response to our many public comments, Letters to the Editor, and visits to supervisors. The commissioners and supervisors were still granting too many variances and road exceptions. Dan pointed out that we were going to have to go to another level when it came to having any impact on the machinery of the prevailing industries—the wine and hospitality industries—and that meant the courts and going to the public through initiatives. "No more Mr. Nice Guy!" he declared.

Donald and I also realized that in acquiring an attorney to deal with the Sinclairs, we too were having to accept *No more Mr. and Ms. Nice Guys!* But how do we proceed with being firm and strong in our advocacy for the savanna and our neighborhood, yet also not hateful? Perhaps it will be like Rilke suggests. "Live the questions now. Perhaps you will then gradually, even without knowing it, one distant day live right into the answers."[121]

CHAPTER 28

Dementia and the Facts on the Ground

MY MIND OFTEN WANDERS back to the verdigris bittersweetness of eternity sensed that one afternoon many years ago now. I see Donald in his white work pants, our long-gone dogs black and white against green, green grass. Nostalgia weakens one's soul; this memory does not. Instead, it is an *omphalos* into the unique archetypal signature of our marriage, experienced early on as falling in love. The experience of this ineffable quality proceeded to expand us in surprising ways. The pattern endures and, tapped into, sustains me and I suspect Donald as well. These days he lives increasingly in another plane, as if transferring his weight from one foot to the other, as one does boarding a canoe. His smiling eyes often glow with an ecstatic wisdom not of this Earth. Each day he takes me aside, confides, as if he has not already told me, "I don't want to cause you unnecessary alarm. Although in the night I am clear, during the day I am not. I need you to help me remember what to do next." I calmly reassure him that I will, but I want to vomit. *Where is this going?* Still, I sense the unique resonance of his soul. Is this new consciousness also that which transcends the tangles and plaques that strangle so-called normal consciousness?

Are we called to become *artists of aging* with increasing years? Jung wrote:

> The creative process . . . consists in the unconscious activation of an archetypal image, and in elaborating and shaping this image into the finished work. By giving it shape, the artist translates it into the language of the present, and so makes it possible for us to find our way back to the deepest springs of life.[122]

The "language of the present": Peggy, a wise friend, told me that my only job is to accept what is right before me. It wastes time to look back sentimentally or to mourn what will not be. *For better or worse,* this is what we sign on to when we marry. Jungian analyst Adolf Guggenbühl-Craig addresses the importance of keeping this commitment.

OPPOSITE: *Gnarly Oak* (Photograph: Bill Hocker)

Marriage is not comfortable and harmonious. Rather it is a place of individuation where a person rubs up against oneself and against the partner, bumps up against the person in love and in rejection, and in this fashion learns to know oneself, the world, good and evil, the heights and the depths.[123]

Dealing with the rigors of Donald's dementia has rubbed me against the hardest parts of myself—and of Donald, too. Dementia is not only loss of memory and judgement, but also personality change. As a psychotherapist, I have the bias that everything can be worked through. With dementia, you learn that is not true. It happened slowly at first. Donald forgot agreements, and we argued, sought couple's counseling, which did not work, until a social worker from the Ray Dolby Brain Health Center showed me how to avoid the head-on collisions. I mourned the feeling of companionship on decision making, but it doesn't matter. That time is over.

When my grandmother was dying, she made notes and stuffed them into vases and taped them under furniture and behind pictures. "This cream pitcher belonged to Aunt Ruth. It was always on her morning tray." "This was the last gift from my father to my mother before he died." A worn envelope: "Small pearl beads and broken clasp. Aunt Ida's." My mother told me that her mother knew Mom would not remember any of this, so my grandmother wanted to make sure the family history of the objects was kept.

Now I feel like my mother did. Donald makes lists over and over: lists of phone numbers—where to order hay, for the plumber, for the electrician, lists of what needs to be done each month on the ranch. I don't want these lists; I want him. But when we run out of hay, or the valve to the irrigation in the vineyard breaks, or we have no idea how to turn on irrigation in the orchard without watering the vines, and Donald doesn't remember the intricacies of the system he designed, I find the lists, accept the *facts on the ground*. It's my job now.

The *facts on the ground* bring us into the present. This is true with a spouse diagnosed with Alzheimer's, and it is also true with the Earth and climate change. We miss the point if we mourn for the past certainty of seasons or eclipse the moment with angst for the future. All esoteric traditions teach that the *point of power* is in the present moment. This is the moment it changes or it doesn't.

But the *point of power* philosophy is tricky! It is so easy to focus on the wrong thing and thereby participate in creating or sustaining it! Many years ago, Donald and I stayed at a cross-country ski resort in which an instructor suggested that I imagine where I wanted to go instead of what I feared hitting. "Picture in your mind where you are going, even if you can't yet see it. The image you hold is what you'll get." To my amazement this worked, and I successfully navigated my way down curvy trails without hitting trees.

In Napa Vision 2050, we struggle with this same concept. Where do we want to be in 2050? What is our vision? Holding this vision within, even in the face of current realities, is our power. If we focus only on the obstacles and transgressions—the oak woodlands and forests cut for vineyards, variances and road exceptions granted, code violations ignored, fragile agricultural watersheds turned into Disneyland for the very wealthy—if we focus only on these, we feed the battle.

Witnessing the withered tree is exceedingly painful, but it is also our only hope. There are things to be done, for sure. Earth needs our advocacy. But apprehending the archetypal pattern of wholeness, whether that be of a marriage or of our Earth, is essential when it comes to witnessing the *facts on the ground* and finding our way into what happens next.

Sea mandala made by my family at the coast during this particularly difficult time

CHAPTER 29

Harmony with Nature

SOMETIMES WHAT SEEMS LOST returns in unexpected ways. Are our lives loops in which we revisit the same territory over and over until we *get* it? Or do our souls have purpose that informs the course, repeating and repeating, a spiraling pattern with a growing gradient that makes our lives make sense?

When I was sixteen, I was chosen to represent our regional United Methodist church youth group in a weeklong United Nations intern program, which would cost $100. Our family neither had the money for this, nor would my parents allow me to work outside the home to get it. *I was needed at home,* they said. The minister of our church offered to have the church pay my way, but my father, I understand now, wisely objected. Every member of our church was as strapped as we were, being farmers. To my father this was charity, asking others to do what he could not, others who also could little afford it. That $100 would have to come from the weekly round of the collection plate.

I was furious. I so wanted to go to the United Nations for this experience! It was only a handful of years since my letter to President Eisenhower, the angst of the Cuban Missile Crisis, the death of Kennedy. I felt inexplicably drawn to working for world peace. New York City and the United Nations were symbols of that. As only a teenage girl can, I threw a fit—tears and drama—but to no avail. My patriarch of a father would not budge!

So it is no mystery that when I was in college and offered a college credit summer internship with Urban Corps in New York City, I snapped it up. This time when I called my father, he asked whether I was *asking* or *telling* him that I was going. I told him that I was *telling* him. I remember his silence on the other end, which oddly saddened me. It was another sign of the end of childhood. I commend him for this reaction. Even being the authoritarian father that he was, he accepted my increasing independence. This wouldn't cost him a cent, I continued. I would receive pay to cover living costs, and my scholarship covered the college credit. I might even come out a little ahead (which, of course, I didn't).

The closest I got to the United Nations building on that trip was the sidewalk past it, but I lived in a Fifth Avenue New York University dorm with international students doing

UN summer internships. I spent all my nonworking hours with them as well as with other interns from Urban Corps. In August when I called my father to inform him that I intended to travel to Toronto and Montreal on my way home with my new French-Canadian boyfriend André (yes, he was a UN intern), my father exploded, probably fearing for my virginity, of which he had regularly expounded the virtues. *"Come home immediately!"* he bellowed. Overloaded with the *zeitgeist* of the times, I returned. It was 1968, the summer of the riots at the Chicago Democratic Convention, which André and I watched with others in the dorm lobby. It was the summer a coke bottle with the note *Get out Whitie!* smashed the window of the Bedford Stuyvesant community center where I interned, and my supervisor had to tell me that, for my own safety, I had to *get out.* Serendipitously, it was also the year that the Napa County Board of Supervisors voted in the first ever Agricultural Preserve in the United States.

After being let go from my internship a week early, Canada had seemed like a good choice for the extra time that I had, even though my father objected. I did not throw a fit this time, however. Perhaps I was beginning to recognize when I was getting into waters over my head! I never saw André again.

But this passion for world peace and the United Nations has endured. Is it the refrain in my soul's song, the one that drove me into the streets in protest of the Vietnam war in the 1960s, or again in 1982 that motivated me, pregnant and with toddler Jesse in tow, to hold hands with thousands of others in a giant mandala around Lawrence Livermore Lab in protest of nuclear proliferation? Were these protests part of the great shift that continues now, from a patriarchal attitude toward each other and the Earth, to one more balanced with the Feminine, in which relationship to the Earth and each other is paramount?

This passion for peace opened me to another invitation some fifty years later to participate in the 2016 Sixth Interactive Dialogue of the General Assembly of the United Nations on Harmony with Nature. The Harmony with Nature project began in 2009 with the purpose to "theorize and strategize" life-sustainable ways for peoples of the Earth as we faced unprecedented Earth change.

As the website for the project stated, this would "require a new relationship with the Earth and with humankind's own existence . . . based on a non-anthropocentric relationship with Nature."[124] In 2012 this was expanded to include recognition of the Rights of Nature at the United Nations Conference on Sustainable Development, held in Rio de Janeiro, Brazil. Heads of state and government adopted the outcome document entitled "The Future We Want." This document recognized "the Earth and its ecosystems are our home," and that this recognition is key in understanding what sustainable development is. Since that year several countries and cities have recognized the legal Rights of Nature. These countries include the following: January 2017, Mexico City's new constitution incorporated the Rights of Nature; March 2017, the Ganga and Yamuna rivers in India were granted human status as well as New Zealand's Whanganui river; and in April 2017, India's Himalayan

Gangotri and Yamunotri glaciers were granted the status of living entities, including water-falls, meadows, lakes, and forests. In 2014, a Colorado State Constitutional Amendment was proposed to allow cities the right to pass laws establishing the Rights of Nature, and Ecuador and Bolivia also incorporated the Rights of Nature into constitutions. In 2019, the Superior Court of Justice of Brazil recognized the rights of non-human animals, stating "the need to change the legal anthropocentric paradigm and replace it with biocentric thinking which advances the interconnectedness and close relationship between human beings and Nature and also recognizes Nature's intrinsic value."[125] One of the more recent rights-based laws passed was in Toledo, Ohio. On February 26, 2019, Ohio voters passed a law in which Lake Erie was granted the legal rights normally granted to humans. It was the first United States rights-based law that protected an entire ecosystem: the lake, all its tributaries, and the many species that call it home.[126] Unfortunately, almost immediately, an agribusiness corporation, Drewes Farms, challenged the ballot initiative, soon joined by the State of Ohio,[127] and a federal judge struck down the Lake Erie Bill of Rights law.[128] Then, in November 2020, in a landslide election, the citizens of Orlando, Florida, granted legal rights to the county's waterways, the ballot measure stating that not only people had the right to clean water, but also the county waterways have a "right to exist, Flow, to be protected against Pollution, and to maintain a healthy ecosystem."[129] This too may well be tested, as a year ago the Florida legislature included an amendment in a clean water bill prohibiting local governments from granting legal rights to nature.[130] The legal Rights of Nature faces resistance, but the tide may be turning.

During 2016, the year that I participated, 127 experts from 8 disciplines and 33 nationalities were each given the same four questions and, starting on Earth Day, April 22, two months to answer. The results were collated and recommendations for implementing strategies presented to the General Assembly in August 2016. In a global way, experts around the world called for very much the same thing: that Earth should be recognized as "as a subject to be communed with"—not an object to exploit—and that we turn to indigenous wisdom still intact in achieving this goal. The feminine values of relationship and nurturance were highlighted over the more so-called traditional masculine ways of power-over, which too often become exploitive and destructive.

The web page for the sixth dialogue ends with the statement that, for the paradigm of nature having rights to grow, "it will require support of laws, ethics, institutions, policies, and practices that have, at their core, a fundamental respect for the Earth and its natural cycles, and a clear understanding that the wellbeing of humankind is co-dependent on the wellbeing of the Earth."

If we are going to survive at all, we have to enter a new period.

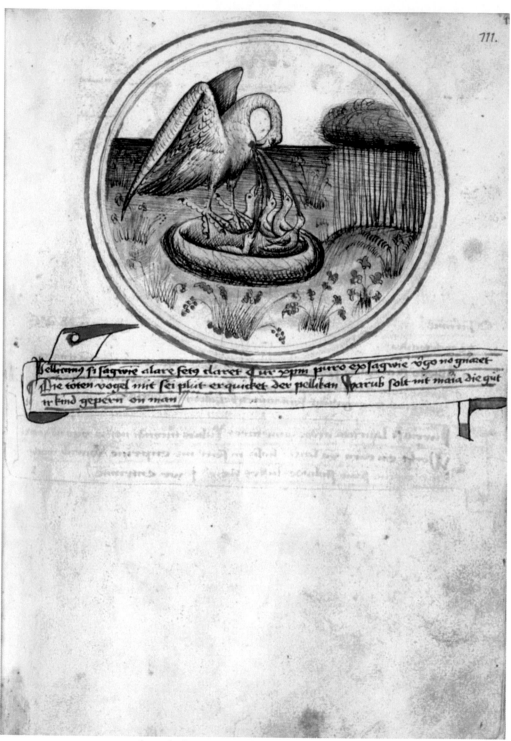

Pelican feeding its young by piercing its own breast for blood, which they drink.

(From Speculum humanae salvationis Memento mori-Texte [u.a.] - BSB Cgm 3974 Creation.
[S.I] Bayern - Osterreich, I: zwischen ca. 1440-1466, II: um Mitte 15. Jh., III: 2. Viertel 15. Jh.)

CHAPTER 30

Another Pelican Dream, Brown Pelican and Dog

In September 2016, *I dreamed that I lived under a bridge in a house on stilts. Others lived nearby. In the dream, I lift a floorboard to see several beautiful brown-spotted pelicans swimming and fishing just below. I call Wesley and Sabien to see this unusual sight. A dog with a woven red blanket over its back trots along the riverbank. At first, I wonder if these are the markings of a wild dog, but realize he is in traditional indigenous ceremonial dress and belongs to one of the campers downstream.*

This dream occurred during a particularly difficult period, both in the county, which I will describe later, and at home. Donald's dementia was worsening. He could no longer manage our commercial property nor make wise decisions on our ranch. People were taking financial advantage of us in ways he would have never allowed before. The doctor told him that he could no longer drive. He was not ready to accept any of this. My attempts to convince him that we needed a property management company and that I needed to take over more of the decision making were met with denial. He said that could happen in time, but that time wasn't here yet. I knew that if this continued, I was going to have to take difficult legal measures that would be exceedingly painful for both of us.

My anxiety rose to the point that I could not sleep. This is when I had the dream. As if to underscore the message, I began to happen across pelican images. One particularly difficult day shortly after the dream, I found an iron statue of a pelican in a favorite store and bought it. It stands on the top of the buffet overlooking our dining room table.

Healing is a process of being restored to wholeness. Dis-ease occurs when we fall away from wholeness. Jung knew this. Shamans know this. Medicine people know this. My senior consultant studied with a Navajo medicine man for years and described to us students how healing happens in that tradition. The medicine man diagnoses a patient and then makes a sand painting representing wholeness, upon which the patient sits. After chants, which may last several days, the sand from the painting is rubbed over the patient's body, restoring him or her to health. In contrast, modern medicine is too often heroic, much like our land-use behavior. Germs are killed. Infected organs cut out. Land is managed for maximum production, often regardless of impact on the environment.

I have the fortune to have a homeopathic healer who listens to the psyche much as an experienced navigator reads a river, or a biodynamic farmer, a vineyard. She often uses my dreams to decide which remedy to use. More than once she has had me collect substances that I dream about to have remedies made to treat various imbalances. So when I consulted her after months of sleeplessness and angst and grief at Donald's increasing loss of memory and personality changes, and my continued anxiety around the encroachment and destruction of the savanna and of our Earth, I was not surprised when she asked for my dreams. After hearing the brown pelican dreams, she prescribed *Pelecanus occidentalis,* a remedy made from a brown pelican feather. It worked; I slept soundly again. Synchronistically, Donald moved from an agitated, controlling state to one of apparent evolved acceptance of his changing brain. Within two weeks of my taking the remedy, he agreed to retaining a property management company. (Of course, this has helped immeasurably with my sleeplessness!) Did the remedy work on returning us to the wholeness of our marriage?

I do not pretend to understand the mystery of this healing. I do know that the way a Jungian analyst understands a dream is quite different from how a homeopath does. As an analyst, I consider several angles. The symbol of pelican is ancient. In alchemy, the *pelican* is known as the vessel in which the alchemical magic occurs. According to Jung, *pelican* represents a distillation of sorts: "The process of realization in which new insights emerge, die, go back into the unconscious and return again."[131] In fact, Jung said that life's greatest problems are not solved, only outgrown.[132] This requires holding opposing and difficult feelings long enough until the change or rebirth happens.

In mythology, it is said that the pelican feeds her young with drops of blood drawn when she pecks out feathers from her breast. In other words, it is a circular, suffering kind of process in which all is held together long enough for transformation, a process necessary for nourishment of the new babes.

James Hillman cautioned about considering only the symbolic nature of an animal in a dream. My Native friends would agree. The animal, in this case, the pelican, is seen as visiting me in the spirit realm and needs to be met on that level. In bringing myself into resonance with the pelican, I am bringing myself into resonance with a particular energy that *is pelican.*

Pelicans fly, fish, and nest in groups. In the weeks after taking the remedy, I found myself relying more on our families and friends to help get Donald and me through the challenges of our marriage. My sons and their families stepped in, concerned, as did some of Donald's children and his sister Norma. The Ray Dolby Brain Health Center met with us, explained the cognitive and neurological changes of Alzheimer's disease and vascular dementia, and coached us on how to deal with Donald. "Don't argue. Stay connected. Be positive." Norma offered me safe refuge during a period of time when I was confused and frightened by Donald's escalating frustration, anger, and fear.

Did the remedy also work on my participation in the community of Napa Vision 2050? Our weekly three-to-four-hour meetings were full of teasing and the sharing of frustrations while fishing for insights on how to address the land-use issues that threatened our community and our environment. As Mary Pipher said at the Women's Congress for Future Generations, "If you are going to be an activist, you had better have fun!"—and we do. I told someone during this period that the frustrating political work I was doing with Napa Vision 2050 is a respite from the rest of my life. The group energy was not only fun but also restorative.

Another kind of animal help is offered in the dream as well, that of dog. Follow your instinct. Sniff out the right direction. Follow your nose—politically: follow the money. Money is energy, and in doggedly following the trail into the campaign donations of our elected officials, we discover where the power is. This is not a wild dog, although perhaps a companion of Lilith, wearing a red blanket, sniffing out the money trail in an intentional way.

In contrast to *dog,* which sniffs out the trail, *pelican* offers perspective. To find the fish, pelicans must rise above the water. Before pelicans dive in to catch fish, they must empty their pouches. Like alchemical distillation, this happens over and over. We need both dog energy on the ground and pelican in water and air. In activism, in order to sniff out the trail, we enter a distillation process of rising above to spot the prize and then emptying our "pouches" of preconceptions to dive in.

Walt Ranch Protests (Photograph: Bill Hocker)

CHAPTER 31

We the People and the Board of Supervisors

Truth is the oxygen of democracy . . . and unless we
see the truth, we are going to run out of oxygen.
BILL MOYERS, "Truth Is the Oxygen of Democracy"[133]

JUNE 2016 BROUGHT JUBILATION—and then rage—to many of us who had
supported the inclusion of the Water, Forest, and Oak Woodland Protection Initiative on
the November 8, 2016, ballot. The initiative extended protections to our Ag Watershed lands
by making many of the provisions of the 2010 Voluntary Oak Woodland Management Plan
mandatory. Although modest in its reach, the initiative inspired fear in the wine industry,
which, having planted out the valley, had moved its sites to the forested and fragile hillsides
of the protected Ag Watersheds.

Almost 6300 signatures were presented to the Registrar's office in mid-May, signatures
gathered by more than 80 volunteers for hundreds of hours over the previous three months.
On June 6, 2016, John Tuteur, Napa County Registrar of Voters, certified the required 3791
signatures, saying that they superseded the required number by 28 percent. Three days later,
June 9, 2016, a bomb dropped: The County Registrar rejected the initiative due to "a very
technical issue." The text of the initiative cited documents that were not available with the
petition on site when people signed. "County counsel believes those documents had to be
included with the petition, and they weren't."[134]

Citizens were outraged. Rumors mushroomed about what really happened: that a
supervisor, compelled by one of the wine industry groups, had ordered the County Counsel
to decertify the ballot initiative in any way possible, that every other initiative making it to
the November ballot had this same technical "flaw." *Sniff out the trail of money,* the wiser
of us said. Follow the money.

Lilith stormed! *We the People will not be suppressed!* Within ten days the supporters of
the initiative appealed the decision of the County Counsel to Napa County Superior Court.

The suit mandated that the Registrar of Voters require the Board of Supervisors either to adopt the initiative as an ordinance or to place it on the ballot. The hearing was set for July 15, 2016. Many of us crowded into the tiny courtroom on the third floor of the County Courthouse. We wondered aloud why a small courtroom had been chosen for a hearing with so much exposure. The bailiff ordered those of us without seats to stand in the hall outside the closed door, which filled as more and more people arrived. We stood in groups, speculating. Occasionally someone would come out and tell us what was happening: Tuteur was looking grim. Perlmutter, the attorney from Shute, Mihaly & Weinberger representing the initiative, was being hammered. It looked good; it didn't.

And Lilith stormed at home as well. Early that spring Casey and Melissa had moved to our ranch with Wesley and Sabien. Given the fact that we were aging, Donald and I had decided to lease the vines. Casey and Melissa would take over the lavender and aromatics and help us generally on the ranch.

The transition was not an easy one. Donald had farmed the ranch since 1982, replanting vines twice and designing the complicated irrigation system. He and I have developed the aromatics and have a close personal relationship with every trail and almost every tree of the forty-one acres that stretch up the mountain from Dry Creek Road to the ridge. Leasing the vineyard was letting go. We felt a sadness when leasees Steve and Jack talked about "their vines"—and they meant ours.

Having Casey and Melissa move to the ranch was a great joy—we were full of hope— but it also turned out to be a rough beginning. They moved to the old house we had lived in while building our home, and it needed more remodeling than anticipated. Donald's expectations became untethered. He forgot unfortunately unwritten original agreements made before Casey and Melissa arrived. When it was time to distill the rose geranium and the lavender in June, Donald effectively forgot that we were stepping out of the farming and Casey and Melissa were taking over.

We all knew Donald's judgement was slipping. This man who designed and built every-thing from the desk in my studio with drawers that glide effortlessly to a Ukiah maternity ward with both function and aesthetics, ordered a replacement window for their living room that turned out to be a foot-and-a-half too short in length and in width and built a kitchen cabinet six inches too short for the pantry. Instead of white stock cabinets in the main kitchen, black cabinets were delivered and had to be repainted.

Even in the light of these errors and his diminishing physical vitality, I misjudged the difficulty he would have letting go of controlling the distillation process. Casey was now to be in charge; Donald decided to enforce his own order and methods. One might think distillation is fairly straightforward, but distillation is an art, unique in many ways to the distiller—the alchemist. *Pelican* steps in. One's soul participates. Remember: "When you set about distilling, you acquire the consciousness of repeating a ritual consecrated by the centuries, almost a religious act, in which from the imperfect material you obtain the essence, the usia, the spirit."[135] Distillation had grown on Donald, and although he said he no longer could do it, he wasn't ready to give it up either.

When things are out of order from how Donald always preformed a task, he increasingly becomes disoriented. Tea making in the kitchen. The timing of the evening meal and what happens next. I thought this was a control issue, but I was wrong. It is neurological. Donald's last testing had shown his executive function, decision making, to be 3 percent of others his age. With the distillation of lavender, this meant that Donald wanted a white cabinet standing beside the still with the quart-sized sterilized bottles in it and everything lined up on the top: one of the brown quart bottles for the oil, a white plastic funnel in the separating funnel beside it, then the clipboard. For Casey, who has his own way of keeping order, this was controlling. Tensions built. We all worried how this was going to work, and it took a year and a half, some breath holding, and a great deal of perseverance on everyone's part to get a workable plan in place, a plan that morphs into another with periodic regularity as Donald continues to lose function, and we adjust.

In early August 2016, the Watershed Initiative received notice that the Napa County Superior Court, which has shown itself to be increasingly unfriendly to the environmental movement, upheld the County Counsel's decision. The initiative would not make it to the November 8, 2016, ballot.

The following Letter to the Editor tells more of the story. Napa Vision 2050's resolve of *No More Mr. Nice Guy* was re-enforced as we matured as an advocacy group. Then the November 8, 2016, the election of Donald Trump to the presidency left the general population reeling in disbelief, fear, and yes, for some 29 percent of our county, elation. What became clear is that we could no longer remain confident that our elected officials would act on behalf of the people. This is true on the national level, and it is true in Napa County as well. We are in a period of great unrest and disorientation, a period described by Jung some seventy years ago:

> . . . a mood of universal destruction and renewal . . . has set its mark on our age. This mood makes itself felt everywhere, politically, socially, and philosophically. We are living in what the Greeks called the *kairos*—the right moment—for a "metamorphosis of the gods," of the fundamental principles and symbols. This peculiarity of our time, which is certainly not of our conscious choosing, is the expression of the unconscious man within us who is changing. Coming generations will have to take account of this momentous transformation if humanity is not to destroy itself through the might of its own technology and science. . . . So much is at stake and so much depends on the psychological constitution of the modern human.[136]

Who is "we" on watershed initiative?

In a recent *Napa Valley Register* article, "State Court Declines to Revive Napa Watershed Measure for November Ballot," Chairman of the Board of Supervisors Alfredo Pedroza was quoted or paraphrased in a number of disturbing statements.[137]

Pedroza claims to be confident that the county, wine, and farming sectors will have whatever discussions need to be had on watershed issues, citing the formation of the Agricultural Protection Advisory Committee (APAC) by the County. Yes, the County formed APAC, but has not followed its recommendations. Watershed protection seems to be lower down the list of priorities, after protecting property rights, elevating direct marketing to an accessory use of Ag, and allowing fragile hillside Ag watershed lands to be clear cut for "great cabs." In our changing climate, we need champions for the environment. This initiative was an agent of those champions.

Pedroza seems to think the formation of Napa Green, the environmental certification programs for wineries and land, fills the bill. Although these programs are good, they are also voluntary and do not limit the use of agricultural chemicals, including glyphosate, whose use has only increased. These chemicals are finding their way into our water.

But perhaps the most egregious of these statements by Pedroza is "We don't need an initiative hanging over our heads."

"We?" Who is he talking about? Certainly not the almost 6300 people who signed the petition wanting to vote on the initiative—more people, I might add, than voted for Pedroza in the June primary. Why is the Board of Supervisors not insisting that Napa citizens get to vote on an initiative shockingly blocked by a small technicality, even after it was certified? What master is this process serving?

We the 6300 people are worried about our climate, our watersheds, and our water. What happens in the watersheds impacts what eventually flows into the faucets of the city of Napa, periodically presenting itself in the smell of the treated, supposedly safe, brown water.

This is nothing less than a moral issue: Suppression of a democratic people's right to vote on an issue that profoundly impacts them now and into the future. When the trees that restore and maintain watershed health are gone, they are gone for a very long time, even if replanted. This suppression of the right to vote is a twin to the moral issue of "should these projects which clear cut our watersheds be done at all?" Not "can they?"

It has never been more important for citizens to insist our voices are heard, or to replace those who do not hear us.

PATRICIA DAMERY

NAPA

CHAPTER 32

"Hall No!"

THE FATE OF THE Watershed Initiative was not the only source of growing citizen discontent and anger. Besides a variety of smaller projects, two large projects drew our attention and work: Walt Ranch and the expansion of the Syar Industries, Inc., mining operations.

Since 2008, Texas entrepreneurs and real estate investors Craig and Kathryn Hall had worked to get vineyard property permitted on the east Napa Valley 2300-acre mountainous ranch that they had purchased in 2005. Their ranch includes two watersheds. About a third of the ranch is part of the Milliken watershed and drains into the Milliken Reservoir, a source of water for the City of Napa and, according to Napa City Water Manager Joy Eldridge, "effectively pristine."[138] The second watershed, the Capell watershed, includes the neighboring community of Circle Oaks, whose citizens fear the proposed Walt vineyard wells will negatively impact their community wells.

Although Craig Hall claimed that "At its basic, Walt vineyard is a vineyard in an agriculturally zoned area," the application suggested another story. As former Supervisor Ginny Simms told supervisors at the November Board of Supervisors appeal hearings, the road and water improvements for Walt Ranch set the stage for a housing project. The local paper reported, "Walt Ranch has 35 parcels, each of which under county law can have a house. Simms said the environmental impact report should address the possibility of houses, given it is supposed to look at the obvious and predictable results of a proposed action."[139]

Walt Ranch attorney Whit Manley countered that the environmental impact report need not look at the possibility of homes, that the improvement of the dirt roads was to reduce erosion. "We have not said anything about our intention to develop estate lots on the property," Manley said. "That's nowhere in our application or elsewhere. The vineyard does not depend on residential development."[140]

Along with the slipperiness of Manley's statement, there are many reasons to question Craig Hall's motives. He is an entrepreneur, not a farmer; moneymaking is his art. His book *Timing the Real Estate Market: The Secrets to Buying Low and Selling High* (2004) reflects his interest. Walt Ranch appears to be an investment opportunity. A November 2013 *D Magazine* article praised his long history of moneymaking, starting in childhood.

> Instead of just one paper route, Hall had several. That led to a thriving lawn-care business that employed his brother and his brother's friends. Hall lied about his age to sell knife sets door-to-door. Meantime, he also went to school and held down jobs ranging from dishwasher to night watchman. At one point, Hall's parents…took him to a psychiatrist, concerned by what they viewed as their son's obsession with money. "The tests were a joke," he says. "I messed with the guy by telling him all the images looked like dollar bills. It was fun."[141]

Was he applying the same coyote "fun" tactics to his recent real-estate venture—Walt Ranch? As Ginny Simms commented, our Board of Supervisors and Planning Commission were clearly not considering the larger picture. In August 2017, the Board of Supervisors would be called out on their repeated failures to comply with CEQA requirements—to look at the "obvious and predictable results of a proposed action"—and this was one of the more blatant examples.[142] Thirty-five potential lifestyle estates, each with a vineyard and a view and possibly a winery, would put added pressure on water supply, traffic, and erosion into and potential contamination of Milliken Reservoir; none of this was considered in the limited environmental impact report. Our governing officials were turning a blind eye to this, perhaps influenced by the $30,000 campaign donations paid to elected county officials just since 2012. During the time the project was working through the county's environment review, the Hall family, including their children who live and work in Texas, also contributed almost $26,000 to Bill Dodd, former supervisor running at the time for Assembly and now state senator.[143]

On June 13, 2016, Walt Ranch received the Planning Commission's tentative approval. The final notice of approval of the Walt erosion control plan came on August 1, 2016. Four groups vowed to appeal the decision to the Board of Supervisors. Many of us spent summer weekend days throughout the protesting in front of Hall Winery's gargantuan chrome rabbit in St. Helena, waving at honking cars and being flipped off by some of the winery-elite's finest executives. Donald; Casey; Wesley, age six; and Sabien, age four; as well as weekend guests, went with me. We wore straw hats and long sleeves to protect ourselves from the hot sun and held signs reading, *No Chainsaw Wines. Halt Walt! Hall No!* Wesley's favorite was a small sign that read *Protect Trees,* which he soberly held. We got to know others in the movement, standing there beside Route 29, one of the two main arteries through the Napa Valley. There was Lisa, a cheery, energetic woman from Circle Oaks; Leonore, former poet laureate of Napa County, whose five-generation-old ranch was a neighbor of Walt Ranch; Steve, a retired psychologist who had worked at the Napa State Hospital; Mike, one of the co-authors of the watershed initiative and a retired commercial airline pilot. The Halls reduced their plan by about a third, some at the insistence of the Planning Department, but they still proposed to disturb 316 acres for 209 acres of vineyards.

The county's environmental impact report (EIR) concluded that the revised development, which still involved cutting 14,281 trees, with mitigations, would have *no significant impact* on the environment. The fact that the Halls were not cutting trees on parts of the ranch was used as mitigation for the 14,281 trees they planned to cut, a reasoning that confounds anyone who thinks about it more than a minute. Although there was much contradictory evidence to the assertion the project would have *no significant impact,* the Planning Commission had okayed the project, something we expected.

Subsequently, the Napa Sierra Club, Living Rivers Council, Center for Biological Diversity, and, jointly, the Circle Oaks County Water District and Circle Oaks Homes Association appealed the decision to the Board of Supervisors. In an August 2016 press release from the Napa Sierra Club announcing the appeal of the county's decision to permit Walt Ranch, Sierra Club chair Nancy Tamarisk wrote the following:

> It is the Sierra Club's position that the County is out of compliance with State laws, including AB 32, which require action to reduce greenhouse gas emissions. Trees are vital bulwarks against climate change, and globally, deforestation is a major driver of climate change. The County's project review process fails to adequately account for and remediate the climate change impacts of woodland destruction, and reflects the County's foot-dragging on the requirement to develop a greenhouse gas control plan.... The County must comply with state law by requiring that Walt and future development projects do not contribute to climate change and environmental degradation. The Walt Project is too big to ignore, and the time for action by the County is long past. We urge the Supervisors to reverse the approval of the Walt project in its current form.[144]

On November 18, 2016, many of us gathered to make public comment and in peaceful protest at the first of the appeal hearings, sporting red t-shirts with large white letters: "Hall No!" Experts hired by the appellants presented reports that challenged the results of the county-approved EIR on erosion control, water, and climate protection. Whereas the Halls were given significant time for their reports, members of the public had to stick to three minutes each. One by one we stepped to the microphone, spoke from our hearts, read statements we had practiced to make sure they were only three minutes. At noon, I am told the Halls were surprised as they watched from the windows of the Board of Supervisors Chamber as over one hundred people, including a number of children, gathered below. Charlie Toledo led a group of local Native Americans in drumming and singing prayers. Musicians sang protest songs, adapted to the occasion. People streamed in over that hour, gathering signs, getting to know each other, the forces gathering.

Nevertheless, in December 2016, without significant consideration of conflicting reports, the Board of Supervisors denied the appeal. Since then, the four appellants have sued the county. In a year-end summary, the Napa Sierra Club wrote:

Above and beyond the Walt project, this fight has galvanized Napa. Literally hundreds of people helped in our effort. The energy spurred the creation of [Napa] Vision 2050, a coalition of concerned residents working against harmful development throughout Napa County. Thanks to the Walt fight, the Napa environmental community is stronger and smarter than ever.

Developers have been put on notice. Attempts to clear-cut Napa woodlands will meet fierce opposition, resulting in huge costs and project delays. Many will decide there are easier ways to make money.[145]

During this time, Syar Industries, Inc., a mining operation in Napa County that supplies aggregate for roads and other projects, also received approval for increasing their mining operation by 106 acres to 497 acres total and gravel and asphalt production from 810,363 tons to 1.3 million tons a year. Volcanic basalt rock is found in layers and is particularly important in road construction. Syar's operation mines basalt, manufactures asphalt, and recycles concrete and asphalt, grinding rock and recycled concrete in the open air.

The quarry has a long history in Napa Valley. Mining originally began in the late 1800s. The quarry was then bought by Leo J. Alexander in 1914 as Basalt Rock Company. Over the years it has employed a number of local citizens. The rip rap from the quarry built up Treasure Island for the 1939 Golden Gate International Exposition.[146] In 1951 Tom Syar founded Syar Industries, Inc., which owned a 50 percent share of Basalt Rock Company. Since 1986, the Syar family has been in control of the entire quarry. Now Syar claimed that if they did not receive approval for expansion, they would run out of the basalt rock. Citizen groups disagreed, saying there was no evidence of this assertion. More concerning were the health risks posed by the mining operations. Crystalline silica has been linked with respiratory problems and cancer. In a letter of public comment, Stop Syar Expansion's Steve Booth quoted a study commissioned by the group that showed the air quality around the mine was contaminated with diesel fumes and silica dust. "PM10 [parts per million] particulate emissions from the quarry are, and will continue to be, in violation of both the National Ambient Air Quality Standard (NAAQS) and the California Ambient Air Quality Standard (CAAQS) if the project is approved as proposed."[147]

The Planning Commission still approved the expansion in November 2015 in a three to two vote. The decision was appealed to the Board of Supervisors by two citizen groups: Stop Syar Expansion and Skyline Park Citizens Association. Despite evidence that Napa County rates of childhood cancer diagnosis in that area had risen to the highest of any county in the State of California between 2008 and 2012,[148] and lack of evidence that the quarry needed to expand, the Board of Supervisors upheld the expansion, four to one, in July 2016, agreeing with the environmental impact report that claimed the blowing dust caused no danger to nearby neighborhoods. Three days of public comment and evidence that the environmental impact report was faulty resulted in the all too familiar decision: with certain steps taken, the expansion of Syar would have "less than significant" impact on the environment. Justifying his yes vote, Chair Alfredo Pedroza said, "I look at the audience and it's almost like it's pro-business and pro-environment. It's about pro-Napa."[149]

Appellants were appalled by the county's dismissal of the health issues. Again, appellants sued the county for approval of faulty environmental impact reports, and Stop Syar Expansion sued Syar for not notifying citizens of harmful dust and emissions (Prop 65[150]) and for nuisance and trespass because of intrusion of harmful material on private property. Stop Syar Expansion asked for Syar's production data. Under the rules governing this request, Syar was required to deliver the information within 30 calendar days; Syar stalled for a year. Once received, the data showed the exposure area was less than originally believed, but not nonexistent. Stop Syar Expansion and the other plaintiffs (Napa Vision 2050, Kathy Felch, and Susanne von Rosenberg) accepted Syar's offer of $5,000 each to settle the case, for total of $20,000. Had Syar been forthcoming, the litigation would very likely have ended a year earlier with less expense to all. Syar's apparent strategy is to make it too expensive for the community to challenge its activities. Reinforcing this apparent strategy is its refusal to pay a court-ordered cost in excess of $58,000 after telling the court it was worth it to Syar to pay $90,000 to get all of plaintiffs' emails. After the settlement, Syar asked the local trial court to relieve it of this cost, which the court did. The Stop Syar Expansion group appealed this decision to the Court of Appeals, which refused to hold Syar responsible for the costs. Again, before the same local trial judge, the Stop Syar Expansion group lost its challenge to the EIR approval. The group appealed the trial court's decision to the 1st District Court of Appeal, which in turn denied the appeal. They then sought review of the decision by the California Supreme Court; review was denied. All of this is paid for by citizens from their own pockets. In the meantime, all concerned are gearing up for the Board of Supervisors' five-year review of the expanded project anticipated to occur in the last quarter of 2021.

The polarity between the planners, commissioners, and supervisors, and the larger citizen groups of Napa County has never been greater. County officials' myopic stance is represented in a quote regarding the Walt Ranch decision by Supervisor Brad Wagenknecht, usually one of the more sensitive supervisors to environmental issues: "I think the applicant has met what we set out as the ground rules and I think in a lot of cases has gone beyond."[151]

The larger perspective of the cumulative impact of these approvals on the watersheds, environment, and the community has been ignored. "I don't get they [the supervisors] have a moral sense of their role in cascading adverse impacts felt by the community," Jim Wilson, co-author of the Watershed Initiative, wrote. His ranch, where he lives with his poet wife,

Leonore, is adjacent to Walt Ranch. "Our tranquil agricultural home is tragically being turned into an alcohol circus. When it comes to the safety and welfare of its citizens, the County Board of Supervisors have averted their eyes, promoting short-term private gains over the long-term protection of the common good."[152]

By the end of 2016, we were saddened by the losses of the year, but we were wiser. We no longer trusted our county officials to act for the common good and for the health and safety of the environment and the residents of Napa County. This was going to take a long time.

LETTER TO THE EDITOR

Napa Valley Register, December 2, 2016

Walt Ranch needs better environmental evaluation.

I'm writing to supplement several important facts from the hours of testimony from the Walt Ranch hearings: "Napa's Walt Ranch Vineyard Hearings Open with Protest" and "Proponents of Walt Ranch Make Their Case."

The Halls, applicants for Walt Ranch, have applied to convert 316 acres of a large 2300-acre tract of land in the Ag-Watershed into vineyards. Although the project has been modified following the protest of various environmental and local groups, it still involves cutting more than 14,000 mature trees, the equivalent of 62 percent of the trees on the city streets of Napa.

As this project started moving through the EIR process, the Halls began contributing large sums of money to various local lawmakers' campaigns. As these hearings began Chair Pedroza asked the supervisors for "disclosures." Each responded by stating any meetings or correspondence he or she recently had. Not one disclosed campaign contributions from the Halls. Can our supervisors make an independent decision that is for the benefit of the community and our environment when the project's applicant has contributed thousands of dollars to his or her campaign?

One of the biggest dangers of this project is the fact that it is a large part of one of the five remaining biologically diverse areas in Napa County in which the original native plants, animals, and soil structure supporting them still thrive. As we face the uncertainties of climate change and a warming Earth, it is critically important that we protect areas still intact and not further exploit them. This project includes cutting the oak woodlands, which will impact the entire ecosystem that these remaining animals and plants populate.

Four different groups, appellants, found fault with the EIR and want the Board of Supervisors to protect our environment by sending the project's contested EIR report back for future study. I was disappointed to see a lack of reporting [by your paper] on the appellants' many reports from biologists, hydrologists, earth scientists, geologists, which took serious issue with some of the findings of the Walt EIR. Attorney Tom Lippe also questioned the process of the EIR in terms of CEQA compliance. Former supervisor Ginny Simms pointed out that the project's 35 blocks of vineyards, each with roads and water supplied to them, are a thinly veiled real-estate development, ready to be sold separately for lifestyle vineyard estates—and wineries. The EIR's responsibility is to anticipate the consequences of such possible future trajectories. This EIR did not consider such future development, which would have significant impact on water and on ecology of the region.

We heard that four novice biologists spent only one day evaluating Walt Ranch for reptiles and amphibians when only one of them is a herpetologist and others could not identify a tadpole from a frog. And hydrologist Greg Kamman reported the proposed deep-ripping of the thin topsoils in order to plant vines, a process recommended by Walt Ranch consultants, does not improve soil infiltration rates, thereby limiting runoff, but in fact destroys soil structure that naturally handles water infiltration. Even the Regional Water Quality Control Board says there is no evidence deep-ripping increases infiltration rates. These are only a few of the many counter claims.

There are too many discrepancies and the stakes are too high. Insist that the EIR be redone. Contact your supervisor to come down on the right side on this: send the EIR back for expert evaluation.

PATRICIA DAMERY
NAPA

"The sun's rays do not brighten the city, which is so near, nor are its lower rays visible beneath the horizon... . This image of the inner sun tells us that becoming more conscious does not result in a state of elation or bliss."

(From Joseph L. Henderson and Dyane N. Sherwood, *Transformation of the Psyche: The Symbolic Alchemy of the* Splendor Solis, Brunner-Routledge, 2003, 169)

PART VI

—

IN SEARCH
OF A LAND
ETHIC

Jesse walks on the beach with Wesley and Sabien on a day the fires lit the sky with orange and the waves reflected the liquid gold of it.

CHAPTER 33

This Is Climate Change

WHEN THE RAINS BEGAN in late 2016, they did not stop. After three years of low rainfall, even the fourth year's average rainfall did not put us out of "severe drought." Valley oaks wearied. Drought-weakened coastal oaks succumbed to oak bore and fell. My faith in the cycles of nature faltered. Now each fall I hold my breath with the first rains, hoping they are not the last—like the great deluge of December 2012 when our world flooded and our ponds filled by mid-December.

This was the December that Donald collapsed at dinner one rainy evening and the paramedics got stuck on the driveway up to our house. Donald was mostly all of himself then. When he recovered consciousness, he directed the paramedics in maneuvering the gurney out the kitchen door to the ambulance.

We were partners. Now, like a widow, I mourn the loss. I depended on him to keep his part of our bargain—operating the ranch and his part in our life together. But after a week of being hospitalized for sepsis and gall bladder removal, and then being hospitalized a second time three weeks later, followed by a TIA (transient ischemic attack—small stroke), Donald and our life would never be the same. Gullies formed in his memory that seemed to widen with each month, washing away what made things make sense. That rainy December I mark as the beginning of the end of life as we knew it.

As copious as rainfall totals were that month, they punctuated the rainfall for the season. That year was followed by two more in which we received a fraction of what we needed. Even after that fourth year of normal rainfall, the snowpack was only 5 percent of average due to warm temperatures, a snowpack that normally provides about 30 percent of California's water supply. We were still deemed in *severe drought*.

But in late 2016 and early 2017, the rains returned in force. We cautiously celebrated the greening of the savanna in October and the filling of the irrigation pond by January 2017. But by late January cavernous holes yawned in the eroding ravine below the goat barn, exposing roots and taking out trees and foot bridges. The goats pouted in their quarters, loathing rain more than confinement. Casey and I walked the three-quarter-mile driveway at all hours during downpours, clearing ditches of debris, our feet squishing in rubber boots. The world liquefied. Each day I emptied the rain gauge, noting it seldom had less than 0.6 inches of rain, day in, day out. Each day I recorded the twenty-four-hour total on a three-by-five card I kept for each season. One week—the sum of ten inches, the next, twelve inches. The brown earth was too soggy to walk on, and our tires slid in liquid clay on the driveway. Rivulets carved cavities around culverts, rendering them useless and diverting the water into new-cut underground channels. A section of the driveway was at risk of collapse.

And across the canyon to the southwest, a landslide caused by a faulty erosion control plan closed the road for a week, taking out power poles and electricity for one hundred homes. The torrential rains filled Northern California's Lake Orville, formed by the tallest earthen dam in the United States. Its emergency spillway, used for the first time since the dam was built in that momentous year 1968, eroded. Nearly 200,000 people were evacuated.

This is climate change—the new normal. Drought and floods are two sides of the same coin. The same February day of the Redwood Road slide, the East Coast experienced its warmest temperatures on record, followed by a massive snowstorm the next day. Tornadoes demolished some of New Orleans's homes rebuilt after Hurricane Katrina flattened them several years earlier. A mere three weeks before this, Donald Trump took office. The term climate change was erased from all federal government websites and a climate change denier was appointed to lead the Environmental Protection Agency (EPA).

As I write this, a series of storms continue to bombard us, threatening hillsides with landslides and the roadways with flash floods. Donald calls from his office in town, where I drop him off for a few hours a couple of days a week. *Tell me again when I see you. Tell me again what is happening today, tomorrow. Yes, I know you wrote it on the journal ledger, but tell me again.* I tell him again, and an hour later, again. I do what I need to do: adapt. Hire a property management company for our downtown commercial property; overlook the operations of the ranch. Check his medications each morning; keep track of where he is. Marriages are, after all, like climate. Circumstances change and impact us.

Some changes—aging and droughts—are simply a part of natural cycles. Some are not. I take comfort in a study out of the Earth Institute at Columbia University that deemed the five-year California drought itself was part of a natural cycle. However, the study qualified that the drought was made as much as 25 percent worse by human behavior, which had caused warming temperatures and more dryness—climate change.[153]

Studies say that 50 percent of eighty-five year olds have some form of dementia. Neuroscience has advanced these last years, telling us much more about the brain, brain trauma, and how our digestive systems and the foods we eat impact our brain. Donald's chronic sleep disorder and the head-first fall off the back of a flatbed truck eleven years ago may have contributed. Chemicals in our foods, the sugaring of processed foods, endocrine systems thrown off by how we eat and exercise and sleep—all these have been shown to be big players in who gets dementia and who does not. Do our earthly habits make aging "25 percent worse"? Or is dementia just part of the natural cycle of living?

Aging is hard, especially if we hang onto ambitions of youth: it can undermine our will to live. Carl Jung wrote, "The afternoon of life is just as full of meaning as the morning; only, its meaning and purpose are different."[154] As he aged, Jung spent more time in seclusion in a stone structure he built on Lake Zurich, a structure he called Bollingen, allowing himself to sink into the state of mind that he said mirrored his soul.

> At Bollingen I am in the midst of my true life, I am most deeply myself.... From the beginning I felt the Tower as in some way a place of maturation—a maternal womb or a maternal figure in which I could become what I was, what I am and will be. It gave me a feeling as if I were being reborn in stone. It is thus a concretization of the individuation process, a memorial aere perennius.... Only afterward did I see how all the parts fitted together and that a meaningful form had resulted: a symbol of psychic wholeness.[155]

Only in old age did he gain this perspective. He described that experience of the "maternal womb":

> At times I feel as if I am spread out over the landscape and inside things, and am myself living in every tree, in the Splashing of the waves, in the clouds and the animals that come and go, in the procession of the seasons. There is nothing in the Tower that has not grown into its own form over the decades, nothing with which I am not linked. Here everything has its history, and mine; here is space for the spaceless kingdom of the world's and the psyche's hinterland.[156]

I understand this. The ranch has immersed me in timelessness through absolute presence. I feel that spaciousness watching the sunrise from the southern edge of the savanna, or when I sit on the kitchen doorstep late summer and fall evenings, listening to the deafening cacophony of millions of crickets, which continues until the fog rolls in at 3:00 or 4:00 A.M. Yet, I also know the bittersweet taste of eternity by the limitations of the incarnate: embodied, we are mortal. Extreme happiness bleeds into grief for the temporal quality of such joy.

Will there be a time when my tears of grief flood the occupied areas of my life, like the rain after the drought? Will there be tears enough to mourn all that was, the traditions that were, the changes that have and will come? For my marriage? For our Earth?

Ground Hog Day at the Planning Commission, again

Anyone who sat through the presentations by the neighbors at the Mountain Peak Winery Planning Commission hearing on Wednesday, January 4, 2017, must also be appalled at the apparent ignoring, AGAIN, by the commissioners of significant comments from informed and thoughtful neighbors about traffic, road conditions, safety, and the meaning of building such an event center (and yes, this is an event center, not just a winery) six-and-a-half miles up a substandard dead-end road originally built for residential use sixty years ago. Videos of speeding cars passing trucks on double lines, photos of lines of trucks and trucks and trucks, and of flash floods inundating the road, water deep as a foot, were shown. Residents raised the specter of the county's liability. Who will be responsible when the county approves a project on a road they know is substandard and there is loss of life due to lack of safe egress during a fire?[157] Two commenters addressed the impact of the spoilings from the caves on the pristine blue-line creek that serves Rector Reservoir. When it silts in, when Napa County is sued, we, the taxpayers, pay—not Mountain Peak Winery.

Going to Planning Commission and Board of Supervisor meetings is like watching the movie *Ground Hog Day* over and over and over. The same things happen: The applicant is helped by the Planning Department to fit their project into the rules; planners recommend approval, certifying that all impacts of the project, after mitigation, are "less than significant." The citizens, noting that the impact on their lives and on the future of the county is significant indeed, protest the recommendation of the Planning Department to the Planning Commission, as they did yesterday. The commissioners effectively ignore citizens' data. When the commissioners okay the project, it is then appealed to the Board of Supervisors, where this process happens all over again: informed citizen comment (3 minutes only, please!), and then, as if it didn't happen, "Wham, bam, thank you ma'am," it is rubber stamped. Those impacted, and that includes all of us in the Napa Valley, are given the choice: do we spend tens of thousands to sue the county?

Our county's elected and appointed officials continue to ignore the cumulative impact of these projects on our environment, on our roads, on the quality and quantity of our water, and on the fabric of our community. If you have enough money, you can do anything. First step is to fund the campaigns of the Board of Supervisors, then do some modifications to your initially inflated plans to show you really are a responsible winery and/or vineyard owner. You'll be allowed to use mitigations, exceptions, and variances to make your square project fit into the round hole of the "rules," rules, that are, it should be noted, crafted by the wine industry to its own advantage. And then you say to those of us who are looking at the larger picture: *I followed all the rules and now I deserve the permit.*

The question is no longer can these projects, which increasingly infiltrate our watersheds and hillsides, be done, but *should* they? Our governing officials appear to lack the will, intelligence, and moral courage to really take this on. Bullied by big (big!) money, they have fallen captive. With an issue as important as the spread of development into our hillsides and watersheds, we citizens need to wake up.

Write or visit your supervisor! Demand that he or she act for the common good of the people and the environment, not that of a few corporate and wealthy interests.

PATRICIA DAMERY
NAPA

CHAPTER 34

The New Babe in the Garden

THIS IS CLIMATE CHANGE as well: The week of the 2017 deluge in Northern California, tens of thousands of people demonstrated at airports after the just inaugurated President Trump banned immigrants from six countries, all Muslim, visas or no, from entering the United States. In Iran, perhaps due to the sympaties of these American protesters, demonstrators did not burn the United States flag as might be expected, although they mocked the president. Seattle Federal Judge James Robart blocked the ban, a decision upheld a few days later by three Ninth Circuit Court judges. Across the country, town hall meetings became lively with citizens' outrage at the administration's cabinet appointments and the threatened repeal of the Affordable Care Act. Citizen groups formed to bear witness and to protest. Veterans joined Native Americans in protesting the executive order resuming operation of the Dakota Access Pipeline despite the incomplete environmental impact report—a pipeline slated to cross the Missouri River just north of the Standing Rock Sioux Reservation. This threatens not only the tribe's treaty rights and cultural sites, but also its water supply as well as the water supply for the millions dependent on it downstream.[158] Daily, the media reported on the administration's conflicts of interest, its ties to the Russians, and the found-intelligence that the Russians interfered with our elections. In Napa County, the Planning Commission sent a proposed winery back to the Planning Department, instructing the applicant "to look at a smaller-scale winery" and to "work more with the neighbors." Perhaps we of Napa Vision 2050 are having an effect.

Is this public participation, fueled by outrage, an aspect of the consciousness of the new babe in the tree of the Garden of Eden? Is this a public reawakening to the rigors of democracy, to the importance of recognizing Nature's sovereignty, and to the need to redefine our place with each other and with the Earth? While we were collectively sleeping, something within ourselves and without has taken over. Corporate interests are controlling the show, and it is time for We the People to take that control back.

The new consciousness necessarily means loving *place* and a renewed sense of belonging to the land, a worldview embedded in the cultures of native peoples everywhere. While researching her book *Love of Country: A Hebridean Journey,* British journalist Madeleine Bunting interviewed Gaelic-speaking peoples of the Outer Hebrides. Culture is embedded within language, she says. The Gaelic word *duthchas,* for example, has no English equivalent. The Gaelic/English dictionary translates the word as *homeland,* but Gaelic speakers told Bunting that it means so much more. "It's a collective claim on the land, which is reinforced and lived out through the shared management of that land. It is a right that is grounded in daily habits and activities, and it is bound up with relationships to others, and responsibilities . . . Gaelic [language] turns notions of ownership on their head."[159]

More than one entrepreneur tried to bring so-called progress to these Gaelic-speaking islands. Two generations of land-right protests ensued, not unlike the battles we are facing in the Napa Valley and in the United States today. The locals Lilith! prevailed. *They would not be suppressed!* In the Hebrides, community land trusts now own half of the land, with two-thirds of all Hebrideans living on community-owned land. The new consciousness necessarily means a feeling of belonging to the land—not the land belonging to us. This is the tension we must hold now: a "progress" that exploits the economic usefulness of land for wealth and a robust sense of sovereignty of all involved—people and Nature. "Capitalism requires a place-lessness to ensure the smooth flow of capital, people and resources to achieve economic efficiency," Bunting says.[160] It is up to each of us, gathering together, to protest this exploitation, and it is going to have to be *over time.*

I return again to the wisdom of my senior consultant. He related a living myth in Bali, analogous to deep analytical work and perhaps to our approach to our planet as well. The demon goddess Rangda fights Barong, a bear-like leader of the forces of good, in a dance reenacted in festivals throughout the calendar year. No one is ever killed off in this dynamic equilibrium, although the myth says eventually Barong prevails and Rangda runs off. Back and forth the dance goes, first one in ascendency and then the other—and the community witnesses.

This dance is part of the creation of a new consciousness that incorporates the battle of good and evil, a battle that must be fought within each of us. Who among us Americans has not profited greatly from our exploitation of Earth's resources? When we don't realize what we project, when we don't own the dark shadow within of greed and entitlement, hidden by *willful ignorance,* then the battle becomes an outer one. At that point, we need enemies who represent these qualities to be whole. But taken as an inner battle, the consciousness of the forces of good and evil, of love and hatred, of self-interest and love of the whole, makes us stronger—like the Biblical David who fought the Angel but never won. As the poet Rilke says, "Whoever was beaten by this Angel / . . . went away proud and strengthened / and great from that harsh hand / that kneaded him as if to change his shape. / . . . This is how he grows: by being defeated, decisively, / by constantly greater beings."[161]

Much is written about why so many Americans still deny climate change. Certainly, the oil and gas industries' agendas enter into it. *The Dallas Morning News* reported that former Texas governor Rick Perry, appointed to be Energy Secretary by former President Trump, "continues to question the extent to which humans are responsible for climate change."[162]

The paper added,

> Perry said during his confirmation hearing this year that humans have a role in climate change, and he advocated for Trump to remain in the Paris deal. But the Texan also has deep ties to the oil and gas industry, and he's since praised the president for ditching the global climate accord.[163]

Will Rick Perry and current Texas Governor Greg Abbott continue to pay lip service to advocating investigation of the "extent to which any activity has a particular level of influence on the climate"? Will the "500-year flooding" of Houston in April 2016, and again in 2017 when Hurricane Harvey hit, have any influence?[164]

And flooding is only one of the recent climate-related disasters in the state of Texas. In 2011, wildfires destroyed more than 2947 homes.[165] In the last ten years, Texas has suffered 67 major weather disasters, more than any other state in the union, damages topping $200 billion.[166] In 2021 Texas's deregulated electric power grid collapsed when the state was hit by a polar vortex, leaving millions of Texans without power and water for several days. Governor Abbott blamed the failure of the grid on renewable power sources, which supply only a fraction of Texas electricity.[167] The delay in acting to reduce carbon pollution in order "to investigate the cause of global warming" and the delay in addressing infrastructure issues to mitigate the impact of our changing climate and sea rise have had disastrous results. At what point do these actions of rolling back protections for taxpayers and our environment become a crime against humanity?

One of Napa County's own versions of this idiocy is reflected in considering uncut trees on one part of Walt Ranch as mitigation for the more than 14,000 trees clear cut in another part. It makes a mockery of Assembly Bill (AB) 32, California's mandate to reduce carbon emissions to 1990 levels by 2020, and the even more stringent Senate Bill (SB) 32, reducing carbon emissions 40 percent below 1990 levels by 2030. We will never make it with these kinds of mitigations. The cumulative impact of these decisions on our county and our world are not taken into account—all for the benefit of industry.

Shortly after the Second World War, forester and environmentalist Aldo Leopold wrote,

> . . . a land ethic changes the role of *Homo sapiens* from conqueror of the land-community to plain member and citizen of it. It implies respect for his fellow-members, and also respect for the community as such.
>
> In human history, we have learned (I hope) that the conqueror role is eventually self-defeating. Why? Because it is implicit in such a role that the conqueror knows, *ex cathedra*, just what makes the community clock tick, and just what and who is valuable, and what and who is worthless, in community life. It always turns out that he knows neither, and this is why his conquests eventually defeat themselves.[168]

Wendell Berry, influenced by Leopold, carries this a little further:

> To live as a farmer, one has to come into the local watershed and the local ecosystem and deal well or poorly with them. One must encounter directly and feelingly the topography of the soils of one's particular farm, and treat them well or poorly. If one wishes to farm well ... then one must submit to the unending effort to change one's mind and ways to fit one's farm. This is a hard education, which lasts all one's life, never to be completed.[169]

How many of us "encounter directly and feelingly the topography of the soils" of the land upon which we live and work? As more and more people move into the Napa Valley, buying views and lifestyle, having no idea what kind of soil or what watershed that soil is part of, as small wineries are bought up by a handful of large corporations—Australian-owned Treasury Wine Estates, Constellation Brands, E.&J. Gallo Winery—that see investment opportunities in the high-end Napa-brand wines, our county's ecological health is increasingly at risk.[170] But in the end, Nature will not be suppressed or cheated. *When will we ever learn* that she will have the final say?

There is another kind of denial, not so opportunistic but every bit as damaging: that of buffering the massive grief of the changes to our Earth by ignoring what is going on altogether. *I don't see it; it doesn't exist.* Denial is a shortcut, a way around that which feels unbearable.

In the Southwestern United States, the Southern Paiute have a cycle of songs, the Salt Songs, which are intimately tied to their physical and spiritual connection to the Earth. The approximately 140 songs must be sung in order. They represent a physical journey through the Southwest in which salt and herbs were collected and the ancestors acknowledged. The songs are sung at funerals to guide the Spirits on their journey. But they are also sung for healing of the community in its largest sense, a reunification of the people with all life and the land, bringing "creation all back together."[171] Kaibab Vivienne Caron-Jake describes the Salt Songs as "the balance between land and people and song and language, and how all of these are interrelated and how you can't do one without the other."[172] The experience of this balance, this intimacy with the land, is an experience of a power the Paiute call *puha,* which comes from confrontation "by a stark and numinous earth."[173] To experience this power is healing, bringing us into wholeness.

Salt Song singer Larry Eddie describes how the Paiute received the Salt Songs: "The great Spirit says, I am going to teach you these songs, but before I teach you these songs, I am going to break your heart."[174]

Having our hearts broken hurts, which is why we resort to the primitive use of denial. But grief is necessary if we are to return to resonance with the Earth, with each other, and with ourselves. I must allow my heart to be broken by what has happened to our Earth, to the savanna, and to my marriage. A broken heart reveals how deeply we love.

CHAPTER 35

The Rights of Nature

"Our democracy's founding ideals were false when they were written. Black
Americans have fought to make them true," Nikole Hannah-Jones declared in her
introductory essay for The New York Times' 1619 Project ... Contained in that bold
statement is the argument that you can do something that is flawed but valuable
because it contains room for revision, because an imperfect gesture can, as we say,
hold space for what is yet to come.
    Rebecca Solnit, "Unfinished Business: John Muir in North America"[175]

IN EARLY FEBRUARY 2017, Napa Vision 2050 organized a gathering of thirty people from
Napa County for a day-and-a-half workshop with Shannon Briggs, founder of Movement
Rights. Movement Rights—a national group of community organizers, attorneys, and
ecological experts—assists communities throughout the country in passing laws that
recognize the rights of people and Nature above the claimed legal "rights" of corporations.
Movement Rights holds that "human activity must take place within the natural system
of laws that govern life on Earth."[176] Not only does the legal recognition of these rights
acknowledge the living presences of all of us, including the non-human, it also establishes
the grounds to sue in case of infractions of these rights.

Despite everything that I have said and written about the legal paradigm shift in recognizing the Rights of Nature, despite everything I believe, the workshop was still a shock.
Perhaps it is always a shock when we stand on the mountaintop with a vista of the path
ahead—or when we peer into that Paradise Lost with the New Babe. It's the realization that
nothing is ever going to be the same again. It can be exhilarating or terrifying. There is no
clear path. It's like hiking in the wilds of the west Ireland peninsulas. You are surrounded
by broad blue stretches of the Atlantic. You reach one signpost and site your path onto
the next, knowing that finding footing through the yellow heather and the deep bogs to
the next post will be treacherous. Does beauty draw us on? Or fear for what happens if we
don't continue? Or does the magnitude of the task tempt us to turn back to what is known,

denying what is before us, like it is said Columbus did when he "discovered" the New World? The story goes that he turned back twice because he knew this changed everything. This was a new continent entirely, and this shocking knowledge would change the recorded maps of the world.

Over the next few hours, the presenters reviewed our country's documents that we hold sacrosanct: the Declaration of Independence, the Articles of Confederation, the Constitution, and the Bill of Rights. They outlined the historic development of corporations. Where is power in our country? In our county? We have the illusion of freedom; we love the idea of the Bill of Rights, and yet, from the beginning of our country, that freedom has been bound up by the economic and corporate interests of a very few, particularly white, wealthy men. Mark you, this workshop occurred during the fourth week of President Trump's term, a term that raised the grain on the inequalities of race, gender, sexual preference, a presidency that was devastating to the environment, to people of color, and to our democracy.

Going around the room that February evening, person by person, *We the People* read aloud the Declaration of Independence with its familiar words and cadence:

> When, in the Course of human events, it becomes necessary for one people to dissolve the political bands which have connected them with another...

Who among us is not stirred by these words? Our higher angels ascribe to them. To read, to hear the words read, is to resonate with a higher governing principle.

> We hold these truths to be self-evident, that all men are created equal, that they are endowed by their Creator with certain unalienable Rights, that among these are Life, Liberty and the pursuit of Happiness...., — That to secure these rights, Governments are instituted among Men, deriving their just powers from the consent of the governed, — That whenever any Form of Government becomes destructive of these ends, it is the Right of the People to alter or to abolish it, and to institute new Government...

As of this writing, the citizens of twenty-six states, including California, have the right of the ballot initiative. When governing officials in these twenty-six states no longer represent the good of the people, then citizens have the right to gather signatures to place a measure on the ballot. This went sadly wrong in 2016 with the Water, Forest, and Oak Woodland Protection Initiative, but ballot initiatives have succeeded a number of times in protecting Napa County's lands and community.[177]

The urgency to use ballot measures to ensure the Rights of Nature has increased due to changes in climate, but the doctrine itself is hardly a new idea. Certainly, this ethic is embedded in First Peoples' consciousness. The First People teachers I have had move in the world in a very different way. When I worked with Lakota Sioux medicine woman Pansy

Hawkwing in learning the ritual of the sweat lodge, I learned that, out of respect, you never step over an object, but instead walk around it. That in preparing to gather stones for the fire, you offer cornmeal in gratitude to Stone People. That once the fire is lit, the ritual has begun. You speak only in prayer.

Still, considering a citizen initiative that advocates for ensuring Nature's rights surprised me. It's so far from where we are, but then, what is our alternative? If our elected and appointed county officials are bought off by corporate and wealthy interests, when the residents are not considered stakeholders, then We the People have the right and the duty to circumvent elected officials and go directly to the people. This is a realization whose time has come.

As we all sat together reading a draft of a possible Rights of Nature ordinance drawn up by Movement Rights, I saw the Rights of Nature dreamed forward:

> We the people of Napa County find that the rural and small-town character and development pattern, which we enjoy and wish to preserve, is threatened by agriculture and agritourism corporations, who are exploiting that rural and small-town character for profits, while ultimately destroying it; and
>
> We the people of Napa County find that agriculture and agritourism corporations are destroying our forested and wooded lands, threatening the species diversity, rural character and ecological function of our community, and
>
> We the people of Napa County…[178]

It was a draft, perhaps only a chimera, but reading it, I saw the next signpost; and in this rarified, philosophical light, the goal shined. Of course, my heart goes to the oak. The possibility of a Rights of Nature document acknowledges the *living presence* of the valley oaks, their right to soils that sustain feeder and structural roots, to *the native forest and meadow conditions, to* the savanna's meadow community of native needle grass and wild blue rye, the bunch grasses, and to the California buttercup and blue-eyed grass that bloom in March. The oaks have the right to protection that their offspring may grow to maturity, the right to groundwater and clean air, to sun and the Mediterranean climate in which they flourish. Redwood Creek, just below our ranch, has the right to the water of the seasonal feeder creeks that flow into it in winter, and the right to flow unimpeded to the Napa River. Our waterways have the right to clean waters without pesticides and herbicides and fertilizers, which kill waterways' native inhabitants. The Rights of Nature doctrine acknowledges the intricacies of the web of life, which, more locally, we call the ecosystem. The establishment of laws that acknowledge these rights is a witness to our growing new consciousness. And the truth is, scientists know that if we don't take this step, we risk the collapse of the systems that support us. Aldo Leopold warned seventy years ago that only in developing an ethic in which we see land as a community to which we belong, will our land be able "to the survive the impact of mechanized man, nor for us to reap from it the esthetic harvest it is capable, under science, of contributing to culture. That land is a community is the basic concept of ecology, but that land is to be loved and respected is an extension of ethics."[179]

The seemingly never-ending fight of Rangda and Barong continues: Later in 2017, after months of collaboration, the original authors of the Napa County Watershed Protections of Oak Woodlands and Forests Initiative, Jim Wilson and Michael Hackett, and Napa Valley Vintners' board president Michael Honig and publicity director, Rex Stultz, filed a revised and stronger watershed initiative with Napa County. The collaborators met with each member of the Board of Supervisors, who celebrated the collaboration and the initiative, the Chair Belia Ramos claiming the Board of Supervisors would make it an ordinance and celebrate its passage under an oak tree in June 2018. But within the week, industry groups that had not been part of the collaboration, including the Winegrowers, Napa Valley Grapegrowers, and Napa County Farm Bureau, officially protested the process and the initiative. As a result, the Napa Valley Vintners, whose board had approved the initiative at every step, rescinded their support. Jim and Mike refiled the collaborated initiative, and we again gathered the required signatures to put it on the June 2018 ballot.

I like to think that the fight of Rangda and Barong, consciously held, creates energy for the shift to a new energized level. In August 2017, the forces of Barong rose when a secret, powerful, wealthy group known as the Alliance for Responsible Governance (Alliance) informed the Napa County Board of Supervisors of repeated violations of CEQA. The Alliance had retained the environmental firm Shute, Mihaly & Weinberger to study the ninety-three winery permits granted between 2013 to late 2016. Only two had required the preparation of an environmental impact report. "The County's insufficient environmental review of these winery applications has resulted in repeated violations of CEQA and a consistent failure to disclose and effectively mitigate the project's environmental impacts, which continue to compound over time...."[180]

The letter from the Alliance promised to take the Board of Supervisors to task. But what became of this? I do not know. Did Rangda get the upper hand? Was some deal cut out of public purview?

Still, this was an act of witnessing. In Rilke's poem "The Man Watching,"[181] the title underscores the importance of witnessing the struggle, of being willing to *feel* the struggle, which Rilke likens to that of the Old Testament wrestlers with the "greater being" of the angel.

What "greater being" will defeat us? Our unprocessed greed, entitlement, and hatred— or the Self, that larger aspect that knows the whole? And what will sustain us during the struggle? Will it be Love? . . . Of Self, of other, of place, and of nature, even love of the struggle itself? Will we bow our heads to these greater beings within ourselves and the world until "my deeper life goes on with more strength, as if the banks through which it moves had widened out"?[182] Can we move from our ego-centered attitudes to ones that encompass the rights to life of all?

CHAPTER 36

The Night Before All Hell Broke Loose

THE NIGHT BEFORE THE fires started, Napa Vision 2050 had a fundraising dinner at Cindy's home on Soda Canyon Road. Although this was our first such event, Cindy is an experienced hostess and took over the details of the evening. Kathy's chef son, Geoff, volunteered to cook the meal for a hundred people. We were at once celebrating the work we had done to date and raising funds to support the legal challenges we were beginning to face.

Cindy's home, surrounded by manicured gardens and hand-tended vineyards, rests in a cup of a valley several miles up Soda Canyon Road. At the time of the fundraiser, the winery/guest house was just east of the house. We met in the upstairs guest house above the small barn-like winery most Monday mornings, winding our way up the flagstone path and stairs to the generously appointed apartment. The structure would burn the next night. I often wonder, what if the fundraiser had been the night of the fires? How would all one hundred of us, panicked, have escaped from the narrow, dead-end, winding road? This is the question *not* seriously considered by our Planning Department and Board of Supervisors when permitting Mountain Peak Winery at the end of Soda Canyon Road the month before, an issue that would drive the project into the courts after the fire. "Cumulative impact is not the question," one commissioner so famously stated. "I think they have satisfied the requirements."

The warm early October evening was clear. Tables with white linen cloths lined the west side of the pool, umbrellas shading us from the late afternoon sun. Several of us arrived early to help.

We were shooed out of the kitchen. Geoff, sweating profusely, was cutting corn from the cob, and Kathy was acting as his sous chef. They were behind schedule. The tables were still to be set, and the wine table set up. I remember feeling disoriented as I wandered among the round white-clothed tables, setting out silverware, napkins, and glasses, Cindy's trained help often beating me to it. We poured glasses of wine and sipped as we greeted guests. Guests pursued the silent auction table: a lavender basket we had donated, two expensive bottles of wine, art. When the food was finally ready, we lined up under the shade structure

outside the kitchen, helping ourselves to chicken or roast, to salads and roasted corn. I had not brought Donald as he was increasingly lost in situations such as this, so I felt a little cut loose, alone, a feeling we dementia-widows grow used to.

I am not sure how Donald would have liked the next part anyway. He has little use for black humor. As we finished dessert, Dan walked to the center of the east side of the pool and began the live auction. First, he auctioned six 10-foot valley oaks, donated by a local propagator, and then a dinner for eight cooked by George at his home on Diamond Mountain. A week in Gary's second home in Hawaii. One by one, Dan auctioned off the donated items until he got to the centerpiece: manure! For this, he called Kathy.

"We live in a valley resplendent in bullshit," she began, holding up a large, dried cow patty the size of a charger plate. "This genuine Napa County bullshit was gathered from a single herd in the Monticello Road area, located at one of the higher elevations of our offerings. Its aged quality makes it an ideal pairing with your tomatoes and onions. "Can I hear $50? $50 over there! Can I hear $75? $75! $100? $100! Gone, to the woman in the maroon sweater!"

A little shocked, the crowd laughed cautiously and then uproariously, which egged Kathy on. Much as one would a premium bottle of Cabernet, she extolled the values of each manure. "In keeping with our preference for estate vintage, this premium chickenshit is from a single flock," she barked, "laid down open-air on a farm, with hints of horse-shit and aged to perfection." She continued to auction off a truckload of horse shit, which didn't get the price we had hoped, as well buckets of goat and llama shit. In all, we brought in over $4000 auctioning off the manure, and we got a great deal of release from laughing.

One poignancy of the evening: George's high-end wine brought in a good sum in the silent auction, but Dan's did not sell. Along with Cindy's winery/guest house and several of the homes of those present that evening, the bottle would burn the next night, along with everything else that Dan and Naoko owned, except the truck they escaped in, their dog, and the clothes on their backs.

OPPOSITE: **Starry night before the fire** (Photograph: Bill Hocker)

CHAPTER 37

Fire

Trauma need not be a life sentence. Of all the maladies that attack
the human organism, trauma may ultimately be one that is recognized as beneficial. I
say this because in the healing of trauma, a transformation
takes place—one that can improve the quality of life.... While trauma
can be hell on earth, trauma resolved is a gift of the gods—
a heroic journey that belongs to each of us.
Peter A. Levine, *Waking the Tiger*[183]

TRAUMA EXPERT PETER LEVINE underscores the importance of reliving traumatic events, but with the awareness of physical sensations and feelings. He emphasizes the importance of human connection in this reliving.

As a community, many of us continue to recover from the trauma of the fires of October 2017, hopefully with the healing that awareness can bring. Otherwise we are at risk of repeating situations that replicate the unresolved feelings, leaving us frightened, angry, and vulnerable to being even more divided as we face the challenges of the coming climate upheavals: fire, flooding, landslides, and now, pandemics.

Instinctively, I relive the events of the fires. I remember the day, October 8, that they began. Donald and I were leaving for Portugal the following evening. Inexplicably, I was compelled to finish packing early, not my usual mode. I had spent the morning hanging laundry on a clothesline that stretches between two valley oaks west of our home and the afternoon preparing notes for watering the garden, the house plants, the lavender, and rose geranium. We ate an early supper at a favorite beer and pizza joint, basking in anticipation of the trip.

OPPOSITE: *Glass Fire, 2020*

But as the sun set, the wind rose. Like demon's breath, the air was uncannily hot and slippery, like nothing I have ever experienced. We put the goats in the barn for the night, and I finished emailing to complete business on the Napa Vision 2050 website and newsletter for the next three weeks. I prepared for bed. Just as I opened the bedroom window to the east around 9:45 P.M., I saw a plume of deep crimson smoke mushrooming into billowing blackness striated in orange on the ridge across the valley. I got Donald, who was in the other end of the house watching TV. By the time he came to the window, the fire had spread south, outlining the ridge top.

At 10:04 P.M., I texted Dan, whom I had just emailed about the website. Dan lived across the valley. "Huge fire, Soda Canyon?"

He texted back almost immediately. "Can you see it? We smell it"—and then: "Wow we see it now. It's on Atlas Peak road above where Gordon lives and the wind is blowing like hell we're gonna pack up thanks."

I called Casey, and within minutes he arrived with Melissa and the boys. We had no idea how big this was to become. By now molten gold was pouring down the mountain like "hot lava," as Wesley put it, seemingly taking everything in its path. Casey and Melissa walked northeast of the house, returned to say there was another fire north on the same ridge. A chill went over us: what was going on?

We reassured ourselves: it was across the valley, some distance from us. Casey and Melissa watched the fires outside as I sat with the boys in the house, monitoring phone calls and watching Channel 2 local TV news to try to get information about what was happening. Winds pounded the house. Casey returned, informed me that the goats had broken out of their barn and were running around the goat pen. I could hear their panicked baas. As we corralled them back in and barred the door, the six goats watched me, anxiously waiting for direction. I told them they needed to stay in. They seemed safe in the confines of those four concrete walls of their barn. It reminded me of securing them in their stalls during winter storms, safe and dry. But rains are so much different from fire. How do you protect from fire?

And then the western sky turned red. Another fire southwest of us—the Partrick Fire— had begun and was within a couple of miles, but downwind. *"We've got to get out of here or we won't be able to!"* Melissa cried. I called Gary, who had phoned me thirty minutes earlier offering help when I didn't think we needed it. His wife, Annie, answered. Gary was now evacuating their horses. Another fire, this one on Mt. Veeder, northwest of us, also flared up. I texted Kathy, who lived south of Napa: "Are you up? Can I borrow your van?" She had equipped her van with hooks to secure her goat herd in case of fire. She immediately texted that she, too, was evacuating. Soon she texted that she was sending her friend David over to evacuate our animals. This was when I received a call from Chris, one of our workers. He was at Casey and Melissa's house down below. He had seen the Partrick Fire, thought we had already left for Portugal, and had come to evacuate the animals. It was 1:30 A.M.

Strange what you remember in times like this: The growing panic and confusion of not knowing *what is going on?* The electricity going out while we were getting collars on the goats. Our questionable decision to walk four goats and Hijo, our llama, down the three-quarter-mile driveway in the whipping winds while transporting two of the goats in our small pickup. Casey's handing me a flashlight, and Donald's insistence that we did not need to evacuate at all, that everyone was hysterical and to just go to bed.

David arrived about the time Chris and I reached the bottom. We managed to load all six goats in his truck, which he delivered to the rescue center that had been hastily set up at Vintage High School Farm. Kathy had already alerted the rescue center to the goats' arrival. David returned within forty-five minutes to take Hijo. Donald and I followed him. We were greeted with hugs from people tending the rescue center, many of them having just evacuated themselves. We were led past sheep, goats, horses. Our goats were in a large stall in the back of the barn, now joined by Hijo. A young woman made notes of our phone numbers and the feeding instructions for our animals, insisting we need not worry about hay. Then Donald and I went to his downtown office in Napa with our lab Leo to sleep for a couple of hours. It was 3:30 A.M. I barely woke when Leo vomited on the office rug. I thought I was dreaming it.

I have been through catastrophes before: Our evacuation during the 1986 flood on the Russian River, the white line outlining the outer edge of our lane erased by churning flood waters. The 1989 earthquake in San Francisco and a woman's screaming in the street, "The Bay Bridge has collapsed! The Bay Bridge has collapsed!" And, of course, the 2014 earthquake in Napa, which challenged my illusion of the permanence of our home.

But this was the worst. Many, like Dan and Naoko, got out with only the clothes on their backs and the family dog or cat. Six people burned alive in Napa County and another twenty-three in Santa Rosa, where the Tubbs Fire, which also ignited that night, burned to ash whole city blocks of homes. Over the next few days, 6300 homes would burn in Napa and Sonoma counties. The air thickened dangerously with toxic smoke and ash.

Emails flew back and forth. Like virtual coyotes, we howled in texts and emails: *Where are you? Are you safe? Did your house survive? Your animals?*

We are safe but mandatory evacuated, I texted, over and over. We had no idea if our ranch would be spared. The fires were widespread, caused by the unusually high winds, called *Diablo* (devil) winds, which damaged power transmission lines and transformers.

Still in shock, Donald and I made the decision to go to Portugal. We had both anticipated this trip for some time, knowing it would probably be our last one overseas, trips that we had always enjoyed. Donald wanted to visit the *Museu Nacional do Azulejo* (National Tile Museum) in Lisbon to study the *azulejos* (tiles) that had been geometrically designed and used to teach math. I knew, given the many challenges that Donald and I were facing, that I had little left in me to stay immersed in a situation that was potentially devastating and that I had no chance of affecting. Besides, I reasoned, we had to go somewhere. Casey, Melissa, the boys, and Leo evacuated to Petaluma. In Milan, I woke at 2 A.M. and 2:30 A.M. and

2:45 A.M. to the pings of texts from Casey on his way to the ranch to evacuate more items, water down the houses, and cut back brush. *Make specific list of items you want removed last chance I am about to lose reception.*

I texted back:

The pearl necklace that I wear all the time.

(The one Donald had made for me.)

Basket by my desk of financial records.

(Why hadn't I thought of this before?)

Any albums of photos.

My computer.

Stay safe.

How do you decide what to save? Just *stay safe.*

For almost a week the wind played ping pong with what became known as the Nuns Fire, buffeting flames back and forth over the ridge between Napa and Sonoma Valley. Donald's son, Lutrell, and his wife, Terry, and Donald's daughter Genevieve were on one side of the mountain; our home, on the other. In the end, none of our homes or properties burned, but we are well aware it is only a matter of time until the forests around us do. Fires are an important part of this ecology; fire suppression policy has been short-sighted. That which is left out is often that which causes the most trouble.

It did not take the wine industry long to assert the role of vineyards as firebreaks. The day the *Los Angeles Times* article "Vineyards May Have Kept Wine Country Fire from Getting Worse" was published was also the day our ranch was most gravely threatened by the Nuns Fire. Casey thought we were goners. The executive director of the Napa Valley Grapegrowers, Jennifer Putnam, was quoted, "Vineyards save lives. They saved property and lives in Napa County. It's as clear as it can be."[184] Cal Fire agreed the vineyards helped provide firebreaks. "'Fire crews use the vineyards to their advantage to ensure that they can stop the spread of the fire or stop the front of the fire from coming through,' said Cal Fire spokesman Jonathan Cox, battalion chief for Northern California."[185]

That same day, October 12, Donald and I were in Lisbon, Portugal, the air also acrid with smoke. Over the next few days Portugal would also be aflame with four hundred fires. A hurricane provided similar wind conditions to those that we had had in Napa: unlike Napa, arsonists had set the fires. Portugal, whose climate is similar to that of Northern California and Napa, farms eucalyptus trees for paper—trees with a high oil content that causes the wood to explode, embers rocketing into surrounding areas. These trees have replaced Portugal's native forests in many places, either on purpose or by their invasive habits. During a cruise on the Douro River to Spain, we choked on the smoke, which obscured the burning mountains along the banks. On our way back to the river's mouth a few days later, we passed through those same mountains, many burned to the river's edge, as well as vineyards extending from the river to mountaintops, mostly unburned, their bare soil and green leaves protecting them.

But this area of Portugal is also monoculture at its worst. Where small farmers once outlined their fields of crops with vines planted to climb trees or high trellises for ventilation, now most of the fields, owned by corporations, are devoid of anything but vines that stretch up denuded mountainsides. Native pine forests, once tended and used for grazing animals and for foraging various fruits, berries, and herbs, were cut to make way for vineyards. As we toured wineries, we were told stories of the past, of workers harvesting grapes in large baskets carried on their backs, of the must of crushed grapes being lugged in barrels onto boats to transport downstream to Porto to age. What I witnessed in Portugal was a country being consumed by corporate greed whose marketing fed on the romantic story of the past. The reality is an ecological disaster that has erased what became a subsistence way of life, leaving a population poor and vulnerable to tourism.

Our trip was like the story of the servant who, after being startled by Death in the marketplace, borrowed his master's horse to escape Death, only to meet her in his hiding place. Just as we cannot get away from the impact when corporations become economically

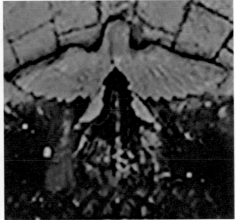

In Lamego, the pelican fountain is at the beginning of the ascent to the healing, a willingness to sacrifice for future generations.

(trabantos/Shutterstock)

powerful and gain "personhood," we cannot get away from fire. Fire is a natural, important force that becomes devastating if excluded. Being in touch with the ecological needs of the West means being in touch with the importance of fire. Fire, like water, unites us.

On November 1, 2017, not even a month since the devastating fires of Northern California, the House of Representatives voted 232 to 188 to allow more "salvage logging" on public lands. House Speaker Paul Ryan asserted that bill HR2936 was needed to protect national forests "from the kind of devastation that California experienced." In fact, analysis shows that this bill takes money away from programs helping homeowners fireproof their homes. Democratic Representative Raúl Grijalva, the ranking member on the House Natural Resources Committee, described the bill as a "shameful giveaway" to the logging business. The Senate introduced their own bill, S2068, "The Wildfire Prevention and Mitigation Act," which would exempt massive logging practices from environmental laws and prevent public participation and comment. Both bills fly in the face of current scientific evidence that shows reducing environmental protections and increasing logging actually accelerate the intensity of fire when it comes, and that "snag forest habitat" is some of the most biodiverse and healthy wildlife habitat in the West.[186]

The last day of our cruise, we toured the city of Lamego. Just above the town's center and atop St. Stephen's hill rests the eighteenth-century *Santuario Nossa Senhora dos Remedios,* a church dedicated to Our Lady of Remedies. People make pilgrimage to this sacred site to be healed. The feeling of the sanctuary was profoundly welcoming and gentle, filled with various paintings and *azulejos* depicting Mary throughout her life. The flights of stairs, 686 steps in all, lead to the church from the city's center, with brief respite from the climb on various levels decorated with *azulejos,* urns, and statues. Was it the feminine feel of the sanctuary that day that woke me to the eternal Present, to *feel* the alive spirit of our Earth, or is it what happened next?

As I was descending the steps onto one of the lower levels on my way to the city center, I came upon Pelican at the top of a three-tiered fountain. She splayed her wings as she pecked her breast to feed the baby pelican stretching up to her. Water spewed from the mother's beak. In Catholicism, the pelican is a symbol of Christ and the Eucharist, a symbol derived from a pre-Christian legend of the bird that sacrifices for her young. In Lamego, the pelican is at the beginning of the ascent to the healing, a willingness to sacrifice for future generations. Later that day I searched the internet again for "pelican," struggling to take in the meaning of her repeated appearances. A spirit animal site summarizes pelican energy in a quote: "Be Still. Allow the world to flow around you for a change. Let its beauty and grace envelope you. Only in the present can we find this state of grace."[187]

In Lamego, I was blessed with Grace, which is the core of deep healing. But Grace often brings a challenge. It can be like walking a tightrope or climbing a long stretch of stairs. You can't anticipate or sink into nostalgia or you lose it. You don't look up, or down, but just keep your eye on the step in front of you. Grace does the rest.

Don't blame the trees

My husband and I have had vineyards in Napa County for over 35 years. Our Dry Creek Road ranch was one that did not burn, thanks to the many first responders and to the temperamental wind. We are certified biodynamic organic farmers and believe agriculture and the native local ecology can coexist in healthy balance, but only with active respect for the needs of the larger ecological system.

To this end, I want to address fire in our zoning-designated Ag Watershed Open Space lands. Even though our own ranch did not burn, we know it's only a matter of time until it does. Fire is an important part of the ecology of Napa County. Our warming planet means we will have even more fire—and we need to plan for it. We need fire, but it needs to move through quickly and with less intensity.

While vineyards acted as firebreaks in a number of circumstances in this last fire, how many of those vineyards were irrigated? In a time of climate change, water will become increasingly scarce, as it has been these last years. Do we have enough water in our Ag Watershed Open Space lands, which have a different geology from the valley floor and much less ground water, to realistically consider using irrigated vineyards as firebreaks?

Farming with the environment means growing what can coexist with the facts on the ground of water, soils, and temperature. At least 80 percent of our vines in Napa were dry farmed before the French blind tasting in the 1970s. Pushing vines for production by irrigation is something we need to reconsider into the future. Do dry-farmed grapes perform as well as irrigated vines for firebreaks?

Our Ag Watershed Open Space lands are key to the water supply of our cities. Oak woodlands and forests restore ground water; irrigated vineyards use it. The reason we had such a catastrophe was not because we have oak woodlands and forests but because we have not managed our so-called wild lands for two centuries, ever since the white man arrived, allowing underbrush and understory to build up. The health of the Napa County environment is dependent on how we manage the forests and oak woodlands.

Oak woodlands and forests do not contaminate our surface and ground water with agricultural fertilizers, pesticides, fungicides, and herbicides. As important organs of the watersheds, they protect the water supply from silt and erosion. Pure, abundant water for our population is dependent on the health of our watersheds.

The fires necessitate that we rethink our approach to the watersheds. There is so much scientific research that says do not cut these burned areas, let them recover—that the best action is no action. This is a time for our governing officials to bow their heads to scientific research, not succumb to political pressure for business as usual.

The health of our beautiful valley begins at the top of the mountains in the Ag Watershed Open Space lands. Our water supply is dependent on this health. Oak woodlands and forests are important components to aquifer recharge, to the health of the Napa River and our reservoirs, and to clean and abundant water for all of us.

Water and Fire remind us of our connection to each other. What we each do on our own land affects us all. Advocate that our county officials pause, allow our burned lands to regenerate, and take steps to manage the understory of our oak woodlands and forests that have not burned. Our population is dependent on it.

Vineyards don't save lives; water does.

PATRICIA DAMERY

NAPA

CHAPTER 38

Fire's Wake

NOW I KNOW HOW Seth felt when he first stared into devastated Eden. We returned from Portugal to a blackened land. Wherever we drove—north, east, west, or south—charred leafless trees, sentinels of shock, stood against blackened hillsides. Here and there ghost trees lay on the ground as if having fainted, only their white ash remembering their shape: the fire had been that hot. When I drove up Soda Canyon Road to Cindy's home the next Monday morning for the Napa Vision 2050 meeting, I passed miles of ashy remains of houses, barns, and sheds. Cindy's was one of the 15 percent remaining.

As I parked in the area outside Cindy's gate, I could not take in the change: Her winery/guest house was a pile of debris, but the lush gardens and verdant green grass that encircled her home were unharmed. Like a voyeur, I could only stare at the carnage. Others were also arriving, and we hugged and shared stories. Among those of us there only Dan's home had burned. However, several living at the dead end of Soda Canyon had to be evacuated by a helicopter that first night, including one of our board members, Diane. Gordon, who lived on Atlas Peak near Dan, had been on a cruise in Europe when he got word of the fire. He checked his security camera from his phone to see the state of his home. Although their home was one of the few that did not burn, his wife insisted that they return, and they did, disembarking the boat and commissioning a $1000 taxi back to Amsterdam for a flight home.

Almost everyone present had been evacuated for at least a week. Some hotels offered lower rates for the evacuees. Jim reported that one of our water warriors, Chris, was still in a hotel with her family as her home had burned and she had nowhere to go. Jim and his wife, Leonore, spent a few days in the same hotel until they could return to their ranch. (In 2020, their home would burn in another devasting fire season.) Cindy told how she had escaped that first night but had to leave her horses behind and then return daily, sometimes sneaking past law enforcement, to feed and water them. Person by person, we accounted for everyone.

We decided to give Dan and Naoko a surprise "fire shower" to replace some of their belongings. So one early November evening, we packed into the back room of Las Palmas, a local restaurant where Gary lured Dan and Naoko for a quiet dinner. We brought gifts

We returned from Portugal to a blackened land. Wherever we drove north, eeast, west, or south charred leafless trees, sentinels in shock, stood against blackened hillsides. (Photograph: Bill Hocker)

of various everyday items: saltshakers and gift certificates for shoes, thermos bottles, and a printer. We drank wine and ate enchiladas and laughed. Afterward, in an email thank you, Dan jokingly complained that after such a rowdy evening, he had to carry in all the contraband from his truck bed into his rented condo, and there wasn't room for it all.

We would soon find out that we were in the eye of a great political storm. Like the aftershocks of an earthquake, we continue to feel the ongoing ramifications of David taking on Goliath and almost winning—or is it that uneasy battle of Rangda and Barong?

On December 1, 2017, I joined a handful of the supporters of the Water, Forest, and Oak Woodland Protection Initiative of 2018 as Jim and Mike lugged boxes of petitions with over 7000 signatures into the county Election Division office and John Tuteur to qualify the initiative for the June 5, 2018, ballot. This was the same initiative that had been co-authored by representatives of the vintners until they pulled out. Among other protections, it would limit the future cutting of oak woodlands to 795 acres, a number calculated from the Napa County General Plan. We stood together as we took pictures of the occasion, John Tuteur joining us. Although we had about twice the number of required signatures, we knew a lot could go wrong. But this time the initiative became Measure C, a ballot measure that would divide Napa County as much as the adoption of the Ag Preserve ordinance had fifty years before. A few days later, George Caloyannidis filed signatures to place Measure D on the ballot prohibiting private landings of helicopters in Napa County, a measure fully supported by Napa Vision 2050. The surrealness of the next months rivaled the nightly news of our national politics.

LETTER TO THE EDITOR

Napa Valley Register, April 25, 2018

Arguments against Measure D are wrong

I want to express my outrage and disappointment in State Sen. Bill Dodd's argument against Measure D (Yes on Measure D prohibits permitting more private heliports).[188]

Dodd argues that under Measure D's terms "Utility contractors, like those working for PG&E, won't be able to use helicopters to replace power poles or service lines as they successfully did after the October fires."

This is dead wrong. Measure D does not change County Code about the use of helicopters to install and maintain distribution lines to convey gas or electricity.

Dodd also states, "Helicopter operators providing essential services may be restricted from landing on private property in Napa County if Measure D is approved."

Again, dead wrong. Measure D does not change County Code about emergency use facility landing sites or emergency medical services' landing sites. (Code 18.120.010/A.9).

Let's be clear: this Measure D does not affect airspace or flight at all. It simply regulates landings of helicopters.

Did Dodd read the text of the initiative? Measure D makes two changes in County Code: 1. prohibiting personal use airports and heliports and 2. prohibiting helicopter landings at vineyards unless unavoidable, such as in emergencies. Aerial applications by helicopter for agricultural production are still permitted.

A *Napa Valley Register* article quoted Dodd as saying that his argument was based on the 9111 report commissioned by the Board of Supervisors to give "independent" legal analysis on the measure. Given the facts above, this analysis, as argued in front of the Supervisors by the Measure's attorney of Moscone, Emblidge, and Rubins, is flawed.

Senator Dodd has been invited to participate at several forums, including the League of Women Voters, to defend his statements but thus far has avoided participation.

Why would a state senator present "facts" that are so wrong? Are perhaps special interest funders behind him? Democracy requires access to the facts. How else can we make informed decisions?

PATRICIA DAMERY
NAPA

EDITOR'S NOTE: *The Register* asked Bill Dodd about the issues raised by the author. He said his legislative schedule has made it difficult to accept invitations to speak on this initiative. He said his opposition to Measure D, and also to Measure C, relates to possible unintended consequences, which would be difficult to fix if the legislation is enacted by ballot initiative. The people and supervisors of Napa County, he said, "are perfectly capable of handling these issues" without resorting to initiatives.

CHAPTER 39

The Election

ON THE EVENING OF June 5, 2018, we gathered at the St. Helena Native Sons Hall for an election night celebration as we awaited the preliminary results of the polls. "Celebrate the incredible work of the Measure C & D teams and Cio Perez for Supervisor," the email read. "Food and treats provided. Bring a bottle to share. 5 P.M. until the results are in, 8:05 P.M."

I arrived a little past 6 P.M. Mike's pickup was parked out front with its large green-and-blue *Yes on Measure C* sign anchored like a shark's fin to the truck bed. I felt an odd sadness when I saw it, thinking *This is the last time!* Over the last months, Mike's truck could be spotted anywhere at any time. The billboard-sized poster announced, in its grassroots way, Protect Our Watersheds, as it navigated its way up and down Highway 29 or the Silverado Highway, or stood in traffic at the intersections in St. Helena, or parked in front of Chris's home or Umpqua Bank's parking lot, for planning and canvassing meetings.

The Native Sons Hall was already packed with people sitting at long tables with paper plates piled high with food or standing in groupings around the perimeter. The evening was warm, especially inside, with at least a hundred people packed together. Only the white-washed walls offered a hint of coolness. On the east side of the room, a long table was generously laid out with plates of deviled eggs, chopped veggies, hummus dips, chips, many salads. Close by, another table offered a cornucopia of homemade brownies, chocolate chip cookies, apple pies, a peach cobbler—all baked by supporters. Excitement, even ecstasy, charged the room, but outside Julia, a strong supporter of the Measure C campaign, and Mike paced nervously. Periodically news media reporters pulled Jim or Mike aside to answer questions and film comments. An old friend from my years in Sonoma County, Jonah Raskin of the *North Bay Bohemian* newspaper, walked around the hall talking with attendees and scribbling notes on a small pad of paper.

Our excitement and anxiety that evening overruled our weariness, many in the room having walked precincts day after day and written hundreds of postcards to mail to homes in more remote areas. Many had penned letters to the editor, delivered and installed signs, and donated funds to counter the outrage of the wine industry. Measure C was also supported and funded by an enlightened group of vintners and growers, organized by Mike and Jim. The No on C campaign outspent Yes on C two to one, stuffing residents' mailboxes with copious amounts of election propaganda weekly and then, just before the election, daily, replete with misinformation and lies. Two of our planning commissioners were pictured on these mailers, claiming that Measure C—and protecting our oak woodlands—would result in more event centers, more traffic, and *allow* the cutting of 795 acres of trees, an evil spin on the limit of cutting *no more* than 795 acres of trees. One brochure pictured members of the Farm Bureau dressed in firefighter uniforms, an activity against state law, which prohibits the use of public uniforms and county equipment for political purposes. PG&E (Pacific Gas and Electric Company) was also cited as coming out against Measure C, a blatant lie. Full page ads were posted in the local paper by the No on C campaign with hundreds of names against the measure, including prominent, respected people who supported C. The No on C campaign played it dirty and without much consequence. The aim was to confuse voters.

And then there was Measure D. State Senator Bill Dodd, a Napa County supervisor until he was elected to the state senate, had written the misinformed No on D arguments for the ballot, again unquestioned by the powers that be. Self-interests ruled. Realtors, who had been against Measure C because of the increased property values of potential vineyard development, were for the passage of Measure D, because heliports in and near residential areas decrease property values.

Cio Perez for supervisor in District 3, a former Farm Bureau board member, ran against incumbent Diane Dillon. His support of Measure C put him at odds with the Farm Bureau board, which had been reconfigured in the last years. Some said a group of powerful vintners staged a hostile takeover. Cio was a real farmer and vineyard manager, but he also supported the protection of the watersheds and our environment.

Napa Vision 2050 endorsed and supported all three: *Yes on C! Yes on D! Yes on Cio!*

Shortly after 8 P.M., Mike grabbed a microphone and announced the preliminary results as they were reported. Measure C was ahead by forty votes! A collective out breath and then great cheering! Measure D by substantially more! More cheering! But Cio was behind—again, not unexpected. The powers-that-be had turned on him for his support of Measure C. We consoled Cio: The ballots counted were those turned in early. Anything could happen.

The next morning the *Napa Valley Register* reported that Measure C was still ahead. "An epic campaign clash over Napa County's Measure C is coming down to an epic, slow-motion finish that will take days, and possibly weeks, to unfold," the paper reported. "The county Election Division released a vote tally at 10:39 P.M. . . . The controversial watershed and oak woodlands protection initiative led 7,191 to 7,149, or 50.15 percent to 49.85 percent."[189]

Measure D had a "commanding early lead of 8,689 to 5,542, or 61 percent." Cio, however, although having given Diane Dillon a run for it, received only 44 percent of the vote. Jonah Raskin's article, also printed that week, "A County Divided: Napa's Measure

C Ahead by a Hair," addressed the rift that had opened. "Napa is so small, geographically speaking—789 square miles, as opposed to Sonoma's 1,768 square miles—and so insular, that political adversaries often work together to harvest the crop that makes the county world famous."[190] In the last line of the article, he quoted me. I read it now with a distance that I did not have that evening when I said to Jonah, and he scribbled word for word on his pad, "After this campaign, I no longer respect some of my neighbors who opposed C. . . . They put up signs meant to confuse people. . . . We will have to forgive one another. The battle for democracy will go on."[191]

By June 28, however, the results were certified: Measure D won, being much less controversial.[192] Cio did not. And Measure C lost by 641 votes, 50.9 percent to 49.1 percent. A *Napa Valley Register* article contrasted comments from both sides:

"It's hard for me to get past the fact that our opponents ran a campaign that essentially tricked voters into voting against their own best interests," [Mike] Hackett said in a post-election press release.[192-1] [Ryan] Klobas saw the No on Measure C campaign differently. "The goal was to educate the public about Measure C's flaws and possible unintended consequences. The initiative process wasn't the best way to address the matter," he said.[193]

Klobas was quoted in this article saying he thought the "message resonated with people. . . . Now that Measure C has been defeated, we can start the work of addressing issues with the Board of Supervisors, where these issues should have been addressed in first place."[194]

We knew what this meant: the Farm Bureau and the wider wine industry would work to firm up their headlock on the Board of Supervisors and their appointed planning commissioners. The fight was far from over.

Coastal live oak

CHAPTER 40

Re-Oaking the Valley

THE COUNTY GOVERNMENT MAY be delinquent and hostile when it comes to protecting our oak woodlands and watersheds, but state-wide agencies and conservation organizations are not. The disconnect between the science of climate change and its impact on water security, severity of drought and flooding cycles, and the increasing intensity and frequency of wildfire with the land-use policies of our local government boggles the mind. At this time (2021) we have nine more years to reach the goal of carbon neutral emissions by 2030 if we are going to limit temperature increases to 1.5 degrees centigrade, yet oak woodlands, conifer forests, and chapparal lands are being converted to vineyards at the rate of about two hundred acres a year.[195] All three are critically important for carbon seques-tration. And at the time of this writing, Napa County still does not have a Climate Action Plan, mandated by the General Plan in 2008. The tourism and wine industries' interests are just too great.

In parallel action with the Napa County government, the Napa Resource Conservation District (RCD) instigated the *Acorns to Oaks* program. During the first eight years of the project, from 2012 to 2019, school children have planted over 5,500 acorns in oak woodland areas, or in areas with soil types that support oaks. Then they have tended the sprouting trees. Acorn *to Oaks* is an extension of the Re-Oaking North Bay program, developed by the San Francisco Estuary Institute, the Napa RCD, and Sonoma Resource Conservation District, and funded by the North Bay Watershed Association. The demise of the valley oak population, valley oaks accounting for more than 65 percent of the oaks in an oak woodland, has sparked deep concern among scientists working for these agencies. Valley oaks are a keystone species; the cutting of valley oaks and the fragmentation of the oak woodland ecosystems that sustain them has serious consequences. The aim of *Acorns to Oaks* is to restore oak woodland habitat in backyards, parks, along streets, farms, creeks, and vineyards.[196] Administrators of the program use acorns that are genetically similar to those in the area. Because our ranch is within a mile of Alston Park, one of the main restoration sites, our acorns are important.

Recently, starting in August each year, Wesley, Sabien, Melissa, and I collect acorns in bags, labeling them as to type of oak—valley oak, black oak, or coastal live oak—and the location collected. Napa RCD showed Wesley and Sabien how to dump the acorns in water to cull those that float and then to rinse the remaining in a light bleach solution to rid the surfaces of mold. When we have done this at home, we then spread the acorns in the sun to dry, carefully guarding so the local squirrel does not load up on our cache, and then bag the acorns and refrigerate them until we deliver them to RCD.

Valley oak acorns drying after being washed

Each year we also make acorn flour. After roasting the acorns in the oven at a very low temperature until their shells are somewhat brittle, we crack them in the hole of a stone found on our property that has been used for millennia for this very purpose, with a wooden mallet that my grandmother used in straining fruit. Although this takes hours, Wesley and Sabien love it. As we work, we speak of the ancestors of the land, how they must be with us as we use their stone. The preparation of the acorns binds us to the land, weaving our souls into history and into a future in which communion with trees is not just revealing in their beauty now and then, or resting in their shade, but is a partnership that literally sustains our bodies. As we boil the acorn meat to rid it of tannins, drain, and then boil again, as we grind the meat into flour and make the flour into muffins, we participate in an ancient rite of working with the *living presences* of the land and valley oaks for sustenance.

After the fires of 2017, we carried the work with the acorns a step further. Napa Vision 2050 joined with RCD in planting acorns on our ranch. Many of us were still in shock from the massive devastation of the fires. An unbelievable number of homes had been lost. Most of us had been evacuated for a week or more. All of us had lived with toxic wildfire smoke for days. Too many of our hillsides were blackened for miles around, oaks burned dead by the extreme incineration of the fires. The act of planting acorns was healing.

In the days before the Saturday event, two women from RCD joined Casey, Melissa, the boys, and me in placing flags on spots to re-oak. We walked the trail west behind our home, finding two areas where oaks would be planted. Sabien, five at the time, was particularly gleeful and careful in the placement of the flags. "We are planting a forest!" he exclaimed.

That November 2017 day twenty of us gathered, including several children; we dug holes by the flags, planting two acorns in each hole, then staked a plastic collar above the planting to protect the emerging shoots from deer or rabbits. We finished by shoveling wood chips around the planting to protect from grasses and to prevent hiding places for rodents. We finished with the prayer poem of Wendell Berry's "*The Sycamore.*" That day valley oak, black oak, and coastal live oak offered us the hope that our lands are resilient.

We planted approximately one hundred acorns that day. Forty-one of these sprouted. Of those which sprouted, thirteen remain. The statistics from RCD about the long-term survival rate of the 5500 planted acorns is about 17 percent.[197] Hopefully these young trees will become strong tall oaks, which our children will visit as adults with their grandchildren.

Oaks restore groundwater, stop erosion, and clean and replenish our air. But as important as this effort of planting oaks, and particularly valley oaks, is, an alarming fact was discovered by Jim Wilson when working with a young Napa Climate NOW! intern, Katie Stillwell. Carbon sequestration of these surviving young oaks is half the carbon sequestration of one 100-year-old oak. Cut one old oak and you undo all the work of these hundreds of school children over eight years.[198] Our county government is expanding vineyards at the cost of our oak woodlands and forests, which are ultimately our greatest hope in mitigating changes in our climate. The disconnect of government and science will be our undoing, unless we fix it.

We must do better on climate change

The second revised draft of the Napa County Climate Action Plan (CAP) coming before the Planning Commission reads more as a document protecting Ag production rather than one protecting our environment and climate.

Projections show that it is unlikely Napa Valley will remain a world-class wine-grape-growing area into mid-century and certainly by the century's end. My husband and I are growers. We know climate change will impact us. We are replanting and have yet to decide what grape can best survive into the future.

Already, Napa County's average temperatures have increased 1–2 degrees Celsius. We as growers will definitely be impacted. But what is more important is not what grape will survive, but what can we do to make those lung organs of our Earth—our forests and oaks woodlands—resilient in the next 100 years. Cutting them is not an option.

This Climate Action Plan falls far short of what is needed. I understand that the wine industry has had a strong arm in modifying the reach of the CAP. I was appalled to hear a representative of the Napa Valley Vintners thank the Planning Commission for doing what the vintners wanted.

In fact, the *North Bay Business Journal* quoted a spokesman for the NVV as saying, "Our goal is to ensure that a final CAP will not be a burden on the wine community, the principal industry here, or cause our members to bear the brunt of ways proposed to remedy [greenhouse gas emissions]."[199]

This neutralizing of effective action is at the cost to all of us and our offspring, vintners and growers included. Perhaps the most notable exclusion in the CAP is that of the importance of stopping deforestation when world scientists are calling for such a cessation. Our forests and oak woodlands in our Ag Watershed lands protect our water supply, sequester and hold carbon in the substance of their growth and in the soils, "breathe in" carbon dioxide and "breath out" oxygen, and prevent erosion. Our native vegetation—including our forests and oaks woodlands—is our greatest hope of resilience into the future.

The Climate Action Plan is potentially one of the most important documents that we as a county can adopt at this time. Our climate is changing, and we need to do everything humanly possible to mitigate the extent of the impacts of upcoming increases in temperature.

Worldwide, scientists are saying we have at most 10 or 11 years to cut our greenhouse gas emissions in order to prevent the worst of the impact those rising temperatures will have on our environment, health, and sea rise. In fact, we are facing the possibility that continuing life on Earth for humans is in question.

In this atmosphere, the time is ripe for another initiative. If the governing bodies cannot or do not act for the common good, then, in California, the people have the right of the initiative. If we cannot protect our environment through the channels of the elected, perhaps it is the next important choice.

PATRICIA DAMERY

NAPA

C H A P T E R 4 1

Planning Commission
Hearing on Sinclair Winery

THE DRY CREEK ROAD Alliance neighbors gathered in the chambers of the Planning Commission. We sat together in clumps for the first of what could well be several hearings about the use permit modification of Sinclair Winery. Donald was not with me. Large gatherings only confused him these days. In fact, that morning when I told him where I was going, he asked, once again, "Now what is it the Sinclairs want to do?" I simplified, "They want to build a winery."

The room quickly filled. Many of us had arrived early to get a seat and to sign a card to get in the cue to make public comment. Mike slipped into the seat beside me. "You have some strange bedfellows," he said softly, referring to our neighbor who posted the No on Measure C signs, now sitting directly behind me. *Yes*, I nodded.

Most of us in the standing-room-only chamber were against the magnitude of the winery's expansion. We were prepared, having spent weeks coordinating our comments. After a presentation of the major modification by the planner and then by the attorney for the Sinclairs, and after questioning of both by the commissioners, we were called one by one to the microphone in the front of the room to make public comment. We used our three measured minutes to address specific issues: fire safety on a long single-lane driveway, for which we had hired a fire safety expert who recommended no more than fifty people at any one event; the fact that the proposed driveway was within thirty feet of two homes, that as "an intensification of commercialization" it was "an egregious taking of our ag lands." A water analysis by a retired NASA physicist showed there was no way the Sinclairs' analysis of water availability worked. There were issues around violations of three easements, in addition to the tree easement, about which the Sinclairs were either initially ignorant or simply ignoring. They planned to cut more than a hundred trees. Neighbors addressed how traffic studies had been done in January at the quietest time of the week and year and how the proposed entry was also on a dangerous curve on Dry Creek Road and would be made especially hazardous when people left the winery after winetasting. After at least two dozen public comments, the Sinclairs' attorney addressed public concerns, basically trying to deem them unfounded. My face burned red when he took swipes at Donald and me, mentioning water usage for lavender (much lower than grapes, by the way) and downplaying our concerns of overspray of non-organic agricultural chemicals so close to our home.

I was relieved when one of the more conservative commissioners expressed his concern for "the very real potential for un-mitigatable neighborhood impacts, including noise, traffic, and the impact on neighboring wells." The hearing was continued from October 2018 to December 2018, and then again to January 2019, and then indefinitely, as the commissioners did not agree with the planners' recommendations that the project was ready to be approved. The Sinclairs were charged to work with neighbors on visitation and gallonage issues, negotiations that turned out to only underscore the great divide.

When the Sinclairs return to the Planning Commission, they will present another revised plan. If the commissioners accept it, and if it is as extreme as it has been, the neighbors will appeal the decision to the Board of Supervisors, and if the decision is upheld, to the courts. If the project is rejected by the commissioners, the Sinclairs will probably appeal. This is how land-use issues go in Napa County. It is a costly process that favors Big Money. How many of us can afford the hundreds of thousands of dollars to endure the years of obtaining a permit? How many of us can afford to go up against such a financial force with citizen-paid consultation for experts, attorneys, and court fees? Such a process has many impacts, including the hit on our democratic process when Big Money makes big campaign donations to our elected and appointed governing officials who make these land-use decisions. But two of the most long-lasting and serious impacts are the unmitigable splintering of our neighborhoods and the damage to oak woodlands and forest lands.

Talk about Chicken Little

On March 6, the Napa County Planning Commission will meet again to take more public comment and make a recommendation to the Board of Supervisors on a watershed and tree protection ordinance. This is the result of Measure C's (Watershed and Oak Woodland Protection Initiative) almost passing.

The wine industry showed up in force at the Feb. 20 Planning Commission meeting, asserting that protecting our hillsides and watersheds any further would result in the demise of the wine industry.

Talk about Chicken Little. The truth is, if further protective measures are not put in place, our environment and water supply will suffer, and with it, the wine industry as well.

The wine industry is robust. Limiting its ability of develop our hillsides and watersheds is not going to be the death of it. However, there is a conflict of interest when any industry insists that a governmental body protect its financial interests at the cost of the environment and water supply.

This is why the Environmental Protection Agency was formed in 1970: to separate out the interests of agriculture's use of pesticides from the needs of the environment. Until then, pesticide usage was governed by the United States Department of Agriculture (USDA), described by Rachel Carson of Silent Spring as a financial "conflict of interest."

We need the planning commissioners and the Board of Supervisors to act on behalf of the citizens of Napa County in protecting our water supply and our environment.

The assertion from some in the wine industry that only a few individuals are pushing watershed protections similar to those of Measure C is absolutely false. A growing number of citizens, vintners and growers are leading the push to protect our natural resource—49.1 percent voted for Measure C in a dirty campaign too often based on the opposition's false assertions and efforts to confuse the voters.

This current effort for the Board of Supervisors to pass an ordinance to protect our hillsides, oak woodlands, forests and watersheds was spearheaded by U.S. Rep. Mike Thompson. Hopefully another initiative will not be needed, but when a governing body does not govern, in California, we the people have that right.

Please contact your supervisor and planning commissioner to encourage them to act on behalf of the environment, not special interest groups.

PATRICIA DAMERY
NAPA

*Entering common ground means listening to the other
and considering the ways we are alike.*

CHAPTER 42

Common Ground

I AM SITTING IN the front row of the Blue Note auditorium in downtown Napa, waiting. Mina Kim of public radio station KQED is interviewing a local author who has written the untold history of the minorities in Napa Valley. I am up next, on a panel with Ryan Klobas, CEO of the Napa County Farm Bureau, addressing post-Measure C and land-use battles.[200] A young female intern then appears and tells me to follow her through convoluted corridors into an elevator. We exchange a few polite words as the elevator takes us up a floor. The door opens into a room painted black. Before us, three people sit on stage at a long panel of controls, with their backs to us. In the center, a stage light illuminates Mina Kim, who is announcing the next segment of the show, the one I am in. A couple of minutes later, I notice a large figure, whom I am soon to learn is Ryan Klobas, exiting the elevator. He wears a short-sleeved plaid shirt and jeans, a man who looks to be in his mid to late forties. Although he looks like a farmer, he isn't. He's an attorney, hired by the local Farm Bureau during the Measure C debacle. Looking out into the audience, I see the auditorium is packed. My only thought? How the hell did I end up here?

Of course, I know the answer! I agreed to! Jim and Mike asked me to be the spokesperson for the Measure C campaign and for Napa Vision 2050. My role as editor of the newsletter *Eyes on Napa* somehow qualified me. I made them promise to coach me.

I study the crowd as Mina makes her introductions. Two halos of red and gold ringlets on the heads of Wesley and Sabien shine about two-thirds of the way back. Casey sits between them. They wave vigorously when they notice I see them, and I wave back. *You are the reasons I am here.*

Oddly, I feel at home sitting next to Ryan. I grew up with the Farm Bureau. My father was a member. In those days the Farm Bureau was a benign presence that supported small farmers, making sure their crops had markets. The American Farm Bureau Federation continues, in rhetoric, at least, to support the farmer but with little regard for the impact of farming on climate and the environment, and, in fact, many would say, little regard for the impact of the changing climate on the farmer. The Federation has strong ties to the oil industry.[201] Although their website says they support "alternative energy sources, which will minimize atmospheric pollution," they also oppose almost any climate change legislation and any regulation of greenhouse gasses by the Environmental Protection Agency, acts that would "put undue costs on American agriculture, business, or consumers."[202] This is the stance of the national federation that Ryan Klobas represents locally—and that I am debating.

Mina Kim begins with essentially the same question that we end with: why did the loss of Measure C not start a process of "mending bridges" around hillside development issues? In fact, spurred by the close vote on Measure C, the county passed a contentious ordinance in April 2019, The Napa County Water Quality and Tree Protection Ordinance.[203] Many of us feel this ordinance falls far short of protecting either our water supply or our trees.

As if answering different questions, Ryan and I respond. Ryan asserts that the No on Measure C campaign was all about "educating" voters concerning the many conservation regulations already in place to plant a hillside vineyard. Like a mantra, he adds for the first of several times throughout the next thirty minutes, "If you can identify a problem, we're more than willing to work with you to identify solutions. Up until now it's been very challenging to have impartial science and data backup to identify a problem."[204]

Mina Kim asks me what I think the problem with vineyard development is and what have we done to back up our concerns.

"Our changing climate," I say. "We can't go on with business as usual. One of the things that we have to do is create resilience into the future." I explain about the importance of biodiversity in creating resilience, including protecting our remaining oak woodlands and forests. "When the valley floor got planted out in vines, people looked to develop the hillsides. But the hillsides are the watersheds. When you buy land in the Ag watershed, you're buying *watershed*."

Mina questions, "What specifically happens with vineyard development that you feel compromises the watershed?"

"Silting of the reservoirs and erosion." I explain the fragility of hillside soils and how easily disturbance of the soils causes erosion. "A little bit of disturbance, and when big rains come, the hillsides hemorrhage liquid mud."

Mina continues: "Why did increased stream setbacks, tree canopy retention, and tree mitigation ratios not settle things?" Most of us in the room knew this ordinance extended the protections of the oak woodlands and forests by only about 3 percent.

I frame the answer this way: that it is a *start* of the conversation. That having common ground where we can talk is the only way we're going to get through this mess. That there is, in fact, a lot of data about water quality and erosion. The statement that there is no science to back claims of water supply and quality and erosion is simply not true. We need to get into an environment where we're not politicizing it. Where we're not buying supervisors with campaign donations. "Are you going to listen to who gave you the donation or are you going to look at the science that citizens are presenting?" I add.

Ryan, of course, is not sitting still for this, saying it's extremely unfair to characterize the supervisors as *bought off*. To say that political contributions influenced the way they voted. In response to his statement, the audience laughs loudly. A tweet broadcast across a large screen facing the audience reads, "Klobas hammered by audience."

For a moment I feel sorry for him. He does not look like a CEO at all, but more like my younger brother, also conservative and in a kind of lock step with the Republican agenda. This is not a friendly audience for Ryan, and our interviewer also has a point of view on the matter, living in Napa herself.

She turns to Ryan. "Explain to me what your response is to the ordinance, because you have also gone on record saying that you feel like it went too far. What's the problem, say, with increasing tree canopy retention from 60 to 70 percent? Why does that specifically hurt Ag, or make it harder for Ag?"

"What it does is begin to create a slippery slope when it comes to regulation. Where do you draw the line?" He continues describing an independent engineer's study that applied existing county conservation regulations on a 10-acre parcel and then added the new ordinance regulations. "You can go from a 10-acre parcel all the way down to maybe 2.3 acres of developable land. Once you add structures, like a house, other structures, and driveway, good luck trying to plant a vineyard. It makes it hard for Ag to be productive. This is Napa County. We are an Ag economy."

Mina turns to me. "Are you hoping that there is no more big development in Napa County, that the valley has been built out, both on the hillsides and on the valley floor?"

"No, and I don't think that a number of Measure C people would feel that way either. But I do think that the issue of planting in the hillsides is, as Ryan says, a slippery slope."

The audience roars with laughter and Mina Kim reminds me under her breath that he was referring to regulation. I nod my head that I am aware of that, but I couldn't resist.

The conversation continues with Ryan saying there is no science substantiating the need for more regulations, my countering with examples of why we need more regulations, then Ryan's counter: "Show me a problem and I will address it." It's exasperating. Mina asks Ryan, "Do you really need to wait for a study to be able to tell you how to move forward? Are there independent studies that both sides would trust?"

"When we threw this into a political arena," I say, "we sacrificed looking at real science. And we're talking about two different things. The conservation regulations, when they're enforced and monitored, are good. Ryan is correct about that. But they're not enforced often enough: code enforcement is a real issue, and they're not monitored when things are put in. We have evidence of that. We have taken pictures of water that's coming off the vineyards and water that's coming off forests right next door. The runoff from vineyards is full of mud and next door it's clear.

"The Napa River is still listed for silt and sedimentation," I add. "It may be taken off for nutrients, but it hasn't been taken off yet. That is a direct result of our development, whether it's a vineyard or residential."

Toward the end Mina returns to the first question. "We were hearing stories about long-term relationships ending between long-time friends, about that inability to figure out a way to come together. How do you think it's become this way?"

This question is the local version of the most important issue of our times. How can we share enough common ground to address issues that impact us all? How can we move past the power struggles of politics to listen to the other and problem solve on issues that may well define how humans can survive in our changing world?

At first Ryan answers as if from the American Farm Bureau Federation playbook. "Throughout the entire process, regulation like this starts to impact a lot of different people from a lot of different walks of life. We want to protect future farming and agriculture in the county. When it comes to small family farmers who are directly impacted by regulation like this, it becomes a politically charged environment."

But this time there's a crack in it. He continues, "There are arguments on both sides of this and at the end of the day, I would believe that we all want the same thing; we're just disagreeing about the way to get there. We all want to be excellent stewards of the land, but the disagreement comes around how do we do that. When we talk about creating law and creating regulation, that naturally starts to become a politically charged environment."

Mina turns to me. "We heard Ryan Klobas say that he's willing to sit down with the other side to try to figure this out. There are also reports of a couple of other things that have been happening in the background, so let me ask you, Patricia, are you going to put another measure on the ballot similar to Measure C?"

I answer honestly. "All options are on the table." The audience applauds.

"Are you in the process?" Mina asks.

"All options are on the table," I repeat to a cheering audience. "And," I add, "I hope we *can* sit down. I do believe there's a lot of common ground. My husband and I are members of the Farm Bureau. I grew up on a small farm in the Midwest and my father was a member of the Farm Bureau. I hope the Farm Bureau helps small farmers, but a lot of these are not small farmers. They're very wealthy individuals who want to capitalize on their investment."

Mina turns to Ryan. "You've talked about forming a political action committee and you're really focused on this proviso of who is up for reelection. Is that your plan or is it truly your plan to sit down and try to figure out another way? Is your plan to try to oust those who you feel are not friendly enough to Ag?"

"The Board of Directors of the Farm Bureau hasn't made any decisions like that," Ryan answers.

"But you're definitely putting that out there," Mina pushes. "So, tell me, what is your next immediate course?"

"Our next tack: we'd like to see if there's going to be another initiative on the ballot, and I'll tell you right now, it's very indicative of an unwillingness to try to work these issues out. When you say you're going to take a blunt-force object like an initiative and you're going to put it on the ballot, then we're going to go through this entire process again. We can take all the money that we've spent trying to beat Measure C and put it to much better uses. So if we're going to go through another initiative process again, I don't think anybody has really learned anything."

Is he correct? If we go through another initiative process, have we learned nothing? I contemplate this as I turn to look at Ryan, like my brother in so many ways. But, unlike my brother, he's not a farmer. He's an attorney, hired to push an agenda.

What does common ground mean? In my mind, it means laying down the weapons of power struggles: the biased slant used to prove one's side as superior, or the lies, in the case of the No on Measure C campaign. Entering common ground means listening to the other and considering the ways we are alike. It means considering science and data and thinking about the good of the whole.

Is common ground an idea whose time must come? Can we afford to consider economic interests when those interests too often threaten the planet that sustains life? Can we afford not to?

And so it ended. When Ryan and I stepped into the elevator to return to the ground floor, I looked him in the eye. "Ryan," I said. "I believe there is common ground."

He turned toward me briefly. "Yes," he said smoothly.

This is not my father's Farm Bureau.

CHAPTER 43

Slipping

SLOWLY I AM ACCEPTING my aloneness in endeavors that Donald and I once shared. It is a strange acceptance, one punctuated with pragmatic resolve and shadowed with grief.

I manage this in different ways. I tell myself that Donald is still Donald and that I must simply meet him where he is. Sometimes this works. Sometimes what I do is more for myself than it is for him. I hate attending social gatherings alone, gatherings that people attend with their mates. I try to think of Donald first, not wanting to put him in an awkward situation. But when Napa Vision 2050 decided to have a potluck the last summer before the pandemic, I was weary from attending so many social events alone, so I suggested to Donald that he join me. He complied, as he almost always does. He is basically binary: answering *yes* or *I will think about that,* which means *no.* Usually, he says *yes,* unless it has to do with exercise, so when I ask, I study his face for the real answer: is he really up for this? Social isolation is deadly for Donald, but overstimulating encounters drown him in a sense of failure to participate in ways that he once enjoyed. In a one-on-one conversation, Donald will warn the other that even though he does not immediately answer does not mean he did not understand what was said. I tell him that when he says this, it makes him more present to everyone. But Donald is slipping. Almost every day he says, "I want to tell you, my memory is not getting better."

"You mean it's getting worse?" I ask.

"Yes," he says. And I am no longer so sure of what he does understand. More often now when he answers, *I will think about that,* it means, *I can't answer.*

The evening of the potluck, I knew almost immediately that I had made a mistake in bringing Donald. The cacophony of conversation was so loud as we entered the outside pool area of Cindy's home that Donald turned off his hearing aids. He cannot stand for long, so I suggested that he sit at the long table by the pool while I got him a glass of Cabernet. I got a glass of sauvignon blanc for myself and returned to sit beside him. "You go on," he said, "I am okay here." And I did, for a few minutes, glancing back at him every so often sitting there alone. I piled two plates high with crayfish and the salads everyone had brought.

When I returned to the table, Dan was sitting close to Donald. Others joined us. Donald could not figure out how to open the shell of the crayfish, so I had to help. I could tell he was retreating into a protected space. Kaleidoscopes of conversations drifted from one end of the table to the other: creeks where people used to fish for crayfish, the political makeup of the Calistoga City Council, Don's trip to Amsterdam. I was torn between the play of conversation and the needs of my husband sitting silently beside me.

Just as we were finishing dessert, Eve appeared. She and Ginna had been discussing our newsletter series, *Everything you wanted to know about Ag Protections but were afraid to ask.* "We want to remind you to underscore that nothing gets done unless it is through a citizen initiative, not by board directive," she said. A little buzzed by the wine and distracted by concern for Donald, I answered, "Text me what you just said." It was time for us to go home.

Once in the car, I tried to explain Eve's statement about the initiative process. Donald listened. I continued about how this series of articles would address the eroding of the protections of the Ag Preserve, how in the last months we learned of a new threat: that of streamlining the permitting process for small wineries. I explained that this proposed ordinance, the Small Winery Protection and Use Permit Streamlining Ordinance, would allow the expansion of at least 40 percent of the wineries in Napa County without the public purview.[205]

Donald was silent. I looked over. "This time of day is not a good one for me," he explained. "You will have to tell me this again later."

"Okay," I answered, staring out at dark Soda Canyon Road, the pool of light before me illuminating only a short distance of pavement ahead.

I am becoming used to not sharing with Donald what also is exciting or current for me. The window on overlapping intellectual pursuits has closed. Yet the business of life and of the county continues, some of it directly pertaining to the oak savanna Donald and I love and live in, walk and breathe in daily. We started this land-use battle together years ago, when we first learned of the Sinclairs' expansion. The erosion control plans within the tree easement that Donald had printed out and commented on bring an ache to my heart. I remember the visits to attorneys and Donald's questions, his comments on the specs of the planned driveway. He knew so much more about this than I. But that was ten years ago, and five years ago. Now I must do this for us both.

CHAPTER 44

What We Know Now

What we know now about land use in Napa County is that basically, over the last fifty years, nothing much has changed. Yes, more than fifty years ago we were lucky enough to have leaders with the foresight to protect our agricultural lands with the nation's first ever Agriculture Preserve, but it was exceedingly controversial then, and forces have worked on eroding it ever since. The public comments from 1989 when the Winery Definition Ordinance (WDO) was being authored and its requisite EIR reviewed, are almost identical with current public comments on almost any winery or vineyard project coming before the Planning Department. EIR reports and their proposed mitigations are treated as only advisory. And while concerns remain the same, traffic, housing, water quality and quantity are dramatically worse—as predicted. In 1989 there were 145 wineries; today, there are more than 500. As reflected in the 1989 annual Grand Jury report, efforts to ameliorate the impact of the wine industry on the county have paradoxically only broadened its reach.[206]

Two of our land-use visionaries, Volker Eisele and Duane Cronk, held that stewardship of Napa County lands is better left to the voters than to the elected officials. At the time the WDO was being authored and its EIR reviewed, Volker and Duane, concerned for the fate of agricultural protections after the 1988 supervisory elections, authored and passed a citizens' initiative, Measure J, ensuring the Ag Preserve would last for another thirty years. "Measure J won in the polls despite all the opposition. What the supervisors who were against us misjudged was that the people of Napa County, when you measured their opinions, were two-thirds in favor of good land use. The voters wanted protection."[207] This protection was extended another fifty years (to 2058) through a second citizens initiative in 2008.

What we know now is that it is only when citizens stay on board and go to Planning Commission and Board of Supervisor meetings and vote and, when necessary, use the tool of the citizen initiative, that the common good, which includes the environment, is served. It's a lot of work, and it's easy to weary from it. In an interview shortly before his death, Volker Eisele, named "The Lion of Land Use," stated that one day he would not be going to Planning Commission meetings and making phone calls, that he would rather be going

It is only when citizens stay on board and go to Planning Commission and Board of Supervisor meetings and vote and, when necessary, use the tool of the citizen initiative, that the common good which includes the environment, is served.

to the opera. But to my knowledge, he continued his land-use work until his death in 2015. As he warned Mike, co-author of the watershed initiatives, the hillsides would be the next fight, again showing his prescience on land-use matters.

One of my favorite stories about Volker tells of his entry into politics when his own ranch was threatened by a proposed motorcycle park nearby. Not only did he organize neighbors and make public comment at the Planning Commission meetings, where the park lost five to one, and when it was appealed to the Board of Supervisors, lost four to one, he also insisted on code enforcement. The Saturday after the park was voted down by the Board of Supervisors, the motorcycles were back at the park. When the county insisted that there was no evidence of this, Volker's wife, Liesel, climbed a tree bearing a 4 × 8 foot sign for the park, ripped it down, and Volker drove the sign to the county administration building, placing it on County Counsel's desk. "Here's your evidence!" he said.

But he didn't leave it at this. When he lamented to county elections officer John Tuteur about the rulings of the dissenting supervisor, asking for a suggestion on how to get rid of this "terrible supervisor," Tuteur replied, "Find a candidate." No simple task, as we have learned, but finding a candidate and supporting that candidate, continue to be important must-do's of activism, even as ephemeral as a candidate's tenure can be. We need people more concerned with service to the community and less with power or staying in power, and we need to not give up on this.

He left a legacy. Sandy Elles, executive director of the Farm Bureau at the time, said, "He taught me more than anything else to enjoy what you do. If you live life to the fullest, you will succeed and you will leave a legacy."[208] This is critically important in these activism issues: to enjoy the ride, because it's going to be a long one!

Sadly, I personally encountered Volker Eisele only briefly. When I first learned that the Sinclairs were purchasing the land next door, I was put in contact with Volker, who, at the time, was a member of a very different Farm Bureau. In fact, he had served as Napa County Farm Bureau president some years before. In a phone call, I explained about the savanna, and he offered to help. In his German accent, he also energetically suggested that I serve on the board of the Farm Bureau. I was so overwhelmed about the extent of involvement this man might require that I did not pursue his help, something I regret. Later at a Farm Bureau picnic, I met him in person. He was a large presence, yes, truly a lion of a man, sturdy with receding white hair. He remembered our phone conversation. "Why didn't you call me again?" he roared. I wonder to this day if it would have gone differently if I had. But it would take a couple more years before I was ready to accept the rigors of land-use battles.

Winter solstice sunrise

CHAPTER 45

Silver Linings and Common Ground

I AM SITTING ALONE on a sofa in the living room of one of our neighbors, whom I will call John, facing a large picture window overlooking the valley. We are preparing for the next hearing of the Planning Commission for the permitting of the Sinclair project. More neighbors arrive, most of whom I didn't know until we formed Dry Creek Road Alliance (DCRA). Residents from the western side of the ridge on Redwood Road have joined us, people especially impacted by the pumping of the wells that the Sinclairs have drilled. Several of their wells have gone dry, and they have to truck in water, some to the tune of $2500 a month in summer. In fact, almost every neighbor around the Sinclairs' property has dry or underperforming wells. The drought has impacted us all, but so has the continued permitting of development in this area now deemed "an area of interest," meaning an area of low groundwater, by Luhdorff & Scalmanini, the hydrologists reporting to the Napa County's Groundwater Sustainability Agency.[209] In the case of the Sinclairs' proposal, for one of the first times, the county Planning Department hired an independent hydrology firm to evaluate their Water Availability Analysis (WAA), citing concerns for the impact of their extraction of groundwater on Redwood Creek and on neighboring wells. We neighbors did not need such a document to tell us about the lack of groundwater in our area.

Just after 4 p.m., Bernie calls us to order. She reads the most recent letter we received from the Sinclairs. The county has begun to recommend that winery applicants work with neighbors to resolve issues. Sally chose Bernie, one of our neighbors, to be the liaison for our group. Unlike the process with another neighbor who talked with us before he bought a small winery and then responded to feedback by downsizing his request for expansion, the Sinclairs have done little to minimize their impact on us. Even the carrot of a revised driveway easement did little to influence them. As our attorney prophetically announced, *when you have 100 million dollars, you think you can do anything.*

We discuss gallonage, the prospect of custom crush, increased truck traffic, the need for an excessive number of road exceptions for the driveway, the requested cave size, and visitation numbers. The county's suggestion that neighbors work it out has the dark edge of pitting us against each other when applicants have little intention of fitting into a neighborhood, only fulfilling their "dream." This is when we need a Planning Department, Planning Commission, and Board of Supervisors to consider the larger picture and the cumulative impact of what they are permitting.

John calls the extent of the Sinclairs winery proposal an "egregious taking" of agricultural land for commercial use. I agree. But he also posted a No on C sign in his vineyard, the one I had referenced in my statement to Jonah Raskin at the election results gathering for Measure C. I am still annoyed by this. Even in this meeting he comments about a Napa City Council member being "a flake" because he supported Measure C. I remind John that I also supported Measure C. This is no secret; I too had a huge 4 × 8 foot Measure C sign facing Dry Creek Road. He quips that I am a flake too, but immediately walks that back.

Yet a week after this DCRA meeting, when he, Bernie, and I escort two planning commissioners along our property lines shared with the Sinclairs, demonstrating the impacts of their project on each of our properties, John explains to the commissioners that planting and irrigating close to the ancient oaks of the savanna could kill the oaks and why. In gratitude, I listen. His words could have been those of any of us who supported Measure C.

As Mike said in the first Planning Commission hearing, John may be a strange bedfellow in some ways, but I find I've changed in my attitude. He is also a good farmer, and one with whom it is possible to find common ground. We differ, I'm sure, on the highest and best use of the land of the Ag Watershed. He would almost certainly say it's agriculture; I would say it's watershed. But I tell John that I hope we can keep discussing these land-use issues, conversations promising to be different from those I have with the choir.

CHAPTER 46

Second Planning Commission Hearing, Sinclair Winery

ONCE AGAIN I DROVE through the shockingly balmy, early February morning to the county administration building, remembering Volker Eisele's avowal that he would rather spend his time going to the opera than to Planning Commission meetings. I would rather have spent my time that morning walking Bramble Berry, our pup, along the trails of our ranch, checking if the milkmaids were blooming, if the pond had filled in the last rain. I wished Donald were with me, remembering the last time that he made public comment to the Napa City Council. He had carefully crafted the statement, had me check it. I had watched him walk to the lectern, stretch to his full 6 feet, 6 inches, and carefully read the words asking the council members to not approve yet another exception to commercial building height in a residential transition zone.

I parked the car in the county garage, hoping not to get a ticket in the three-hour zone, and walked to the county building, the familiar anxiety that had awakened me at 2 A.M. to revise my three-minute comment again swirling in my gut like an eggbeater.

In January 2020, we had received notice that the next hearing for Sinclairs Winery was scheduled for this day. County planners' recommendations were as expected: "Adopt the Mitigated Negative Declaration and approve the Exception to the Napa County Roads & Street Standards, the Variance, the Viewshed, the Use Permit modification, and the Agricultural Erosion Control Plan, as conditioned." As with many such projects before, this project was deemed to have no significant impact on the environment with these "mitigated negative declarations." But oddly, the staff report added the caveat that the extent of the project may not be appropriate for the site.

To date, the Sinclairs had held firm to their wish to increase their gallonage to 50,000 (50K) gallons from the previously permitted 30,000 (30K). They had scaled down their visitation request to a little over 13,000 per year with several large events of 100 and 200 persons, in spite of the fire expert's recommendation of no assembly with more than 50 persons, given the location and egress. Bernie's last negotiating contact with Sally had proven unfruitful as the DCRA had suggested the average visitation for a 30K winery, about half of what they were asking. My own letters to the county regarding the savanna remained unanswered until the county confirmed in the staff report sent out before this hearing that easements were a civil matter to be determined between parties, not the business of the county.

Again, we neighbors had divvied up our talking points. Steve would address the commercialization of our ag lands by this oversized project in a remotely accessed area; Betsy would

Bobcat hunting in the oak savanna

address the increased truck traffic that a custom crush facility would bring. Walt reevaluated the water analysis, suggesting that even at 30K it was not clear if there was enough water to irrigate more vineyard and also run the winery. Bernie would address the history of our negotiations with the Sinclairs. Some would address neighbors' dry and underperforming wells, visitation, and the cave size, which would be one of the largest in Napa County. I would ask that the erosion control plan be held until we understood why there was so much more runoff onto our land from the Sinclairs in two locations, and until it was clear there was enough water for both the winery and increased irrigation for more vineyard.[210]

Again, we worked to keep within our three-minute limit. Bernie would decide our speaking order. I contacted members of Napa Vision 2050 as well as other friends who have followed me on this journey, asking them to be present at the hearing. I took pictures of the ten-to-fifteen-foot-deep gullies, one of which had already been classified as a Class II stream, to show during my comments.

When I reached the third-floor chamber of the administration building, the room was filling. Almost everyone was against the project. I hugged friends as they arrived from Sonoma County and Berkeley, Marin, and, of course, Napa: Jimalee and Eric (from my writers' group) and Leah (from Berkeley and the Jung Institute), Kathleen (a graphic designer from Marin), Debbie and Charlotte, Gary and Kellie (from Napa Vision 2050), Bill (from Save Rural Napa). DCRA members sat together, exchanging notes. There was a rumor the Sinclairs had changed their ask on gallonage. My anxiety became excitement in the presence of these many supporters.

The chair of the Planning Commission asked Walt to lead the Pledge of Allegiance. We stood, supposedly united, with hands over our hearts. Then the planner and the attorney for the Sinclairs spoke. There were two surprises. The Sinclairs proposed a lot-line adjustment to avoid the need of a variance, and they dropped their request for increased gallonage, accepting the already entitled 30K gallons. Instead of continuing the hearing to another date so all parties could consider the impact of these changes, the protocol under such circumstances, the commissioners soldiered on, accepting public comment, then giving time to the Sinclairs' attorney to answer/discredit neighbors' concerns about water, fire safety, visitation, erosion, and the abnormally large cave proposal. Then, for the last hour or so of the five-hour hearing, the commissioners engaged in what they described as horse-trading: deciding among themselves the appropriate visitation for a 30K winery, about half of what the Sinclairs asked but the average for a 30K winery. Despite one commissioner's suggestion that, given location and accessibility, the visitation numbers be less than average for a 30K winery, and another's suggestion that the erosion control program not be permitted until after three years of the winery's operation to ensure enough water, the project was approved unanimously. Commissioners patted each other on the backs for involving the neighbors so successfully in the process of coming to terms with the conditions of the approval of such a complex and contentious project.

I sat in disbelief. As of yet, there was no agreed upon ingress. The almost half-mile flag-pole substandard driveway had barely been discussed at all. What about the proposed bridge to be built on Donald's and my property line after clearcutting sixty old-growth blue oak and bay on the steep erosion-prone hillside, or the alternate option of the commercializing of the residential easement over the neighbor's property without his consent? What about the cutting of 130 trees in order to develop such a project when deforestation is the one thing we are supposedly trying to stop for climate disruption? In effect, in the rush to move this project through, the commissioners had just approved a major modification and erosion control plan without an entry to the project, leaving it, again, to the neighbors to work out.

As I walked to my car, I tried to reconcile the results. Was this as good as it could get?

The gallonage was not increased, and the visitation limited. Is this all that we can expect from our local government? More vineyard was just approved in a precious oak savanna in an area with landslides and severe erosion. Yes, water would be monitored, and if there was not enough, the project would have to be scaled back, but the county has a bad track record for following up on making public the monitoring of problematic wells, if done at all, as one of our neighbors had delineated in her comments that morning. A quote went through my mind from one of the commissioners:

> I've heard several comments today about the "remote" winery issue. As a reminder, a remote winery has not been defined by policy that I am aware of.... We don't have a policy regarding remote wineries ... it is not my place to define a remote winery based on concerns or needs or whatever else is going on....[211]

Except, there is a policy from the 2010 revision of the Winery Definition Ordinance, section III, and it is not based on the "concerns and needs" of a few neighbors, but is an attempt to protect the environment and community from the rapacious reach of a wine industry out of control:

> To ensure that the intensity of winery activities is appropriately scaled, the County considers *the remoteness of* the *location* and the amount of wine to be produced at a facility when reviewing use permit proposals, and endeavors to ensure a direct relationship between access constraints and on-site marketing and visitation programs.[212]

Driving home after the five-hour hearing, I thought of Eve's statement that nothing gets done unless it is through a citizen initiative, not board directive. You can't count on elected and appointed officials. I thought of Volker Eisele's story of his own brand of code enforcement, placing "the evidence" of an eight-foot signboard on the County Counsel's desk. And I remembered David Brooks's statement that only a well-governed people have the luxury of not caring about politics, and even then, not caring is risky.[213]

I have empathy for Eisele, that he would rather go to the opera than fight another land-use battle. I remember the golden days when my walks through the ranch were unburdened by worry for the survival of the savanna and all that sustains it. But it's another time. Yet, I also know Volker Eisele never quit fighting.

CHAPTER 47

Intent to Appeal

The present is not a time for desperation but for hopeful activity.
THOMAS BERRY, *The Great Work: Our Way into the Future*[214]

The Board of Supervisor's office is quiet, the front desk vacant. It is 11:42 A.M. on the last day that an intent to appeal can be filed. A young woman comes forward from somewhere in the back. "Can I help you?"

"I want to file an intent to appeal," I say. She disappears into a warren of cubicles and reappears with a gently balding man who asks, "Can I help you?"

I repeat, "I want to file an intent to appeal."

He studies me. "For what?"

I scramble through the words swimming in my mind. This is the first time I have done this. Words float to the top. "A Planning Commission decision on a major modification." He disappears to get a stamp and receipt book.

When he returns, I ask to whom I am to write the $1000 check. "The County of Napa," he replies.

The young woman questions him on procedure. He shows her how he stamps the original paper I am filing, the one that Kathy, my dear Napa Vision 2050 colleague and attorney, filled out for me. He tells her how to complete the receipt. "Don't stamp the check," he instructs. "We will then walk this to County Counsel's office." I tell him my attorney needs a copy of the check. "Of course," he says. This must be standard procedure. He disappears to make a copy. The woman is meticulously following his guidance on filling out the receipt. We wait. He is gone a long time.

"Are you training for a new job?" I ask.

She smiles. "No, I just want to know what to do when the secretary is gone." We wait some more. She glances toward me, asks a little shyly, "Is this next to your home?"

"Yes," I reply. Sadness swells, threatens to breach the banks. "It makes the difference of whether we can continue to live there."

"How long have you lived there?" she asks.

"Twenty-five years."

Her head juts slightly backward in consolation. She doesn't make eye contact, says nothing more.

The man returns, hands me a stack of papers stapled together for my attorney. Almost apologetically, he warns, "If your check bounces, the appeal is off."

"It won't bounce," I say.

Valley oak and usnea, which only grows in clear air

"Your attorney has until 5 P.M. on March 5 to get your appeal in," he continues. "If it is not in here by 5 P.M., the appeal is off."

"Okay." I thank him and turn to leave. I let out a deep breath as I walk to the elevator and push the button for the lobby.

I have ten working days to file the actual appeal that will delineate the issues. Those issues include the lack of safe access to the site and the fire danger of approving an event center in a medium to high danger area; the cutting of trees, mostly oaks, without mitigation, when we need to stop deforestation; whether there is enough water for both the winery, which they have never operated onsite, as well as for irrigation for more vineyard. The list goes on. Kathy will use her legal language to make our case. Anything not listed in the appeal cannot be brought up in the hearing. We will collect and list witnesses, some experts, some neighbors. I have to notify all neighbors within 1000 feet of the project by getting the list from the title company, another $500. Then there are various assorted charges for labor by the county, mailing costs of the notices. There will be a pre-appeal hearing. Then the date for the hearing with the Board of Supervisors will be set.

I know I am not the first to file an appeal, and I will not be the last, but this day I cross a threshold into a new world. I have to go to the mat: for the ancient oak savanna that has

Valley oak branches and grass

molded me like clay these many years, for the oak woodlands around it, for these tender hillsides with their rich diversities. I have to fight for the at-risk salmonoid populations still in Redwood Creek, threatened by the pumping of wells on the ridge, for the coyotes and mountain lions who inhabit the nights and for the usnea hanging from the oaks like Spanish moss on our still-pristine mountainside. These living beings can't fight for themselves, and if we don't start fighting for them, for the right to life for all, human and non-human, none of us will be able to continue to live on our dear Earth. It is simply that dire.

Treat the climate as the emergency it is.

For many of us attending the downtown Napa Climate Strike on Friday, Sept. 20, the event was energizing if also poignant. Such enthusiasm.

I could hear cheering and chanting from several blocks away as I parked and walked down Main Street to Veterans Park, the beginning of the march: "We're students, united, we'll never be divided! We're students, united, we'll never be divided!"

As new groups of students arrived carrying signs and chanting, they were greeted with raucous cheers and clapping. So much excitement. So much optimism. That's where the poignancy comes in.

We older folks stood in the back, in the shade. A *Napa Valley Register* reporter approached me: "Why are you here?" I gestured toward the whooping, even joyous, crowd of kids, ages from kindergarten through high school, and said, "They need us. They need our support because they are facing a huge burden: climate change. And the actions of many of our governing officials do not reflect this."

Yes, we are in a climate emergency.

As I was telling my son Casey and daughter-in-law Melissa about the march that evening, Casey showed me the most recent *National Geographic* magazine, subject: Extinction.

On the front cover was a man kneeling over the last white rhino on the planet, dead. Opening the magazine, I came upon a picture of a giraffe, the largest living ruminant on the earth, lying on its side, shot. What would ever motivate someone to kill such a beautiful animal?

"This issue is too sad to show Wesley and Sabien," Casey said, and then added, "Yet I have so much respect for *National Geographic* reporting as they are."

When is a child able to take in the severity of our situation? At what age can they handle knowing the facts? At what age will we adults take in the facts that foreshadow doom for human life on earth—and act? We have yet to have a county Climate Action Plan, although it's been in the works for 10-plus years. Our Board of Supervisors allowed prevailing industries to modify it.

Actions to protect our water and our environment have been neutralized by these same industries. Witness Measure C, which was heavily opposed by the wine industry.

As I watched classroom after classroom arrive for the downtown climate rally, chills ran up and down my arms as I listened to the shrieking and cheering of children welcoming each group: the little ones, the teenagers. My heart hurt to listen to their "yes we can" attitude. Yes, they are optimistic. Yes, that is good, because it will carry them a distance. But the truth is, I have some idea of what a distance there is to go if we make it at all.

But we need to have their backs. Why are we letting them carry an adult load? We all have to act as if this is a climate emergency—because it is.

PATRICIA DAMERY
NAPA

CHAPTER 48

The Numinous Light of Being

WHEN DID WE STOP venerating the oaks and oak woodlands? I ask that each time I enter the savanna. It's been said that early loggers, when first entering the virgin redwood forests, experienced awe, as if they were in a holy temple. That is how I feel in the savanna, that it is a holy place. To be in the presence of these majestic giants is to be before the goddess herself. For millennia people knew this. Trees were portals to other dimensions, old guardians of the Earth. My ancestors the Celts and the Druids held their rituals in sacred groves. Trees, with their lofty boughs and deep roots, connect heaven and Earth. The shaman travels the world tree, up and down its trunk, to restore the patient to wholeness.

In those gentle breezes, we floated in timelessness where trees and animals, including humans, communicate and work together in harmony.

The Dodona Oak in northwestern Greece, considered by many to be the oldest oak in Europe, served as an oracle millennia before Zeus claimed it as his own. Ancient people consulted the oak, listening to its leaves whisper in the breezes and winds, foretelling who would be king; will I conceive? Doves, nesting in the branches, cooed, their voices speaking the wisdom of She who transcends time.[215] It is that portal of perception that Charlie Toledo and I entered within the circle of valley oaks on the evening of the September blue moon so many years ago now. As we lay on our backs under the oaks where Jesse and Lisa married, Charlie drew my attention to the rustling leaves as we leisurely conversed. "See?" she said. "They agree!" In those gentle breezes, we floated in timelessness where trees and animals, including humans, communicate and work together in harmony. In these oaks I hear the messages from not only ring-necked doves but also acorn woodpeckers who colonize oak woodlands, chattering and bickering with each other as they flicker about in the boughs. It was the woodpeckers who informed me—It is now! Your father is passing now!—that day I hung laundry as my father died 2000 miles away.

They say Zeus claimed the oak at Dodona sometime before the Common Era. Thunderstorms frequented the area perhaps more than any other place in Europe.

Reliefs depict Zeus throwing his thunderbolt followed by life-giving rain and fertility.[216] It appears that the ancients understood the synergy of rain and forests in a way scientists are only now rediscovering. Through transpiration, our forests are responsible for "rivers in the sky" that then fall as rain.[217] As my sister Judy said, 50 percent of rain comes through a tree. Cut plants like trees, you cut rainfall.[218]

In 2021, we in the West are again experiencing drought, the worst ever. After two years of low rainfall, our vegetation is dangerously low in moisture, our forests neglected from years of fire suppression. We fear we are in the beginning of a megadrought. And I wonder, is our lack of reverence of the spirits that animate the natural world to blame? There is no greater way to anger the gods! In Napa County and the larger West, Zeus's thunderbolts start fires, but no rain follows. Oh, where is that Taoist rainmaker from China, the one who was called in during another time of severe drought? After three days in a hut, he emerged, and it snowed. When asked what he did, he claimed that he came from another land where things are in order. Here, he said, they are not in order and he also was not in the natural order of things because he was in a disturbed country. He had to wait until he was in order and then naturally the rain came.[219] Perhaps now he would suggest we stop cutting trees.

We too are not "in order." As Jung wrote more than a half century ago,

Thunder is no longer the voice of an angry god, nor is lightening his avenging missile. . . . No river contains a spirit, no tree is the life principle of a man. . . . No voices now speak to man from stones, plants and animals, nor does he speak to them thinking they can hear. His contact with nature has gone, and with it has gone the profound emotional energy that this symbolic connection supplied.[220]

"It appears, through all our progress and accomplishments," Jean Houston wrote, "western culture seems to favor the diminishing of being. More and more we are less and less consciously present in the present."[221]

And yet that symbolic connection served by the gentle art of respectful listening to the needs of oaks and rivers, of coyotes and wood rats, is there to be relearned. It does mean giving up the illusion created by Judeo-Christian traditions of viewing ourselves as "conquerors of nature"—unless, of course, the nature we are addressing is that of our own. And even then, may we learn to be more accepting and open to those aspects of ourselves we would rather project onto others and deny.

CHAPTER 49

Peace in Lavender

When despair for the world grows in me ... I go and lie down
-where the wood drake rests in his beauty on the water....
WENDELL BERRY, "The Peace of Wild Things"[222]

WHEN DESPAIR FOR THE world grows in *me,* lavender grounds me. One July day in 2017, Donald and I distilled lavender together, Donald insisting that he do it just once more. I worked with him, not trusting he could safely light the propane turkey-cooker or keep track of how long to keep the flame going. When we first started distilling many years ago, we had a trailer that Donald occupied thirteen hours a day for the three-week period we were distilling. I loved taking him food in the evening as he finished one last distillation. He was always a little in the ethers when I got there, having read German philosopher Immanuel Kant for most of the day. As I unpacked wine glasses and the supper, he woke as if from a dream. He would tell me that he is able to communicate spiritually with Kant because he recognizes in Kant the projection of being an excessively rational individual, yet, also realizing, this not to be so.

"Jung and Kant are not in significant disagreement," he would say. "Both are telling me there is present a *feeling function* in the natural state of our philosophical and psychological being. Kant allows me to know that although my *thinking* is most apparent, to the dismay of some of my children and stepchildren, that my *feeling* function is present, but not, so to speak, 'up front.'"

He would look at me in his sweet early morning way, the time he says he is the most clear-headed these days. "You and I are not *thinking/feeling* opposites, but are, as Kant and Jung have it, geometrically adjacent: a *sensation* type [himself] and *intuitive* [me], with significant overlap. Both Jung and Kant allow me to rationalize this closeness we have, but to also understand that sometimes either one of us may not have it exactly correct, and disagree, but for only slightly different philosophical or psychological reasons. As Kant put it, we should not dismiss any one as being completely wrong because, in doing so, we may throw out that portion which we love most."[223] In the end, is relationship that subterranean stream of love that unites us, the elixir that might fortify us for the turning to the devastation around us, the devastation we have caused?

Donald is still a philosopher as much as he was an architect and is still an artist. It was all there in the beginning, that brushstroke of a man and of a relationship that would fill in the detail and color, a marriage we continue to grow into. That early exhilarating Eden experience expanded me and us, enchanting us to continue. A taste of Eden can go a very long way.

What is Eden, anyway? You may think Eden to exist in only myth, but after living on our ranch, I know myth in another way and Eden to be a place in time *and* eternity. The graceful boughs of the valley oaks, the delicate slender stands of wild blue rye, the first green golden glow of blades of grasses and budding grapevines, all ripped the veil from my eyes. Apprehended, Eden is frightening. You think you must be dead to be seeing the life force in this way. Everything is of one piece.

Death is part of the equation, for Eden is a forbidden fruit experience. Certainly, the grape was the fruit of my eviction! When the serpent Lilith tempted Eve to eat of the fruit of the Tree of Knowledge even though God forbid it, Eve and then Adam were condemned to the distillation of being mortal. As James Lovelock wrote,

> I see through Gaia a very different reflection. We are bound to be eaten, for it is Gaia's custom to eat her children. Decay and death are certain, but they seem a small price to pay for life and for the possession of identity as an individual. It is all too easily forgotten that the price of identity is mortality.[224]

When I remember the brilliance of that early spring photo, Donald in white pants against spring grass, I feel the bittersweetness that has only ripened over a quarter of a century. Now Donald is too frail to walk the road. He is present, even though his memory and judgement no longer orient him. (He tells me this is not as bad as it sounds.) Elsie and Cincinnati are long gone, and Leo too. The road leads to the house we built together and is lined with slabs of the ancient valley oak that graciously missed the old house when it fell. Fallen trees populate the forest, weakened during the last five years of drought. I ask questions I did not consider before: will the species of valley oaks and madrones survive in our Napa County until 2050?

Was the presentation of the grape—or perhaps the fruit of the underworld, the pomegranate—an invitation to act as gods with the unintended consequence of a curse of such impudence? On every level, we are experiencing the impact of our human behavior on our planet. We have acted as if we owned the place, but like the sorcerer's apprentice, we have created havoc. Any feeling we have had of living in Eden is paradoxically delusional and absolutely true.

Perhaps it is always this way, whether it is in raising children, meeting our mate, or discovering the land that feels like a lost piece of one's soul. We *fall in love*. In this state, we feel wholeness. We pierce through the temporal qualities to what endures, the divinity of the other and of ourselves. In those early meetings, our souls merge. Is there such a thing

Lavender and valley oak at sunrise

as soul intercourse? When souls swell in recognition and hope, strengthened by the experience of wholeness?

In time, we get down to the particulars, the bones, of the matter: we see the flaws in ourselves and the other, part of this experience of differentiated wholeness—what Jung called *individuation*. In the case of our ranch, after seventy years of fire suppression, our forest is not in healthy balance. Downed wood and brambles tangle its stream banks, drought-weakened oaks succumb to oak bore, hillsides damaged by cattle hemorrhage silt into streams during winter rains. The sheltering canopy of madrone, oak, and overabundance of bay in the ravine through which the driveway snakes suffers from neglect. No one has thinned the bay and tended the brush since Vallejo's vaqueros killed off or enslaved the Indians. Our task is to address this, that the forest may be resilient as temperatures warm and wildfire returns.

The trick, I suppose, is to remember the larger vision while also recognizing the mortal on-the-ground qualities of the beloved—the perspective of Pelican and the nose-to-the-ground of Dog. For me, that possibility dawned the day Nature's first green glowed golden against the white of Donald's pants and of Elsie and Cincinnati's dark contrast. Did the shadow of sadness passing like a dark wing across the sun herald a growing consciousness? Although Eden apprehended is eternal, the price of that apprehension is to suffer the pains of incarnation. "They wished to flower, and flowering is being beautiful: but we wish to ripen, and that means being dark and taking pains."[225]

Deer watching the killing of young oaks in the savanna (Photograph: Melissa MLaughlin)

Qualified Successes

Across the world, the environment is in peril. Forests are being
stripped, stressed and burned. Natural habits are vanishing. Deserts are advancing....
The atmosphere and ozone shield are under assault....
All these alarms, and more, have been widely sounded. There is no
reason to belabor them. What we need now is answers.
CHRISTOPHER D. STONE, *Should Trees Have Standing*[226]

THE DANCE OF CREATION persists; the choreography is predictable: Barong has some wins; Rangda erodes them. But through the tensions of the encounters, a tender shoot of consciousness is growing, one we must protect. As I finish writing this book, I report some of the most recent successes, small or large, which happen more often. I might also add that the Coronavirus pandemic—and climate change—have impacted the wine and hospitality industries far more profoundly than any of our political actions, humbling us all. In the end, Nature will have the last say.

SINCLAIR WINERY

The appeal date for the Sinclair Winery was delayed and continued twice until almost a year after the Planning Commission's approval, in part, due to the Coronavirus pandemic. The Board of Supervisors denied the appeals, made by several appellants, disqualifying much of the presented material as "new" and unable to be considered. Material disqualified included evidence of enormous, erroneous cave-tailing calculations, revised recommendations for protection of the root systems of the valley oaks based on a soil filtration study in the savanna by a retired California Fish and Wildlife employee, a map showing the condition of neighboring wells, and the field report from the National Resources Conservations Service and California Fish and Wildlife estimating erosion damage to our land caused by the driveway construction by William, the previous owner of Sinclairs' land, to potentially require $100,000 of stabilization in the area of the proposed bridge. Work on the bridge and driveway extension could undo this.

The next steps will be defined as we proceed. We can't trust our local government. We appeal to relevant state agencies to intervene, agencies less controlled by the wine industry, and resolve to waste less time on the Board of Supervisors and Planning Commission and spend more on the citizen initiative and the courts. The stranglehold of the wine and tourism industries is just too strong. Again, citizens have sued Napa County, this time for granting some of the exceptions as well as on water issues. The situation is likely to stay in the courts for a while, at great expense to all.

WALT RANCH

After the December 16, 2016, Board of Supervisor's denial of the appeal of the Planning Commission approval of Walt Ranch (see Chapter 32, "Hall No!"), the appellants (Napa Sierra Club, Center for Biological Diversity, Living Rivers Council, Circle Oaks County Water District, and Circle Oaks Home Association) sued the county. When Napa County Superior Court upheld the approval, these groups then appealed the decision to the 1st District Court of Appeals. In September 2019, citizens experienced a qualified victory when the court remanded the case back to the Napa County Superior Court on greenhouse gas matters. You cannot mitigate for 14,000 trees by saying you are not going to cut 14,000 trees elsewhere on undevelopable or already protected land. This was a big win for those of us working to stop deforestation. Disappointingly, though, the Court of Appeals sided with the lower court on several issues, including that the county-approved environmental impact report adequately addressed groundwater and protected rare species.[227]

MOUNTAIN PEAK WINERY

After the October 2017 Atlas Peak Fire burned 82 percent of the structures on Soda Canyon Road, killing six residents, after helicopters evacuated people trapped by the flames from a landing site near the remote Mountain Peak Winery, the Soda Canyon Group challenged the decision of Mountain Peak's permit, saying that the permit should be reconsidered in the face of the harrowing experiences of fire evacuations of residents on the road. A tug of war between the Board of Supervisors, who did not want to reconsider the project, and the Napa County Superior Court judge ensued. In the end, the judge remanded the case back to the county, stating that "truly new evidence of emergent facts" must be considered. The fire experiences must now be taken into account in a new court hearing.[228] The Board of Supervisors again upheld the permit. Citizens again appealed the decision to the Napa County Superior Court on January 19, 2022. The tentative decision may require an environmental impact report concerning traffic, safety, and surface and ground water.

THE OAK SAVANNA

At the time of this writing, the oak savanna remains mostly intact, but until the valley oaks and coastal life oaks, until the meadow and forest conditions that support them have legal standing, these battles will continue. There is a time for the arm of the law, and that time is now, when we are transitioning between world views, one in which humans have dominion over Nature, and one in which humans are only one member of a community that includes Nature.

The stretches of the savanna continue to grow my soul and to define my path. I must use my voice to protect this land that I hold dear, land that has no voice in this current consciousness. But the shift is in process, the shift to the Rights of Nature.

LETTERS TO THE EDITOR

I CONTINUE WRITING LETTERS to the Editor, the *Napa Valley Register*'s limit being one per month. Here are two of the most recent ones, spurred by the drought, over development, and our drying well. Letters to the Editor continue to help me process my own feelings and thoughts. My focus continues to be on *showing up* and *telling the truth*. I like to think this may also serve a citizenry of informed voters.

LETTER TO THE EDITOR
Napa Valley Register, June 3, 2021

No more development in water-stressed areas

An open letter to the Groundwater Sustainability Agency and Napa County Groundwater Sustainability Plan Advisory Committee (GSPAC): I am writing to update GSPAC on the water security situation on Dry Creek Road.

We are alarmed by the decrease in groundwater levels. This is becoming an emergency situation. My husband and I have lived on lower Dry Creek Road for 39 years. Last year our largest irrigation pond (2½ acre-feet) did not fill at all for the first time. This year it did not fill again.

And this last week, our 350-foot deep well on Dry Creek Road had no water to pump for several days. For the first time we have lived here, we had to truck water. Ten days later, we ordered another truckload. Almost every neighbor around us has to truck water. Bingham Potable Water said they have been swamped the last two months and expect this to be a long summer of hauling.

The drought stressed our old vines, and we had to pull them several years ago. Now, without reservoir water, we cannot replant. We have never used groundwater to irrigate vines, but many around us do, which appears to be part of the problem. Isn't it time we restrict irrigation with groundwater?

Until the mid-'70s, 85% of vines were dry farmed. The North Bay is now designated to be in extreme severe drought, yet the county continues to permit more development, including in our neighborhood. What is your plan as our wells run dry, as the state decreases water allocations from the North Bay Aqueduct, as the county reservoirs' water levels drop, and Napa City needs to also draw on groundwater reserves?

Will the city continue to sell water to trucking companies that fill our tanks?

Isn't it time we have a county-wide plan? Do you have a plan? Isn't it time to limit new well permits and development in these water-deficient areas, to restrict the use of groundwater for irrigation?

PATRICIA DAMERY
NAPA

The water wars have begun

Those of us who attended the city of Napa's Zoom meeting outlining the proposed changes to the hydrant meter usage starting Aug. 1, 2021 (to be voted on at the Napa City Council on July 20) witnessed the beginning of what promises to become a contentious and challenging transition into water rationing.

We agree with the city's clear-eyed attention to the water emergency in our county, planning to meet the needs of city residents. However, we are alarmed at the county's apparent blind eye to the needs of residents outside of the city.

Since 2009, the trucking of water to rural customers from the city of Napa hydrants has increased. Rural wells have become underperforming or dry due to increased development, the drilling of more wells, and climate changes and drought. This year trucking reached an all-time high. Between January and June, the amount of water trucked has doubled from the same period last year, going from 24 acre-feet (AF) in 2020 to 47 AF in 2021.

Napa city gets 59% of its water from the North Bay Aqueduct, reserving Lake Hennessy reservoir for use should the city need this water in coming years. Currently, the lake is at 63% capacity. Last season's low rainfall added only 1,000 AF to the reservoir. The city of Napa has asked city residents to reduce water by 15% voluntarily, but usage has increased. To make up for this, residents must reduce water usage by 20% from August through October or until the rains begin. Irrigation of landscaping will be further restricted. A goal is to keep Lake Hennessy at 54% of capacity by November 2021 as insurance against another dry winter.

But what does the county plan for our water emergency? What about those whose wells have been heavily impacted by the county's addiction to development and the permitting of more and more wells, resulting in the need for trucked water? As of Aug. 1, rural residents will be limited to 4,000 gallons of trucked water a month for indoor purposes only. Outdoor irrigation with trucked water is prohibited. For a family of four, the 4,000 gallon limit per month means 33 gallons a day each. The average person uses 80–100 gallons a day. There is no leeway for farm animals.

When confronted with this situation, Napa County Director of Planning, Building, and Environment David Morrison stated that those living in rural areas must accept that we don't have the amenities of those living within the city limits—like sidewalks—implying access to drinking water is an amenity.

Director Morrison, access to water is not an amenity. It is a right. And the county is culpable. In too many cases, our wells have been dried by the county's refusing to consider the cumulative impact of development and well drilling in areas where neighbors report water problems. These reports are effectively ignored and dismissed as anecdotal. Groundwater is a complex issue, Director Morrison asserts. The lack of it, though, is not complex. Maybe it's time for a moratorium on development until the complexities of groundwater are figured out.

Rural residents are not the only ones who are impacted. Trucked water may not be used for commercial purposes or for construction on property outside Napa city limits. There will be a cap on the amount of water a trucking company can haul. Those vineyards and wineries receiving "interruptible Ag water" will be required to cut back by 20% of 2020 usage. And while all of this is going on, the Groundwater Sustainability Agency Advisory Committee is trying to prove that there is no overdraft of the Napa County subbasin.

Please, isn't it time we look at the larger picture? In the June 9 meeting, Director Morrison stated there are 70-some water providers within Napa County. Napa city and American Canyon both purchase water from the North Bay Aqueduct, which the state has cut back to 5% of the usual allotment. Will there come a time when Napa city also needs to draw on groundwater? Isn't it time we have an agency that coordinates all the water in Napa County? All of us will be making sacrifices and learning to live within our water budget, but let's get our planners and builders on board as well. Otherwise, we will not all have adequate access to drinking water.

PATRICIA DAMERY

NAPA,

DEMOCRACY

Until we understand in our deepest core the dynamics of the functioning of money in our county, in our state, in our nation, and in our world, we are doomed to these struggles that I have described, struggles that grossly favor the wealthy at the expense of the middle class and the poor. Campaign reform is necessary.

In October 2019 Gavin Newsom, governor of California, signed into law (effective January 1, 2021) a modicum of campaign reform applying state campaign donation limits to city and county governments that do not yet have such limits. Will this help, or will dark money find its way around these limits?

Our democracy is at stake, and it's on all of us to act: candidates, the elected and appointed, voters and residents. Groups like Napa Vision 2050 have the responsibility to bring the facts before the people, and citizens are responsible for learning about the issues—and for voting. At times we will be called to the streets and to the courts. There is just too much at stake. Courage is required from all of us: those running for office with allegiance to the issues and not the donors, those willing to fight for what is right, and those charged to serve the common good. This is a crisis of consciousness, after all. There has never been a time of such "auspicious . . . conditions favorable to progress along the path of higher being."[229] This is it; we are in that time.

And a New Babe

On January 24, 2020, Jesse calls shortly after 7 A.M. Lisa is in labor, her contractions three to five minutes apart, and they are heading to the hospital. I find myself shockingly emotional. When we receive an update that she is eight centimeters dilated, we head to the hospital, fifty minutes away. Casey and Melissa, Wesley and Sabien, and I, all arrive at the same time. I text Jesse from the hospital lobby. He texts back, "It's a girl!" Their long-awaited babe is here, my first granddaughter. We wait three hours to meet her, eating a celebratory lunch, wandering through shops, biding our time. When the nurses allow us in, she lies swaddled in Jesse's arms beside a tired but exuberant Lisa. It will be two days before they decide on the name of this feminine bundle just descended through gossamer ethers to this earthly plane. When they speak her name, it is like finding the missing piece that absolutely fits. Her name is Grace.

I have a new photo I love. In the photo, Donald cautiously holds newborn Grace to his heart, his large lined face smiling sweetly as he peers at her smooth sleeping one. It's all there: that which has lived out a life and that which is just arriving and is yet to be revealed.

(Photograph: Bill Hocker)

ADDENDUM

ON THE MORNING OF Saturday, December 11, 2021, Donald passed from this world, surrounded by his family. As he took his last breaths, "Jesu, Joy of Man's Desiring" came over the airwaves, the single piece of music that Donald had been practicing on his saxophone over the past two years.

"....a journey that gathers light from a descent into darkness, a pilgrimage of knowledge that penetrating deeper seemingly turns away the light, which yet reappears—and yet vanishes...."
Dante Alighieri, *The Inferno of Dante*

Acknowledgments

A BOOK IS ALWAYS a chorus of voices who bring it into being. I thank those many voices.

First, I thank my husband, Donald, and our ranch for the halcyon days that opened and then matured me. I thank my family for their support during difficult times: Jesse Pizzitola and Lisa Murgatroyd, Casey Pizzitola and Melissa McLaughlin, Wesley and Sabien McPizz, Norma Carr, and Norma Churchill. I would never have continued in my writing had it not been for my writing group of these thirty-six years: Jan Beaulyn, Norma Churchill, Jimalee Gordon, and Elizabeth Herron. Former writing group member Dianne Romain hosted me in her home in Guanajuato, Mexico, during the week that I began writing the book. We shared adventures that brought great laughter and joy. Thank you! Leah Shelleda, Leonore Wilson, Casey Pizzitola, Jimalee Gordon, and Debby Fortune have all read early versions of the book and offered wise and important counsel in its formation.

The incredible people who have moved in and out of Napa Vision 2050 over the years have mentored and accompanied me onto the path of activism in Napa County. We have had fun while learning the ropes of local government. I especially thank Dan Mufson, Kathy Felch, Debby Fortune, Eve Kahn, Jim Wilson, Gary Margadant, Ginna Beharry, Charlotte Williams, Laura Tinthoff, Beth Nelson, Cindy Grupp, George Caloyannidis, Mike Hackett, Bill Hocker, and Kellie Anderson. I apologize for not including all of your names. Bill Hocker and Lowell Downey, photographers and stewards of the movement, generously shared their photographs. I thank our neighbors in Dry Creek Road Alliance who have reminded me of how important neighbors are.

My gratitude to Dyane Sherwood for her openness and caring in publishing this account of my activism and for her keen eye for threads of themes I often miss in the unconscious passion that can drive me. My gratitude too for LeeAnn Pickrell's careful editing through this book's several iterations.

Last, but not least, I thank Oak. Throughout my life Oak has come, a teacher, a healer, a Zen master. May I return the favor.

APPENDIX:

PERTINENT NAPA COUNTY LAND USE ORDINANCES AND BALLOT MEASURES

Following are the ordinances, voter initiatives, and ballot measures discussed in this book. Ordinances are approved and can be changed by the Board of Supervisors. California citizens have the right of the initiative, which must receive a percentage of voter signatures to be approved for the ballot. Land Use Ballot Measures are voted in by a simple majority of voters and can only be changed at the ballot box.

1968 NAPA COUNTY AGRICULTURAL PRESERVE

The County Board of Supervisors created the Napa County Agricultural Preserve, the first in the nation. Its stated purpose was to protect "the fertile valley and foothill areas of Napa County in which agriculture is and should continue to be the predominant land use, where uses incompatible to agriculture should be precluded and where the development of urban type uses would be detrimental in the continuance of agriculture and the maintenance of open space which are economic and aesthetic attributes and assets of the County of Napa." This action, highly controversial at the time, was fueled by concerns about urban sprawl, which was occurring in other areas of California. Restrictions included a twenty-acre minimum parcel size in the Agricultural Preserve (*https://sodacanyonroad.org/docs/Ag_Preserve_Ordinance_1968.pdf*).

1973–1976

Extension of agricultural protections to the watersheds through the Agricultural Watershed and Open Space district classification (AWOS). The AWOS district classification is intended to be applied in those areas of the county where the predominant use is agriculturally oriented; where watershed areas, reservoirs, and floodplain tributaries are located; where development would adversely impact all such uses; and where the protection of agriculture, watersheds, and floodplain tributaries from fire, pollution, and erosion is essential to the general health, safety, and welfare (*https://www.countyofnapa.org/DocumentCenter/View/3391/Ordnance-511-Agricultural-Preserve-July-27-1976-PDF*).

1990 MEASURE J, AGRICULTURAL LAND AND PRESERVATION INITIATIVE

Extends protections of Ag Preserve for thirty years, or until December 31, 2020, stripping the Board of Supervisors of its ability to change the Ag Preserve during this period. Measure J limits the intensification and commercialization of the areas zoned Ag Resource (now AP) or Ag Watershed and Open Space (AWOS) in the General Plan. Any change of intensification of use must be approved by two-thirds of the voters. It also imposed a minimum parcel size of 40 acres in the AP and 160 acres in the AWOS. Measure J was upheld at three court levels in California: Trial, Appellate, and Supreme Court (*https://www.napagrowers.org/uploads/1/3/6/4/136481570/measure_j_text.pdf*).

1990 Winery Definition Ordinance (WDO)

The WDO placed limits on new wineries and uses including limits on tours and tastings. This ordinance defined a winery as an "agricultural processing facility" for "the fermenting and processing of grape juice into wine." Seventy-five percent of grapes must come from Napa County. The ordinance also allowed for wineries to sell and market wine, but such marketing activity must be "accessory" and subordinate to production (*https://napavision2050.org/wp-content/uploads/2019/07/Winery-Definition-Ordinance.pdf*).

1991 Conservation Regulations Adopted

The regulations require an Agricultural Erosion Control Plan for agricultural/vineyard or development plans on slopes over 5 percent. The review includes conforming with the conservation regulations and with CEQA (*https://library.municode.com/ca/napa_county/codes/code_of_ordinances?nodeId=TIT18ZO_CH18.108CORE_18.108.020GEPR*).

2008 Measure P

Extends protection of Measure J for fifty years, or until 2058. One of the key phrases in Measure P is "to protect the County's agricultural, watershed, and open space lands, to strengthen the local agricultural community and preserve the County's rural way of life." By expanding what is allowed (whether by right or by permit), the rural way of life is/can be destroyed. The number of unintended consequences is significant (*https://ballotpedia.org/Napa_County_%22Save_Measure_J_Initiative%22,_Measure_P_(November_2008)*).

2008 Updated General Plan

In 2008, the Napa County General Plan (GP) was updated for the first time since 1984. The Steering Committee for the 2008 update was comprised mostly of industry representatives and winery owners eager to expand their business options. The updated GP, approved by the Board of Supervisors on June 3, 2008, expanded the definition of agriculture to include not only the raising of crops, trees, and livestock, but also the production and processing of agricultural products and related marketing, sales, and other accessory uses. Agriculture also includes farm management and farmworker housing. This change was to reflect the 1990 WDO (*https://www.countyofnapa.org/1760/General-Plan*).

2010 Winery Definition Ordinance Revision

After the 2008 economic downturn, the wine industry pressured the Board of Supervisors to include direct marketing as an accessory use of agriculture. The board approved this in 2010. This means that visitation, wine and food pairings, and related events, are consistent with "accessory use of a winery" (*https://www.napagrowers.org/uploads/1/3/6/4/136481570/winery_definition_ordinance.pdf*).

2016 Water, Forest and Oak Woodland Protection Initiative

This initiative gathered 6300 signatures to be put on the November 2016 ballot but was disqualified by the county due to a technicality (*https://sodacanyonroad .org/forum.php?t=1227*).[230]

2017 Revision of the Napa County Code Definition of Agriculture

By state law, the General Plan and County Code (ordinances) must conform. In 2017, the Board of Supervisors revised the county code definition of agriculture to conform with the 2008 changes to the definition of agriculture in the General Plan. Now the definition of agriculture includes, with the grant of a use permit: "1. Production and processing of agricultural products, including agricultural processing facilities; and 2. Marketing, sales, and other accessory uses that are related, incidental and subordinate to the main agricultural processing use." This change was highly controversial.[231]

2018 Measure C, Napa County Oak Woodland Watershed Protection Initiative of 2018

This initiative was originally authored by the Napa Valley Vintners and two members of the original 2017 initiative, Mike Hackett and Jim Wilson. The measure would have amended the Napa County General Plan and zoning code creating water quality buffer zones within the Agricultural Watershed (AW) zoning district and restricting tree removal within those zones; strengthened oak removal remediation standards and established a permit program for oak tree removal once 795 acres of oak woodland were removed. It was approved at every step of the way by the Napa Valley Vintners Board until the last minute, when the Vintners Board chose to stop supporting it. Hackett and Wilson chose to continue on with the initiative, which became Measure C. Heavily opposed by the Farm Bureau, Winegrowers, Napa Valley Grapegrowers, and then the Vintners, the measure narrowly lost in the June 2018 election, 50.9 percent to 49.1 percent (*https://www.countyofnapa .org/DocumentCenter/View/8123/Full-Text-of-Measure-C-PDF*).[232]

2018 Measure D

Measure D strictly prohibits landings for private helicopters on private property. Helicopter landings by public service providers are already protected in existing County Code and are therefore exempt. Measure D won by a large margin, 61 percent to 39 percent, and was then contested by two vintners but settled with clarifications, including definition of "unavoidable landings," in March 2020 (*https:// napavision2050.wpengine.com/wp-content/uploads/2018/03/INITIATIVE-TEXT-1.pdf* and *https:// www.countyofnapa.org/DocumentCenter/View/14392/Napa-County_FAQs-Regarding-Measure-D*).

2019 Water Quality and Tree Protection Ordinance

After the loss of Measure C, the Board of Supervisors did a series of community meetings and authored an ordinance that was supposed to protect the watersheds and trees. Influenced again by the wine industry, the ordinance reduces total developable area in Napa County Ag Watersheds by only 3 percent, leaving grasslands and chaparral, important to the health of our ecosystems, unprotected as well as 28,700 acres of forest. In all forest and grasslands, 70,000 acres remain at-risk (*https://sodacanyonroad.org/docs/W&TP_Ordinance_4-9-19 .pdf*).[233] Schools for Climate Action students have begun petitioning city councils and the county government to place a moratorium on tree cutting until this ordinance is updated. To date, the City of Calistoga unanimously voted to support this action.

NOTES

1   Thomas Berry, *The Great Work: Our Way into the Future* (New York: Bell Tower, 1999), 13. Excerpt(s) from *The Great Work: Our Way into the Future* by Thomas Berry, copyright © 1999
by Thomas Berry. Used by permission of Bell Tower, an imprint of Random House, a division of Penguin Random House LLC. All rights reserved.

2   John O'Donohue, *Divine Beauty: The Invisible Embrace* (New York: Penguin Random House, 2010).

3   David Michie, *Buddhism for Busy People: Finding Happiness in a Hurried World* (Ithaca, NY: Snow Lion Publications, 2008), 85.

4   Demeter USA is the certifier for biodynamic products in United States.

5   Wendell Berry, "A Native Hill," in *The Long-Legged House* (Berkeley: Counterpoint, 2012), 220.

6   Paracelsus quoted in C. G. Jung, "The Unconscious as a Multiple Consciousness," *Spirit and Nature: Papers from the Eranos Yearbooks,* ed. Joseph Campbell (Princeton: Princeton University Press, 1982), 404.

7   Ibid.

8   Ibid., 405.

9   "Nothing Gold Can Stay" by Robert Frost from *The Poetry of Robert Frost* edited by Edward Connery Lathem. Copyright © 1923, 1969 by Henry Holt and Company. Copyright © 1951 by Robert Frost. Reprinted by permission of Henry Holt and Company. All Rights Reserved.

10 Jung quote from *A Matter of Heart,* directed by Mark Whitney, written by Suzanne Wagner (New York: Kino International, 1986; DVD, 2004).

11 C. G. Jung, *The Red Book: Liber Novus,* ed. Sonu Shamdasani, trans. Sonu Shamdasani, Mark Kyburz, and John Peck (New York: W. W. Norton & Co, 2009), 233.

12 *Milk fever* is an archaic term for *mastitis.*

13 C. G. Jung, "Psychological Aspects of the Mother Archetype" (1939), *The Archetypes and the Collective Unconscious,* in *The Collected Works of C. G. Jung,* Vol. 9i (Princeton: Princeton University Press, 1968), 172. References to Jung's *Collected Works* will hereafter be referred to by title, date, volume number, and paragraph number.

14 Nathan Schwartz-Salant, "Ancient Mysteries of Union in Clinical Perspective," from a tape of a presentation given at the C. G. Jung Institute of San Francisco, on November 1, 1985.

15 *Samskara* is a Hindu word meaning actions well thought out and performed with full awareness.

16 Roger J. Woolger, *Other Lives, Other Selves: A Jungian Psychotherapist Discovers Past Lives* (New York: Bantam Books, 1988), 148–149.

17 Louise J. Kaplan, *Oneness and Separateness: From Infant to Individual* (New York: Simon and Schuster, 1978), 40.

18 Names have been changed.

19 Wendell Berry, "The Sycamore," in *Selected Poems of Wendell Berry* (Berkeley, CA: Counterpoint, 1998).

20 Ibid.

21 Ibid.

22 All About Heaven, Symbols, s.v. "Pelican," accessed September 14, 2017, *http://www.allaboutheaven.org/symbols/1032/123/pelican.*

23 Lynda V. Mapes, *Witness Tree: Seasons of Change with a Century-Old Oak* (New York: Bloomsbury, 2007), 14.

24 Ibid., 32.

25 Aldo Leopold, *A Sand County Almanac*

(Oxford: Oxford University Press, 1949), 246.

26 Matthew 6:25–27. Revised Standard Version.

27 Rachel Carson, *Silent Spring* (New York: Houghton Mifflin Company, 1962).

28 Environmental Protection Agency, "DDT: A Brief History and Status," accessed September 21, 2017, *https://www.epa.gov/ ingredients-used-pesticide-products/ ddt-brief-history-and-status.*

29 Michael Ruse, "Rachel Carson and Rudolf Steiner—An Unknown Debt," *Huffpost,* July 23, 2013, with updates on September 22, 2013, *http:// www.huffingtonpost.com/michael-ruse/rachel- carson-and-rudolf-_b_3639684.html.*

30 C. G. Jung, *Psychological Types,* 1921/1971, CW 6, 709.

31 Aldo Leopold, Foreword to *A Sand County Almanac* (Oxford: Oxford University Press, 1949).

32 "Gaia Theory: Model and Metaphor for the 21st Century," *http://environment-ecology.com/ gaia/ 711-gaia-theory-model-and-metaphor-for-the- 21st-century.html.*

33 James Lovelock, "Gaia: A Model for Planetary and Cellular Dynamics," in *Gaia, A Way of Knowing: Political Implications of the New Biology,* ed. William Irwin Thompson (Great Barrington, MA: Lindisfarne Press, 1987), 93, 95.

34 Lynn Margulis, "Early Life: The Microbes Have Priority," in *Gaia, A Way of Knowing: Political Implications of the New Biology,* ed. William Irwin Thompson (Great Barrington, MA: Lindisfarne Press, 1987), 109.

35 Berry, *The Great Work,* 173.

36 David C. Korten, *The Great Turning: From Empire to Earth Community* (Oakland, CA: Berrett-Koehler Publishers, 2006). *See also* People-Centered Development Forum, *http://davidkorten.org/about-the-forum/*

living-economies-forum/.

37 George Lakoff, *Don't Think of an Elephant! Know Your Values and Frame the Debate* (Vermont: Chelsea Green Publishers, 2004, 2014).

38 John Muir, "A Wind-Storm in the Forests," in *The Mountains of California* (Mineola, NY: Dover Publications, 2017), 252–254.

39 Muir-Hanna Vineyards, "Muir's Legacy," accessed September 21, 2017, *http://www.napawineproject.com/ muir-hanna-vineyards/*

40 Bill McKibben, *Eaarth: Making a Life on a Tough New Planet* (New York: St. Martins, 011), 219.

41 Joanna Macy and Chris Johnstone, *Active Hope: How to Face the Mess We're in without Going Crazy* (Novato, CA: New World Library, 2012), 113.

42 Meredith Sabini, ed., *The Earth Has a Soul: The Nature Writings of C. G. Jung* (Berkeley: North Atlantic Books, 2002), 154.

43 C. G. Jung, "Transformation Symbolism in the Mass" (1942/1954), in *Psychology and Religion, East and West,* 1969, CW 11, 408.

44 C. G. Jung, "Psychology and Religion (The Terry Lectures)" (1938/1940), CW 11, 126.

45 C. G. Jung, "Paracelsus as a Spiritual Phenomenon" (1942), in *Alchemical Studies,* 1968, CW 13, 145–238.

46 *Farming Soul: A Tale of Initiation* (2014), *Between Heaven and Earth: A Jungian Look at the Use of Biodynamic Compost Preparations* (2014); "The Enclosed Garden: Underlying Principles of Jungian Analysis and Biodynamic Agriculture" (Jung Journal: Culture & Psyche 5, no. 2); "Patricia Damery on Water. . . .and Fire" (Jung Journal: Culture & Psyche 9, no. 1).

47 Rudolf Steiner, *Agriculture* (Junction

City, OR: Bio-Dynamic Farming and Gardening Assoc., 1993), 10. Translated from *Geisteswissenschaftliche Grundlagen zum Gedeihen der Landwirtschaft,* vol. 327 in the *Rudolf Steiner Gesamtausgabe* (Dornach, Switzerland: Rudolf Steiner Verzog, 1984).

48 Ibid., 10.

49 Guy H. Cooper, "Coyote in Navajo Religion and Cosmology," *The Canadian Journal of Native Studies* VII, no. 2 (1987): 181–193, *http://www3.brandonu.ca/cjns/7.2/cooper.pdf.*

50 Barry Eberling, "Supervisors Approve Woolls Ranch Winery," *Napa Valley Register,* November 22, 2014, *https://napavalleyregister.com/news/local/supervisors-approve-woolls-ranch-winery/article_76152ac3-7ced-5fe5-ae2f-56bd77b37d3c.html.*

51 This property touches the tip of our ranch to the northwest and was originally owned by Clarence. This is not to be confused with the southwest property line shared with the Sinclairs, who own the land once owned by William.

52 Paula Gunn Allen, quoted in Diane Wolverton, "We'd Form a Society Based on Partnership," in *If Women Ruled the World: How to Create the World We Want to Live In,* ed. Sheila Ellison (Makawao, Maui, HI and San Francisco, CA: Inner Ocean Publishing, 2004), 118.

53 Barbara Black Koltuv, *The Book of Lilith* (York Beach, ME: Nicolas-Hayes, Inc., 1986), 8.

54 Robinson Jeffers, "Science," in *The Collected Poetry of Robinson Jeffers: Volume One: 1920–1928,* ed. Tim Hunt (Stanford, CA: Stanford University Press), 113.

55 Kelli Kendricks of Project Coyote, Carolyn Parr Nature Center, Napa, California.

56 Wendell Berry, "The Purpose of a Coherent Community," in *The Way of Ignorance and Other Essays* (Berkeley, CA: Shoemaker and Hoard, 2005), 72.

57 Epistle 26, Lessons in Tanya, Igeret HaKodesh.

58 C. G. Jung, *Mysterium Coniunctionis,* 1970, CW 14, 592.

59 Patricia Damery, "The Soul Is a Riddlemaker: Three Lessons," in *Marked by Fire: Stories of the Jungian Way,* eds. Patricia Damery and Naomi Ruth Lowinsky (Carmel, CA: Fisher King Press, 2012).

60 James W. Mavor, Jr. and Byron E. Dix, *Manitou: The Sacred Landscape of New England's Native Civilization* (Rochester, VT: Inner Traditions, 1989), 2.

61 Adapted from Patricia Damery, "When an Old Friend Dies," *Psychological Perspectives, A Quarterly Journal of Jungian Thought* 58, no. 2 (2015): 162–171, *https://doi.org/10.1080/00332925.2015.1029414.*

62 Berry, "The Sycamore," in *Selected Poems of Wendell Berry.*

63 Dennis Klocek, *Climate: Soul of the Earth* (Greater Barrington, MA: Lindisfarne Books, 2011).

64 Lovelock, "Gaia: A Model for Planetary and Cellular Dynamics," 83–97.

65 Albert Einstein, "Atomic Education Urged by Einstein," *New York Times,* May 25, 1946.

66 Dennis Klocek, *Sacred Agriculture: The Alchemy of Biodynamics* (Greater Barrington, MA: Lindisfarne Books, Greater Barrington, 2013), 349–370.

67 Ibid.

68 The *prima materia* is the alchemists' beginning coarse material to be transformed.

69 Kenneth Grahame, "Dulce Donum," in *The Wind in the Willows, http://www.cleavebooks.co.uk/grol/grahame/wind05.htm.*

70 Deirdre Bair, *Jung: A Biography* (Boston: Little, Brown and Company, 2003), 8, 651–652.

71 C. G. Jung, *Memories, Dreams, Reflections* (New York: Vintage Books, 1989), 83.

72 Steiner, *Agriculture,* 10.

73 Alzheimer's Association, 2017 Alzheimer's Disease Facts and Figures, *http://www.alz.org/facts/.*

74 Primo Levi, *The Periodic Table,* trans. Raymond Rosenthal (New York: Schocken Books, 1984), 57, 58.

75 Carolyn Raffensperger, Congress Organizer, Women's Congress for Future Generations, Minneapolis, Minnesota, November 2014, from a dream.

76 See the Science and Environmental Health Network at *https://www.sehn.org.*

77 Norma Smith Olson and Kathy Magnuson, "Future First and the Women's Congress," *Minnesota Women's Press,* October 2, 2014, *https://www.womenspress.com/future-first-and-the-womens-congress/*

78 *https://monarchconservation.org/karen-oberhauser/*

79 Karen Oberhauser, Monarch Lab, University of Minnesota, *https://monarchlab.org/about/staff-and-students/karen-oberhauser.*

80 Opening, Women's Congress for Future Generations, November 11, 2017.

81 The first recording of the 7th Generation Principle is in the Great Law of Peace of the Iroquois Confederacy created in the twelfth century. It is a principle embedded in the cultures of most indigenous peoples worldwide. Molly Larkin, "What Is the 7th Generation Principle and Why Do You Need to Know About It?" *Molly Larkin, Ancient Wisdom for Balanced Living,* May 15, 2013, *https://www.mollylarkin.com/what-is-the-7th-generation-principle-and-why-do-you-need-to-know-about-it-3/.*

82 Sandra Steingraber, *Raising Elijah: Protecting Our Children in an Age of Environmental Crisis* (Boston: Da Capo Press, 2013) 27–55.

83 Ibid.

84 Mary Pipher, *The Green Boat: Reviving Ourselves in Our Capsized Culture* (New York: Riverhead Books, 2013).

85 Robin Grossinger, Ruth Askevold et al., *Napa Valley Historical Ecology Atlas* (Berkeley, CA: University of California Press, 2012), 42.

86 Jon Bonné, "After the Leap: His Celebrated Winery Sold, Warren Winiarski Ponders His Legacy—and His Next Move," *San Francisco Chronicle,* March 28, 2008, *https://www.sfgate.com/wine/article/After-the-leap-His-celebrated-winery-sold-3289903.php.*

87 Stett Holbrook, "Napa's Water War with Big Wine," *Food & Environment Reporting Network,* June 20, 2016, *https://thefern.org/2016/06/of-water-and-wine/.*

88 Barry Eberling, "Winery Appeals Stacking Up before Napa County Board of Supervisors," *Napa Valley Register,* August 14, 2017, *https://napavalleyregister.com/news/local/winery-appeals-stacking-up-before-napa-county-board-of-supervisors/article_713ec3a2-4a14-5ee3-a869-5f9354d9cf87.html.*

89 Paraphrased quote from Aldo Leopold, *A Sand County Almanac.*

90 Amy Goodman, "Blue Covenant: Maude Barlow on the Global Movement for Water Justice," *Democracy Now!,* February 27, 2008, *http://www.democracynow.org/2008/2/27/maude_barlow_on_the_global_movement.*

91 Vine Deloria, Jr., *Jung and the Sioux Traditions: Dreams, Visions, Nature, and the Primitive* (New Orleans: Spring Journal Books, 2009), 115.

92 "2015 Annual Statewide Pesticide Use Report Indexed by Commodity: Napa County," Department of Pesticide Regulation, *http://*

www.cdpr.ca.gov/docs/pur/pur15rep/ comcnty/napa15_site.pdf.

93 "Childhood Cancer Diagnoses," kidsdata.org, https://tinyurl.com/uzozrav.

94 State Cancer Profiles, National Cancer Institute, https://tinyurl.com/wdvypj5.

95 From the "2015 Annual Statewide Pesticide Use Report Indexed by Commodity: Napa County."

96 David Brooks, "Joint Venture Silicon Valley: State of the Valley," KQED Public Radio, March 29, 2017, http://www.kqed.org/a/radiospecials/ R201703292000, minute 21.

97 Amber Manfree, "Napa County Conservation Policy: Existing Conditions and Proposed Policy Impacts," March 22, 2019, https:// napavalleyregister.com/napa-county-conservation-policy -existing-conditions-and-proposed-policy-impacts/pdf_2ee4fb94-3cd1-5aed-a186 -66bc238c94af.html.

98 C. G. Jung, Symbols of Transformation, 1967, CW 5, 652.

99 Deloria, Jung and the Sioux Traditions, 115.

100 C. G. Jung, "Man and His Environment, Interview with Hans Carol, 1950," in C.G. Jung Speaking: Interviews and Encounters, eds. William McGuire and R. F. C. Hull (Princeton: Princeton University Press, 1977), 202.

101 Gerbert Gohmann, The Plant, vol. 2., trans. K. Castelliz and Barbara Saunders-Davies (Milwaukee: Bio-Dynamic Farming and Gardening Association, Inc., 1989), 155.

102 This quote is from the thirteenth-century Kabbalistic, The Zohar.

103 Barbara Hannah, The Archetypal Symbolism of Animals (Wilmette, IL: Chiron Publications, 2006), 155.

104 The ad hoc committee formed after the March 10, 2015, hearing.

105 Jung, Symbols of Transformation, CW 5, 368.

106 C. G. Jung, "The Philosophical Tree" (1954), Alchemical Studies, 400.

107 Ibid.

108 Jung, Mysterium Coniunctionis, 1970, CW 14, 512.

109 C. G. Jung, "Letter to Père Lachat" (1954), The Symbolic Life.

110 Berry Eberling, "Supervisors Tackle Winery Regulations," Napa Valley Register, December 8, 2015, http://napavalleyregister. com/news/local/supervisors-tackle-winery-regulations/article _f3064fe0-9c41-5c82-b8d9-d76ca3734d0e. html.

111 Howard Yune, "Battle Over Napa County Watersheds Plays Out Before Supervisors," Napa Valley Register, March 26, 2019, https:// napavalleyregister.com/news/local/battle-over -napa-county-watersheds-plays-out-before-supervisors/article_969eceeb-872b-53df-8d51 -b37e1be08115.html.

112 Berry Eberling, "Supervisors Tackle Winery Regulations," w, December 8, 2015, http:// napavalleyregister.com/news/local/ supervisors-tackle-winery-regulations/article _f3064fe0-9c41-5c82-b8d9-d76ca3734d0e. html.

113 Howard Yune, "Napa Asks, How Many Hotel Rooms Are Enough," Napa Valley Register, February 19, 2017, http://napavalleyregister. com/news/local/napa-asks-how-many-hotel-rooms-are-enough/article_d71fd679-3ff1- 550f-bb09-c1237c48fe59.html.

114 Bill Bryson, Neither Here nor There: Travels in Europe (New York: William Morrow and Company, 1992). Quoted on Goodreads, https://www.goodreads.com/ author/quotes/7.Bill_Bryson.

115 Barry Eberling, "Report Says Well-Heeled Napa Valley Tourists Love Wine and Scenery," Napa Valley Register, July 19, 2017, http:// napavalleyregister.com/news/local/ report-says-well-heeled-napa-valley-tourists-love-wine-and/article_11edd5ee-

de58-5c7a-82ee-f6afd796722d.html.

116 Barry Eberling, "Napa County Supervisors Side with Raymond Vineyards," *Napa Valley Register,* August 16, 2017, *http://napavalleyregister.com/news/local/napa-county-supervisors-side-with-raymond-vineyards/article_9df18d4f-27d7-5f70-85f8-deaf8726685c.html.*

117 Tahir Shah, *House of the Tiger King: The Quest for a Lost City* (London: Secretum Mundi Publishing, 2004).

118 However, things have changed! In the *Express,* a September 27, 2017, article, "'WE WON'T BE BACK!' Furious Tourists React after Majorca Demands Britons GO HOME," tells a new story. Two-thirds of the residents say there are too many British tourists in Majorca and the number of visitors should be capped. See *https://www.express.co.uk/news/world/858926/Limit-British-tourists-Majorca-Mallorca-Ibiza-Balearic-Islands-weather-restrictions.*

119 Eben Fodor, "Better, Not Bigger," YouTube, December 14, 2010, *https://www.youtube.com/watch?v=uv619NexIYw.*

120 Ecclesiastes 3:1

121 Rainer Maria Rilke, *Letters to a Young Poet,* trans. Reginald Snell (Dancing Unicorn Books, Kindle), Letter 4, July 16, 1903, 21.

122 C. G. Jung, "On the Relation of Analytical Psychology to Poetry" (1922), *The Spirit in Man, Art, & Literature,* 1966 CW 15, ¶130.

123 Adolf Guggenbühl-Craig, *Marriage: Dead or Alive,* trans. Murray Stein (Woodstock, CT: Spring Publications, 2001).

124 Harmony with Nature, United Nations, *http://harmonywithnatureun.org.*

125 Rights of Nature Law and Policy, *http://www.harmonywithnatureun.org/rightsOfNature/.*

126 Jason Daley, "Toledo, Ohio, Just Granted Lake Erie the Same Legal Rights as a Person," *Smithsonian Magazine,* March 1, 2019, *https://www.smithsonianmag.com/smart-news/toledo-ohio-just-granted-lake-erie-same-legal-rights-people-180971603/.*

127 "Press Release: Lake Erie Bill of Rights and Rights of Nature Argued in Federal Court," Community Environmental Legal Defense Fund, February 6, 2020, *https://celdf.org/2020/02/press-release-lake-erie-bill-of-rights-and-rights-of-nature-argued-in-us-federal-court/.*

128 Nicole Pallotta, "Federal Judge Strikes Down Lake Erie Bill of Rights," Animal Legal Defense Fund, May 4, 2020, *https://aldf.org/article/federal-judge-strikes-down-lake-erie-bill-of-rights/.*

129 Rebecca Renner, "In Florida: A River Gets Rights," *Sierra Magazine,* February 9, 2021, *https://www.sierraclub.org/sierra/2021-2-march-april/protect/florida-river-gets-rights.*

130 Ibid.

131 Jung *Aion,* CW 9ii, 1975, 377, note 58.

132 Richard Wilhelm, *Secret of the Golden Flower: A Chinese Book of Life,* with a foreword and commentary by C. G. Jung (1929), trans. from German to English by Cary F. Baynes (New York: Harcourt Brace & Company, 1962), 91. Originally published in London in 1931.

133 "Bill Moyers: Truth Is the Oxygen of Democracy," *Amanpour,* CNN, Jung 9, 2020, *https://www.cnn.com/videos/tv/2020/06/09/amanpour-bill-moyers.cnn.*

134 David Stoneberg, "Tuteur rejects 'Water, Forest, and Oak Woodland Protection' Initiative," *Napa Valley Register,* June 10, 2016, *http://napavalleyregister.com/news/local/tuteur-rejects-water-forest-and-oak-woodland-protection-initiative/article_2e55cc27-5afa-5f30-bc74-f9dd1b659d74.html.*

135 Levi, *The Periodic Table,* 58.

136 C. G. Jung, *The Undiscovered Self: The Dilemma of the Individual in Modern Society* (New York: Signet, 2006), 303.

137 Barry Eberling, "State Court Declines to Revive Napa Watershed Measure for November Ballot," *Napa Valley Register,* August 11, 2016, *http:// napavalleyregister.com/news/local/state-court -declines-to-revive-napa-watershed-measure- for-november/article_a0430b26-7536-5df6 -8a3c-054012facd66.html.*

138 Barry Eberling, "Decision on Walt Ranch Project Expected in June 13," *Napa Valley Register,* April 4, 2016, *http://napavalleyregister.com/ news/local/decision-on-walt-ranch-expected- june/article _64658252-36f4-52e1-af15-963599132b88. html.*

139 Ibid.

140 Ibid.

141 Christine Perez, "Craig Hall: The Reluctant Entrepreneur," *D CEO Magazine,* November 2013, *https://www.dmagazine.com/ publications/d-ceo/2013/november/craig- hall-the-reluctant -entrepreneur/.*

142 California Natural Resource Act, *https:// www.wildlife.ca.gov/Conservation/CEQA/ Purpose.*

143 John Harrington, Letter to Kelli Cahill, Planner III, Napa Planning Building and Environmental Services Department, November 6, 2014.

144 "Sierra Club Appeals Napa County's Walt Ranch Decision," Press Release, Sierra Club Redwood Chapter, August 22, 2016.

145 "Walt Ranch Litigation," Sierra Club Redwood Chapter, *https://www.sierraclub.org/redwood /napa.*

146 Barry Eberling, "There's Valuable Rock in Them Thar Hills," *Napa Valley Register,* April 18, 2015, *http://napavalleyregister.com/news/ local/there-s-valuable-rock-in-them-thar- hills/article _ebf18a8b-bffd-5abb-9ba7-408c4e9aa31e. html.*

147 Steven Booth, Letter to Donald Barrella, Stop Syar Expansion, October 19, 2015, *http://www .stopsyarcoalition.com/wp-content/ uploads/2015/10/10-19- 15StevesSyarEIRComments21.pdf.*

148 Kidsdata Advisory, Childhood Cancer Diagnoses Rise in Northern California Counties, Lucile Packard Foundation, September 23, 2015, *http:// www.kidsdata.org/advisories/cancer_2015. html.*

149 Barry Eberling, "Napa Supervisors Tentatively Approve Syar Quarry Expansion," *Napa Valley Register,* July 11, 2016, *http:// napavalleyregister.com/news/local/napa- supervisors-tentatively -approve-syar-quarry-expansion/article_ d86e2d8a-a8d5-5b9f-a26f-6c8f38c7146f. html.*

150 Proposition 65 mandates that businesses inform Californians of the release of significant amounts of listed chemicals known to cause cancer, birth defects, or reproductive harm so they can make informed decisions to protect themselves. OEHHA, "Proposition 65 in Plain Language," *https://oehha.ca.gov /proposition-65/general-info/ proposition-65-plain-language.*

151 Barry Eberling, "No. 1 Story of 2016: Wine Industry Under Fire," *Napa Valley Register,* December 30, 2016, *http://napavalleyregister. com/news/local/no-story-of-wine-industry- under-fire /article_21223b42-3c7c-5510-828f- 200a9707075a.html.*

152 From email correspondence with Jim Wilson, April 26, 2017.

153 Haya El Nasser, "California Drought Is Up to 25% Worse Because of Climate Change," *Aljazeera America,* August 20, 2015, *http://america. aljazeera.com/articles/2015/8/20/california- drought -is-25-percent-more-severe-because-of- climate-change.html.*

154 C. G. Jung, "The Personal and Collective Unconscious," *Two Essays on Analytical Psychology,* 1953/1966, CW 7, 114.

155 Jung, *Memories, Dreams, Reflections,* 225.

156 Ibid., 225–226.

157 The October 2017 fires in Napa burned up and down Soda Canyon Road. Very few structures were left. Six people in Napa lost their lives that night due to the fast-moving fire, two of them on Soda Canyon Road.

158 "The Standing Rock Sioux Tribe's Litigation on the Dakota Access Pipeline," Earth Justice, accessed November 30, 2017, *https://earthjustice.org/features/faq-standing-rock-litigation.*

159 Madeleine Bunting, "Language of the Land," *Resurgence &Ecologist,* issue 300 (January/February 2017): 14.

160 Ibid.,15.

161 Rainer Maria Rilke, "The Man Watching," in *News of the Universe: Poems of Twofold Consciousness,* ed. and trans. Robert Bly (San Francisco: Sierra Club Books, 1980), 121–122.

162 Tom Benning, "Energy Chief Rick Perry Says It's 'Inappropriate' to Label Climate Change Skeptics Neanderthals," *Dallas Morning News,* June 19, 2017, *https://www.dallasnews.com/news/texas-politics/2017/06/19/energy-chief-rick-perry-says-inappropriate-label-climate-change-skeptics-neanderthals.*

163 Ibid.

164 Nadja Popovich and Claire O'Neill, "A '500-Year Flood' Could Happen Sooner Than You Think. Here's Why," *New York Times,* August 28, 2017, *https://www.nytimes.com/interactive/2017/08/28/climate/500-year-flood-hurricane-harvey-houston.html.*

165 Texas A&M Forest Service. "2011 Texas Wildfires: Common Denominators of Destruction." *https://tfsweb.tamu.edu/uploadedFiles/TFSMain/Preparing_for_Wildfires/Prepare_Your_Home_for_Wildfires/Contact_Us/2011%20Texas%20Wildfires.pdf*

166 "Texas leads the US in weather disasters," Houston Chronicle. *https://www.houstonchronicle.com/politics/texas/article/Texas-leads-U-S-in-weather-disasters-Biden-s-16095032.php*

167 David Montgomery, Simon Romero, and James Dobbins, "'Now It's Coming Back to Bite Them': Democrats See an Opening in GOP Oversight of Texas Grid," *New York Times,* February 17, 2021, *https://www.nytimes.com/2021/02/17/us/texas-electric-grid-failure.html.*

168 Leopold, *A Sand County Almanac,* 240.

169 Wendell Berry, "Imagination in Place," in *The Way of Ignorance and Other Essays,* 46.

170 Henry Lutz, "Big Wine Companies Are Snapping Up Napa Valley Producers and Vineyards," *Napa Valley Register,* June 19, 2017, *http://napavalleyregister.com/news/local/big-wine-companies-are-snapping-up-napa-valley-producers-and/article_b48e32e7-f100-5f25-8c07-9427b1cafe43.html.*

171 William Logan Hebner, *The Southern Paiute: A Portrait* (Logan, UT: Utah State University Press, 2010), 14.

172 Ibid.

173 Ibid., 20.

174 Ibid., 14.

175 Rebecca Solnit, "Unfinished Business: John Muir in Native America," *Sierra Magazine,* March/April 2021, 43.

176 See Movement Rights, *https://www.movementrights.org.*

177 Two successful ballot measures include Measures J and P, which protect the integrity of the Ag Preserve until 2058. See appendix.

178 From Movement Rights, Draft, Sustainable Development Community Bill of Rights.

179 Leopold, *A Sand County Almanac,* xviii–xix.

180 Alliance for Responsible Governance, letter to Board of Supervisors, Napa County, August 11, 2017.

181 Rainer Maria Rilke, "The Man Watching," in *News of the Universe: Poems of Twofold*

Consciousness, ed. and trans. Robert Bly (San Francisco: Sierra Club Books, 1980), 121–122.

182 Rilke, "Moving Ahead," in *News of the Universe,* 120.

183 Peter Levine, *Waking the Tiger: Healing Trauma* (Berkeley, CA: North Atlantic Books, 1997), 12.

184 Geoffrey Mohan, "Vineyards May Have Kept Wine Country Fire from Getting Worse," *Los Angeles Times,* October 12, 2017, *https://www.latimes.com/business/la-fi-vineyards-firebreak-20171012-story.html.*

185 Ibid.

186 Chad Hanson, "Congress, Trump Exploit Fire Tragedy to Promote Logging Agenda," *Sierra,* November 14, 2017, *http://www.sierraclub.org/sierra/congress-trump-exploit-fire-tragedy-promote-logging-agenda.*

187 Spirit Animal Totems, s.v. "Pelican Symbolism," accessed December 1, 2017, *https://www.spirit-animals.com/pelican/.*

188 "Napa County—Measure 'D': Argument in Support of Measure 'D,'" Napa Vision 2050, *http://napavision2050.org/wp-content/uploads/2018/03/INITIATIVE-ARGUMENT-FOR-AGAINST.pdf.*

189 Barry Eberling, "Napa's Measure C Fate May Be Unknown for Days--or Weeks," *Napa Valley Register,* June 6, 2018, *https://napavalleyregister.com/news/local/napa-s-measure-c-fate-may-be-unknown-for-days/article_699d333f-1511-5128-bd72-5da408d3b965.html.*

190 Jonah Raskin, "A County Divided: Napa's Measure C Ahead by a Hair," *North Bay Bohemian,* June 6, 2018, *https://m.bohemian.com/northbay/a-county-divided/Content?oid=6270173.*

191 Ibid.

192 Measure D was challenged by a vintner, but a March 2020 settlement resulted in a clarification of the term "unavoidable landings." The county subsequently posted a fact sheet about Measure D. See *https://www.countyofnapa.org/DocumentCenter/View/14392Napa-County_FAQs-Regarding-Measure-D.*

192-1 Mike Hackett, "A Good First Step, but Not Enough," *The Weekly Calistogan,* May 7, 2019, *https://napavalleyregister.com/community/calistogan/opinion/a-good-first-step-but-not-enough/article_1e2c973a-3d39-55a7-87f1-18dd995fb4e7.html.*

193 Barry Eberling, "Napa's Final Election Results Make It Official—Measure C Lost," *Napa Valley Register,* June 25, 2018, *https://napavalleyregister.com/news/local/napa-s-final-election-results-make-it-official--/article_2dba1948-9f97-5f56-9046-21000c22f6d5.html.*

194 Ibid.

195 Amber Manfree, "Napa County Conservation Policy."

196 "Re-Oaking North Bay: A Strategy for Restoring Native Oak Ecosystems, Focusing on Napa and Sonoma Valleys," San Francisco Estuary Institute, Aquatic Science Center, August 1, 2020, *https://www.napawatersheds.org/news_items view/13136.*

197 Email, from Eric McKee, Education Project Manager, Napa County Resource Conservation District.

198 Research done by Jim Wilson and Katie Stillwell in 2020.

199 Gary Quackenbush, "Napa County Has Taken a Decade to Create a Climate Action Plan," *North Bay Business Journal,* July 10, 2018, *https://www.northbaybusinessjournal.comhome/8503956-181climate-change-napa-wine.*

200 *Forum* on the Road: Land-Use Battles Continue as Napa County Passes Controversial Tree-Water Ordinance," hosted by Mina Kim, KQED, April 26, 2019, *https://www.kqed.org/forum/2010101870749/forum-on-the-road-land-use-battles-continue-as-napa-county-*

passes-controversial-tree-water-ordinance.

201 Georgina Gustin, John H. Cushman, Jr., and Nella Banerjee, "The Farm Bureau: Big Oil's Unnoticed Ally Fighting Climate Science and Policy," *Inside Climate News,* December 21, 2018, *https:// insideclimatenews.org/news/20122018/ american-farm-bureau-fossil-fuel-nexus-climate-change-denial-science-agriculture-carbon-policy-opposition.*

202 American Farm Bureau Federation, *https:// www.fb.org/issues/regulatory-reform/ climate-change/afbf-policy-on-climate-change.*

203 Napa Country Water and Tree Protection Ordinance, FAQ, *https://www.countyofnapa. org/DocumentCenter/View/12143/Water-and-Tree-Protection-Ordinance-FAQs-PDF?bidId=.*

204 Ryan Klobas, *Forum* on the Road.

205 The proposed ordinance, the Small Winery Protection and Use Permit Streamlining Ordinance, is not about protecting our hillsides, watersheds, and Ag lands; it is all about, once again, giving the wine industry carte blanche to expand without the bother of hearings before the Planning Commission and the annoyance of public comment. These permittings would become ministerial, meaning granted without public participation.

206 Statement from the 1988–1989 Grand Jury report: "The proliferation of non-conforming and accessory uses, and the participation of the Board of Supervisors, the Planning Commission, and the Conservation and Planning Department in the current further redefinition of a winery appears to accede to the very commercial and urbanizing pressures the County General Plan has committed to avoid and keep separate from agriculturally zoned land. The danger is that each redefinition allows a new level of commercial, cultural, or promotional activity occurring on Agricultural Preserve or Agricultural Watershed land which in turn establishes precedent and legal foundation for expanding future agricultural uses." See "General Government Committee: Land Use," *https://napavision2050*

.org/wp-content/uploads/2019/07/87-88-Grand-Jury-copy.pdf.

207 Peter Jensen, "Measure J Made Napa County Voters Protectors of Agricultural Lands," *Napa Valley Register,* March 4, 2012, *https:// napavalleyregister.com/news/local/ measure-j-made-napa-county-voters-protectors-of-agricultural-lands/ article_0d4aeeca-65bf-11e1-a220 -001871e3ce6c.html.*

208 Ibid.

209 The Sustainable Groundwater Management Act requires that local agencies manage groundwater so that recharge rates balance with pumping of groundwater. The Groundwater Sustainable Agency (GSA) in Napa County is responsible for this. Unfortunately, the Board of Supervisors has appointed themselves to be the GSA. See California Water Boards, The Sustainable Groundwater Management Act, *https://www. waterboards.ca.gov/water_issues/programs/ gmp/.*

210 The National Resources Defense Council (NRCD) had arranged for both California Fish and Wildlife and the State Water Control Board to visit the sites of concern in March to determine the cause as well as mitigation measures.

211 Transcript of the Second Planning Commission Meeting, February 5, 2020.

212 Resolution No 2010-48, "A Resolution of the Napa County Board of Supervisors, State of California, Establishing Interpretative Guidance on Marketing Activities for Wineries," *http:// sodacanyonroad .org/docs/2010_WDO_guidance_appendix. pdf.*

213 Ibid.

214 Berry, *The Great Work,* 19.

215 "Sanctuary of Zeus at Dodona," Warwick: Classics and Ancient History, *https://warwick.ac.uk/fac /arts/classics/intranets/students/modules/ greekreligion/database/clukcw.*

216 Wikipedia, s.v. "The Golden Bough/Worship of the Oak," from *The Golden Bough* by

James Frazier, accessed July 22, 2021, *https://en.wikisource.org/wiki/The_Golden_Bough/The_Worship_of_the_Oak*; Tracy Boyd, "The Oracular Oak at Dodona," Sacredthreads.net, 2004, *http://www.sacredthreads.net/www.sacredthreads.net/oak_at_dodona.html*.

217 Fred Pearce, "Rivers in the Sky: How Deforestation Is Affecting Global Water Cycles," *Yale Environment360*, July 24, 2018, *https://e360.yale.edu/features/how-deforestation-affecting-global-water-cycles-climate-change?fbclid=IwAR1jFLbUwSkjNN41anrY1KWP64jOXqfnOULOn9u0HBe8Fv-fQlqVlZdNfBM*.

218 Personal communication with Dr. Judy Damery Parrish, Professor Emeritus of Biology, Millikin University, Decatur, IL, July 19, 2021.

219 Jung, *Mysterium Coniunctionis,* 1970, CW 14, fn. 419–420.

220 C. G. Jung, Approaching the Unconscious, in *Man and His Symbols,* ed. C. G. Jung (London: Aldus Books, 1964), 95.

221 Jean Houston, *The Wizard of Us: Transformational Lessons from Oz* (New York: Atria, 2012).

222 Wendell Berry, "The Peace of Wild Things," in *Selected Poems of Wendell Berry*, 30.

223 This quote was adapted from Damery, *Farming Soul: A Tale of Initiation.*

224 Lovelock, "Gaia: A Model for Planetary and Cellular Dynamics," 96.

225 This quote has been attributed to Rainer Maria Rilke.

226 Christopher D. Stone, *Should Trees Have Standing: Law, Morality, and the Environment* (Oxford: Oxford University Press, 2010), 125.

227 Barry Eberling, "Napa County Approval of Walt Ranch Appealed Again," *Napa Valley Register,* May 5, 2018, *https://napavalleyregister.com/news/local/napa-county-approval-of-walt-ranch-appealed-again/article_09816ed3-6c03-5eca-926c-d0f3390cff24.html*.

228 Barry Eberling, "Judge Says Mountain Peak Winery Fire Issues Need New Look from Napa County Supervisors," July 1, 2019, updated January 8, 2021, *https://napavalleyregister.com/news/local/judge-says-mountain-peak-winery-fire-issues-need-new-look-from-napa-county-supervisors/article_eecd3f8c-f102-523e-b070-dfe7eee6f8b1.html*.

229 Michie, *Buddhism for Busy People*, 85.

230 Forest Unlimited, *Forest Communiqué,* Fall 2016, *https://www.forestunlimited.org/wp-content/uploads/FU-Newsletter-Fall10-16.pdf.*

231 Barry Eberling, "Napa County's New Definition of Agriculture to Include Marketing," *Napa Valley Register,* April 9, 2017, *https://napavalleyregister.com/news/local/napa-county-s-new-definition-of-agriculture-to-include-marketing/article_8de8538b-ff1b-51b0-b205-6d3cf5e0f307.html*.

232 Barry Eberling, "Napa's Final Election Results Make It Official—Measure C Lost," *Napa Valley Register,* January 25, 2018, *https://napavalleyregister.com/news/local/napas-final-election-results-make-it-official—measure-c-lost/article_2dba1948-9f97-5f56-9046-21000c22f6d5.html.*

234 Quote in caption from Dante Alighieri, *The Inferno of Dante,* trans. R. Pinsky (New York: Farrar, Straus & Giroux, 1994), 311.

ABOUT THE AUTHOR

PATRICIA DAMERY is a retired analyst member of the C. G. Jung Institute of San Francisco living near Napa, California, where she and her husband farmed a biodynamic organic ranch for years. She has published numerous articles and four books, including *Marked by Fire: Stories of the Jungian Way*, which she co-edited with Naomi Ruth Lowinsky. A board member of the activist group Napa Vision 2050 and co-editor of its newsletter, *Eyes on Napa*, she also served on the Executive Committee of the Napa Sierra Club and is also an active participant on the Sierra Club Redwood Chapter's Northern California Forest Committee, Oak Working Group. She maintains a blog at *www.patriciadamery.com*.

Patricia with Agaleah, the queen
(Photo: Cristin McDonnell)

Made in United States
Orlando, FL
30 August 2022

21747360R00150